A NOTE TO THE READER
This publication has been electronically reproduced from digital information. Jossey-Bass is pleased to make use of this technology to keep works of enduring value in print as long as there is a reasonable demand to do so. The content of this book is identical to previous printings.

MAKING GOVERNMENT WORK

Martin A. Levin
&
Mary Bryna Sanger

MAKING GOVERNMENT WORK

*How Entrepreneurial Executives
Turn Bright Ideas
into Real Results*

Jossey-Bass Publishers • San Francisco

Copyright © 1994 by Jossey-Bass Inc., Publishers, 350 Sansome Street, San Francisco, California 94104. Copyright under International, Pan American, and Universal Copyright Conventions. All rights reserved.
No part of this book may be reproduced in any form—except for brief quotation (not to exceed 1,000 words) in a review or professional work—without permission in writing from the publishers.

Substantial discounts on bulk quantities of Jossey-Bass books are available to corporations, professional associations, and other organizations. For details and discount information, contact the special sales department at Jossey-Bass Inc., Publishers. (415) 433-1740; Fax (415) 433-0499.

Manufactured in the United States of America. Nearly all Jossey-Bass books and jackets are printed on recycled paper that contains at least 50 percent recycled waste, including 10 percent postconsumer waste. Many of our materials are also printed with vegetable-based ink; during the printing process these inks emit fewer volatile organic compounds (VOCs) than petroleum-based inks. VOCs contribute to the formation of smog.

Library of Congress Cataloging-in-Publication Data

Levin, Martin A.
    Making government work : how entrepreneurial executives turn bright ideas into real results / Martin A. Levin, Mary Bryna Sanger. —1st ed.
      p. cm.—(The Jossey-Bass public administration series)
    Includes bibliographical references and index.
    ISBN 1-55542-658-1
    1. Public administration. 2. Entrepreneurship. I. Sanger, Mary Bryna. II. Series.
JF1351.L468 1994
350—dc20   94-381
                                                                                      CIP

FIRST EDITION
HB Printing   10 9 8 7 6 5 4 3 2   *Code 9466*

The Jossey-Bass
Public Administration
Series

Contents

Preface xi

Acknowledgments xxi

The Authors xxvii

1
Government Can Work:
Learning from Successful Executives 1

2
Management Matters:
It's Where Policy Succeeds and Fails 33

3
Using Old Stuff in New Ways:
The Sources of Innovation 87

4
Not from Blueprints:
The Process of Innovation 127

5
Bureaucratic Entrepreneurs:
A Bias Toward Action 149

CONTENTS

6
The Crucial Role of
Organizational Culture 171

7
Balancing Innovation
and Accountability 213

8
The Chief Executive Role 239

9
Cultivating Bureaucratic Entrepreneurs:
Lessons for Success 269

Conclusion:
Pointing the Trains in the Right Direction:
Public Management Is About Values 311

Index 327

Preface

Government Can Make Things Work

Imagine for a moment that we pick up the newspaper tomorrow morning and read that a fully effective AIDS vaccine has been discovered. When this happens, everyone's response will be one of joy. We all will suppose this to be the happy ending to the long nightmare of AIDS. Unfortunately, nothing could be further from the truth.

The discovery of an effective AIDS vaccine will be not the beginning of the end but rather only the end of the beginning. The discovery is not the cure. Bright ideas are not enough; attention to management is needed to succeed. The day after an AIDS vaccine is discovered will only usher in the next chapter of the ordeal. It will be the start of an equally difficult period: the implementation of the campaign to inoculate all Americans with an AIDS vaccine.

We predict the following scenario. This period will be marked by management problems and delays resulting from many serious conflicts: scientific controversy over the vaccine's effectiveness and safety; threats of lawsuits over side effects and demands from manufacturers for indemnification from lawsuits; professional and institutional timidity by health care providers; media sensationalization of rare cases. All these conflicts will discourage the public from embracing the vaccination program.

During this time Americans will continue to die of AIDS. Many billions will be spent on treating cases of AIDS that continue to develop after the discovery of the vaccine. This is because management matters. And management is not a routine task. This is one of the main themes of *Making Government Work*. We show how executives make a difference. The successful executive strategies and skills that we describe here are critical to effectively meeting the challenges of public policy.

Making Government Work

Indeed, there is increasing evidence that government can make things work. In recent years, a wide range of innovative initiatives have developed at all levels of government. These achievements were accomplished, even during this time of cynicism about government, through executive skills, through management. Using success stories drawn from a broad range of innovative public programs and agencies over the past twenty years, this book reveals how executives create public sector innovation and the ways in which even ordinary public managers can improve government performance. We show how executives can make a difference. Clever ideas and policy choices grab all the attention. But clever ideas—even a breakthrough like an AIDS vaccine—are not enough to produce policy success. Management is so important because that is often where policy and programs fail *and* succeed.

Years of government bashing have left even committed

PREFACE

public managers uneasy about the prospect for a revitalized public sector. Indeed, more fashionable today is a glorification of the benefits of allowing the market to do the government's business. Students of public policy and management have been discouraged by the generalized cynicism about the value of their skills and training to create productive improvements in public performance.

Our book is positive and hopeful. It is designed to dispel the myths of an impotent and incompetent public sector by revealing a multitude of concrete and visible public successes and examining how they were achieved. We offer a refreshing and invigorating view of the possibilities for innovative and effective public enterprises and the appropriate strategies to realize them.

By showing that successful public enterprises are operating at all levels of government, *Making Government Work* seeks to inspire and boost the spirits of practitioners in government and students of public management. Not only do we describe and explain how effective public managers realized innovative policy and management goals, but we also provide an explicit road map and directions for applying their lessons. The trick to reinvigorating the public sector is not to replace it with the market, though there may be areas where the market can contribute. Rather, it is to redirect the focus toward management and reeducate public executives to appreciate the need for the strategies and skills that we spell out here.

Making government work does not require genius. What it requires is an executive—an active, focused, flexible, and adaptive executive—who pursues particular strategies and approaches. This book shows how successful executives make government work by examining their strategies and approaches. But these are not presented as maxims for innovation. This is a book about real life, not theoretical principles. We present flesh-and-blood lessons from actual success stories.

In *Reinventing Government,* David Osborne and Ted Gaebler draw a striking picture of a transformed public sector.[1] But Osborne and Gaebler's "entrepreneurial spirit" is not enough to change recalcitrant bureaucracies. Osborne and Gaebler do not provide an adequate road map and do not spell out the managerial skills necessary to produce this change. In *Making Government Work,* we reach beyond the desired outcome to show the path that must be taken by focusing on executives—the people who are going to carry out these strategies to improve government. Entrepreneurial government does not spring forth on its own. It would be nice if the world worked that way, but it doesn't.

Ours is a more realistic view of the difficulty of getting things done in government in general and of innovation in particular. Bureaucracies fight back. For every control mechanism, there is a countercontrol response. Innovations are produced by the constant tending and nurturing of executives. Real success in government derives from executives' attention to line decisions. Successful executives tenaciously attend to implementation—where most innovation develops—using the skills and strategies that we describe. We provide the road map that aspiring public managers need.

A Brief Overview of the Book

In Chapter One, we introduce several inspiring success stories that feature ordinary public managers engaged in highly innovative and effective activities. We advance our view that success is achievable in government but that it depends primarily on the active direction of an entrepreneurial executive. Attention to management can show us how to succeed. With a bias toward action and a willingness to take risks, bureaucratic entrepreneurs succeed by being focused, flexible, adaptive, and opportunistic. They build on existing practice, using old stuff in new ways.

In Chapter Two, we make our central argument that management matters. We describe the difficult management challenges that executives face in the public sector and what makes their role different from private sector managers: their multiple, often contradictory goals (more complex than efficiency and profit maximization), are set in an environment where executive discretion is severely constrained.

In Chapter Three, we examine a wide range of innovative public initiatives, exploring their character and sources. Chapter Four goes further to analyze the process by which innovative public programs are brought about. Eschewing the prevailing models of policy development, which stress formal analysis of a comprehensive set of options ahead of time, Chapter Four reveals that successful initiatives, from welfare reform to environmental protection, are more likely to derive from field-based learning. Successful public managers, flexible and adaptive, are shown to move quickly to test good ideas in the field and alter and adapt programs in response to informal experiential learning. Innovation does not emerge from blueprints but from an often messy process under the careful direction of a vigilant executive.

Chapter Five looks specifically at the characteristics and approaches of executives who have carried out successful and innovative programs. Rather than deriving from a charismatic leader, a genius, or a manager possessing a unique set of qualities, innovations are more often the result of ordinary executives who employ specific strategies. These bureaucratic entrepreneurs act quickly, take risks, and intentionally underestimate the obstacles that may lie in their way. Above all, they are driven by a well-defined mission.

As entrepreneurs, they are opportunistic, taking advantage of both available resources and crises. They capitalize on crisis situations, often turning what seem to be intractable situations into attractive opportunities. Crisis opens new options, removes opposition to change, and provides the freedom to experiment. Innovative executives scan the environment, seize a good idea, and build momentum for its implementation. Unlike most cautious public sector executives, they have a bias toward action. And they act quickly, applying a trial-and-error process known as "ready, fire, aim," their goal being to create visible and marked achievement early. This provides an enhanced public image for them and their enterprises, and the reputation for action facilitates future initiatives. These are lessons that can be learned by ordinary public managers.

One highly effective strategy for successful public managers is managing the organizational culture. Chapter Six explores this approach through a range of cases. It systematically identifies the characteristics of the approach and the reasons why managers who use it can achieve significant and lasting change.

Chapter Seven is a reflective look at the potential costs of these strategies. We explore the dilemmas of seeking to promote innovation while maintaining oversight and democratic accountability to citizens for government actions. We suggest practical ways of developing a balanced system that nurtures innovation while subject to oversight and accountability.

Chapter Eight identifies the two central roles that executives and managers need to play in order to ensure both innovation and accountability. Program executives take ownership of a policy or management idea. Through their management and energy, they develop a program and get it implemented. But chief executives are also necessary to maintain a broader set of interests and responsibilities. They provide stewardship and oversight for the overall enterprise. Because we seek both innovation and accountability, these two different management roles are needed to create a balanced system.

In Chapter Nine, we use the lessons of success revealed in the earlier chapters to instruct practitioners in how to improve their performance. Further, we draw implications for the training of students of public management. By summarizing the common practices of successful executives and managers and providing a guide for applying them,

PREFACE

Chapter Nine provides the road map for anyone aspiring to make public organizations innovative.

Our Conclusion offers a caution and a reminder. Although improving public performance and achieving effective public activity are worthy and important objectives, public managers must not neglect a more fundamental imperative—ends. Making the trains run on time is important; seeing to it that they run in the right direction is even more important. Public managment is fundamentally a political endeavor; it is concerned with ends as well as means, questions of values and virtue as well as of power and action. Management is value-driven rather than value-free. Hence, it is a moral activity. Getting things done is not the same thing as choosing the right things to do. With all the attention currently devoted to improving government performance, we wish to conclude with a reminder that no more important imperative exists for public servants than ensuring that the direction of their efforts is moral and just.

In addressing the needs of beleaguered public managers, the lessons of this book suggest that pursuing an ambitious public agenda does not depend on rare managerial talent. Rather, it depends on specific strategies and approaches that we can identify. Managers can be taught to be bureaucratic entrepreneurs. This book is a user's guide for all who seek to make government work.

March 1994

Martin A. Levin
Brookline, Massachusetts

Mary Bryna Sanger
New York, New York

PREFACE

Note

1. David Osborne and Ted Gaebler, *Reinventing Government: How the Entrepreneurial Spirit Is Transforming the Public Sector* (Reading, Mass.: Addison-Wesley, 1992).

*For Gordon Chase,
Jeff Pressman, and
Aaron Wildavsky*

Acknowledgments

These acknowledgments are not mere ritual. The myth of the lone scholar is just that—a myth. As Plato knew, "The older I grew, the more I realized how difficult it is to manage a city's affairs rightly. For I saw that it was impossible to do anything without friends." Research and writing, like most pursuits, are done best in community.

We have been very fortunate to be members of many fine communities in our research. We have had help and support from our respective institutions, from wise and generous colleagues, and from a community of practitioners and academics who are engaged in a critical collaboration to improve the quality of public management.

The Gordon Public Policy Center at Brandeis University and the generous support it receives from the Gordon Foundation provided an ideal home for our research. The Gordon Center has been for us, as it has for so many others, a community of scholars and practitioners, with shared interests and diverse experiences, who interact and provide stimulating audiences for each other's work. Their generous feedback and suggestions on many drafts created a continuing dialogue on policy and management issues central to our work. First among this band of colleagues has been Marc Landy, whose always wise and perceptive advice helped us at critical stages. We had the fine research support and administrative assistance of the Center's energetic staff: Vanessa Ferber, Brian Herman, Jennifer Kang, Megan King, Lu Ouyang, J. D. Siegel, Amir Weiss, Jonathan White, Tammy Whyman, Amy York, and Gongli Xu. We are grateful for outstanding research assistance on Chapters Two through Six from Stephen Rockwell, David Cromley, Allen Kamer, and Richard Davies.

The Graduate School at the New School for Social Research provided strong administrative support for the project throughout the research and writing and, through a funded sabbatical, supported our collaboration at Brandeis. Dean Jack Krauskopf provided continuous encouragement for the project. The innovative activities of the graduate school, which provides active involvement in the life and problems of public institutions, has been a wonderful laboratory for testing our insights and raising additional hypotheses.

Beyond the walls of our respective institutions is a community of scholars and practitioners who have been essential in developing an intellectual environment that stimulated our thinking and subjected our work to productive criticism. Bob Behn's management panels at the annual Association for Public Policy Analysis and Management (APPAM) Research Conferences and the conferences sponsored by the Ford Foundation on Innovations were two such special arenas. Bob and Alan Altshuler (co-organizers of these conferences) have contributed much to our field through their writing and their academic entrepreneurial skills.

Aaron Wildavsky, an early supporter of our decision to look at successes, encouraged us throughout the process and reviewed the entire manuscript, offering many wise suggestions. Indeed, his life's work was a continual inspiration to us. His ideas and personal and intellectual generosity were of enormous help.

Martin Shapiro expanded our reach and our appreciation of subtle issues raised by our argument, and made many suggestions that made our arguments better, clearer, and more accessible to a wider audience. His emphatic intuition about how different actors think and behave is uncanny.

Thomas Glynn and Ellen Schall, two inspirational public managers, both served as exemplary cases of success and of highly reflective practitioners who helped us to understand the value of using academic research for highly applied objectives. Both are practitioners who are equally at home and adept in the world of ideas and the world of action. For over twenty years, Tom's friendship and professional example have served as a beacon to those discouraged by the declining esteem in which public service has been held. He stayed the course. His clear and unwavering dedication to improving public management taught us a lot and his help and support have been invaluable.

Lee Freidman provided us with important substantive advice on an early draft of our research findings as editor of the *Journal of Policy Analysis and Management*.

ACKNOWLEDGMENTS

Many friends helped us at various stages of research and writing. Art Klebanoff provided incalculable assistance on multiple issues related to publication. Our many friends and colleagues at the University of California's Graduate School of Public Policy in Berkeley provided lively formal and informal settings for our work during many visits there. The school's dean, Gene Smolensky, and his able staff provided a congenial and supportive environment for writing and thinking. Alan Altshuler, Mark Zegans, and Meryl Libbey of the John F. Kennedy School of Government generously provided us with all the available documents on the finalists and winners of the Innovations in State and Local Governments Award. Gene Bardach, Mike O'Hare, and Bob Behn have been good friends and colleagues. Their own work helped and inspired us significantly. Joe Quinn, Sid Milkis, Jim Gomes, and Shep Melnick were terrific colleagues at the Gordon Center.

As we thank Gordon Center colleagues, we want to emphasize our appreciation to our oldest friends there and its founders—the trustees of the Gordon Foundation of Chicago: John Adelsdorf, Sandy Bank, Burton Feldman, Robert Green, and David Silberberg. Their faith in this project, as well as the other endeavors of the Gordon Center, has been so steadfast and enduring.

We are grateful to all the executives who talked to us either directly or through their work and lives. Their energy and exceptional commitment inspired us. They were the real source of our education and the lessons of our research findings, and are the real heroes of the public sector.

ACKNOWLEDGMENTS

The Citizens Budget Commission provided us with a congenial home in New York during a sabbatical. Cindy Green, Chuck Brecher, and Ray Horton shared their insights on state and local management. Other colleagues, Norman Fainstein and David Howell in particular, were constantly available to talk or simply to try out our ideas on—always to useful ends.

Finally, we appreciate the exceptionally intelligent and well-managed editorial process provided by Jossey-Bass's consummate professionals. They not only improved the product greatly but also graciously smoothed the procedure. Alan Shrader is an academic's dream: realistic, patient, and substantively perceptive at every step along the way. Frank Welsch, Susan Williams, Noelle Graney, and Danny Gromfin added to the quality of our work as well.

Working on a collaborative project where the authors have management responsibilities in addition to their academic work means working nights and weekends, long phone conversations, and travel. All these posed burdens on our families. But, our spouses, Marilyn and Harry, were exceptionally supportive. Becca and Jesse, and Margo and Meredith, our respective daughters, as always were warm sources of comfort and joy. For all of their support, help, and indulgence we are very thankful.

While many have helped us, we take full responsibility for all remaining errors or omissions.

This book is dedicated to three of our young but late friends: Gordon Chase, Jeff Pressman, and Aaron Wildavsky. They were great scholars and great managers who

ACKNOWLEDGMENTS

meant a lot to us. We miss their wisdom and their friendship. But their words and deeds stay with us. As Aaron Wildavsky once said, "Moses was a leader who taught his people to do without him by learning how to lead themselves. This is the highest stage of leadership."

—M.A.L.
—M.B.S.

The Authors

MARTIN A. LEVIN is founding director of the Gordon Public Policy Center, a multiuniversity and interdisciplinary research center located at Brandeis University. Founded in 1987, the center's mission is to analyze domestic policy to improve the implementation of public programs through research and direct practical service to government. The center is the research home of social scientists from Brandeis, MIT, Boston College, Boston University, Harvard, and Wellesley College.

Levin is also professor of political science at Brandeis University, specializing in policy implementation, criminal justice, and the presidency. He served as chairman of the Urban Studies Program at Brandeis from 1976 to 1984. He has taught at the University of California's Berkeley and Irvine campuses as well.

In 1991, Levin was elected president of the Association for Public Policy Analysis and Management (APPAM), the leading national association of academic and government policy analysts and managers. Earlier he had served on APPAM's executive committee, as chairman of its New Roles Committee, and as its vice president.

Levin is author of *The Political Hand: Policy Im-*

THE AUTHORS

plementation and Youth Employment Programs (1985), which was described as "breaking new ground by discovering programs that actually work and finding out what makes them work." His earlier book, *Urban Politics and the Criminal Courts* (1977) has been called "the best piece of work" on trial judges and one that "must be read by any serious policy analyst concerned with the criminal courts." Levin is coeditor of *The New Politics of Public Policymaking* (1994). He has also contributed numerous book chapters and journal articles.

Levin is a Phi Beta Kappa graduate of Cornell University and holds a doctorate from Harvard University. He is married, has two daughters, and lives in Brookline, Massachusetts.

MARY BRYNA SANGER is associate dean for academic affairs and professor of urban policy analysis and management at the Graduate School of Management and Urban Policy, New School for Social Research, New York City.

A former chair of the Master's Program in Urban Policy Analysis, Sanger's research interests are broadly based in both public policy and management. She works in the area of social welfare policy and policy implementation and management.

Having served on the editorial boards of both the *Journal of Policy Analysis and Management* and the *Policy Studies Journal,* Sanger currently sits on the Policy Council of the Association for Public Policy Analysis and Management, chairing its Nomination Committee and serving on its Committee on Governance, Organization, and Membership.

THE AUTHORS

She is author of *Welfare of the Poor* (1979), *Designing Social Protection Systems* (forthcoming, with L. Hausman), and numerous journal articles and book chapters. She is currently working on a new project with Martin Levin which explores the role executive management plays in the success of public health initiatives.

Sanger is an honors graduate of Vassar College and holds a doctorate from Brandeis University. She is married, has two daughters, and lives in New York City.

MAKING
GOVERNMENT
WORK

1

Government Can Work
Learning from Successful Executives

In recent years, politicians have found it increasingly profitable to "bash government." They join ordinary citizens in describing government as the problem rather than the solution. Nevertheless, evidence is growing that government can make things work. Indeed, broad and diverse innovations have emerged at all levels.

Long on problems and short on solutions, the 1980s nevertheless witnessed an impressive range of creative responses to public need: employment and training for welfare mothers, school-based health and social services for at-risk high school kids, tax amnesty for revenue generation, and comprehensive health care for the children of the uninsured working poor. Necessity really is the mother of invention!

How were these achievements accomplished, even during a period of marked cynicism? This book explains how public sector innovation can succeed and the ways in which even ordinary public managers can improve public performance.

Management Matters

Success in the public sector depends on skillful executives: management matters, and, as this book reveals, executives are key to innovation. New concepts and policy debates monopolize the headlines. But new ideas—even those developed through formal analysis—are not sufficient in themselves. Management makes the difference between success and failure.[1]

Attention to management is essential. Successful bureaucratic entrepreneurs use an activist style to build on existing practice, using old stuff in new ways. They intentionally underestimate the roadblocks thrown up by bureaucracy and politics.

Successful innovation depends on bureaucratic entrepreneurs who grab a good idea and build momentum for its implementation. Skilled executives evaluate the operational success of their initiatives in the field. Relying on an iterative process to reveal what works and what does not, they use the lessons from their field experience to correct, adapt, and refine their original programs. This is the messy and imperfect process, repeated over and over, that produces successful program development and effective management.

By contrast, the public policy schools have long taught aspiring public managers to use policy analysis and program planning ahead of time to reveal the optimal choices.

But our study of the most successful operating programs teaches very different lessons. Our lessons, more realistic and more effective, suggest that government efficacy can be greatly enhanced by teaching aspiring public managers to manage through experiential learning rather than simply through prediction. Policy decisions are the essential first steps, but they depend on management to be realized. Successful government performance depends far more on confronting the challenges at this management stage.

Successful public outcomes are not solely the domain of charismatic leaders. Nor are they mainly the result of formal policy analysis. There is a real difference between choosing the right thing to do and getting things done. Even wise policy choices made with the benefit of sophisticated policy analyses are not self-effectuating. Management matters most. Our message is that the skills and approaches necessary to launch successful public initiatives can be taught and learned. Some innovators may be born, but others can be trained.

How Innovative Executives Get Things Done

This chapter highlights how management matters and how innovative executives get things done. The innovative government solutions described throughout this book illuminate some simple but important themes. They point to the central role that management plays in getting things done. The current generation of practitioners and students of public management, frustrated by the difficulty of accomplishing much in government, should find comfort in these success stories. Inspirational and stimulating, they provide incentives to continue the good fight.

Frustration was especially high during the Reagan-Bush era. But these administrations' message that "government is the problem, not the solution" has deep roots. It started with George Wallace's national candidacies and went on through Jimmy Carter's critique of Washington and government, which continued even after he became president. This critical view of government also has academic origins. Since the early years of Lyndon Johnson's Great Society, many scholars—and not only neoconservatives—have suggested that "nothing works" in the public sector, that nothing can get done in government. Though academics and politicians continue to debate the value and competence of government intervention, our research provides rich and inspirational examples that government can indeed work.

Using Old Stuff in New Ways

Bureaucratic entrepreneurs are the key to program and policy success. Their results are often exceptional, but many times their initial idea is just a decision to combine familiar bits and pieces—to use old stuff in new ways. Program and policy elements that fuel effective initiatives are rarely original. Innovators make them so. Old stuff becomes new in a different context, often yielding what we call "prosaic profundities"—such as the effort to deliver social services to youths in a juvenile justice detention center.

For Ellen Schall, Commissioner of Juvenile Justice in New York City, the innovation centered on just such a combining of familiar bits and pieces—a simple change in the bureaucratic schedule. Her department's detention center was a tension-filled warehouse for kids awaiting trial when Schall decided to make use of that unproductive time. Instead of waiting weeks or months for the recommendations of the juvenile judge, she started a process to evaluate each child's needs and provide educational and rehabilitative services immediately after the kids were arrested. The impressive results won the program a prestigious Innovations in State and Local Government award from the Ford Foundation and Harvard University's John F. Kennedy School of Government.

Creating New Missions

Often the bureaucratic entrepreneur's first step is to create or redefine a new mission for the agency. In creating the now nationally renowned Employment and Training (ET) Choices program, Massachusetts Welfare Commissioner Charles Atkins and Deputy Commissioner Thomas P. Glynn assembled old stuff in new ways to redefine their department's mission: from providing clients with correct and timely welfare checks to developing routes out of poverty. They merged training and employment with support services, including child care and transportation, to build a sequence of steps for clients to invest in their own futures. ET Choices was highly successful. It attracted large numbers of participants and led to a large number of job placements at good wages.[2]

A Bias Toward Action: Ready, Fire, Aim

These bureaucratic entrepreneurs have a bias toward action. Executives in the public sector are typically cautious, constrained by political factors, legislatures, and more restrictive budgets than in the private sector. Further, broader oversight and accountability mechanisms in the public sector discourage risk taking. But these public sector managers' bias toward action helped establish their agency's credibility with the public. Emphasizing rapid and visible success and concrete and measurable results, these managers preempted the formal prior analysis of policy options advocated by the public policy schools.

When Ira Jackson became head of the Massachusetts Department of Revenue (DOR) in 1983, the agency was so demoralized by scandals that it was barely functioning. Error correction and adaptation were essential to his evolutionary, iterative process of innovation. Jackson focused on adjusting and trying to make up for the department's past errors—first by simply making it an honest and efficient agency. But then he moved fast and tried to compensate for a historical error of too little tax enforcement by pursuing a "ready, fire, aim" approach.[3] Without much pause or prior analysis, he picked up one of the most obvious and familiar things lying around for a revenue department—enforcement of tax collection—and initiated a series of decisive actions. His dramatic enforcement activities—closing popular restaurants and seizing the yachts of wealthy tax evaders—were pursued iteratively, with a lot of learning by doing. There was more firing than aiming.

As he increased enforcement, little time was taken out for formal policy analysis. As he continued firing, he began to take better aim and learned about his targets and the woods surrounding them. Then he moved forward, sometimes sideways, and developed newer policies such as aggressive enforcement and criminal prosecution.[4]

Soon he had developed new and bigger targets and an even more aggressive vehicle—a tax amnesty plan. Jackson's many innovations at the DOR garnered public support for an agency that seldom gets it in any jurisdiction, new powers to enforce revenue collection, and over $60 million in back taxes through the tax amnesty program. The program brought national attention to the governor and became a model for other states.

The Entrepreneur as Opportunist

Opportunity is a great engine of innovation. Crises present problems but also great opportunities. They furnish the fuel for change and often silence natural opponents and provide political and organizational support for innovation.

Gordon Chase, head of New York's Health Services Administration (HSA) under Mayor Lindsay, opportunistically turned crises besetting the city and the HSA to his advantage. He used media and public outcry to allow the HSA to initiate pioneering public health programs that were uniformly successful and often became national models. Public outcry over the heroin epidemic softened resistance to his bold and highly controversial methadone maintenance program. Large and difficult to implement, it was the first in the nation.

Government Can Make Things Work: Learning from Success

Recent years have witnessed tremendous public disillusionment with the public sector. The common perception is that it can't get anything done and that policy and management failures are inevitable. In fact, routine public policy treatments have not proved adequate to the problems that society faces. Indeed, it is commonly the failure of routine responses of other institutions, such as the market and the family, that creates the public sector's work. So now practitioners and students must look for innovative solutions. But increasingly they are frustrated by bureaucratic obstacles.

We argue that there are in fact successful innovations in the public sector: government *can* make things work. But too few people know about these successes, and too little has been learned from them. These innovations are largely the result of executive skills: management matters because that's where policy often fails. Executive skills are essential to policy success. What we often observe in government is not the scarcity of executive talent, though this is the conventional view today. Rather, we find that executive talent is often suppressed and discouraged by the deadening demands of bureaucratic routines and regulations and by political disincentives for risk taking.

Our inspirational stories of successful innovative public programs demonstrate the importance of executive skills. Our findings are derived from more than thirty successful public programs and agencies at all three levels of government. From them we have developed lessons that can be taught and learned. Using a model broader than leadership, we reveal the critical role of an executive in an environment that encourages and supports initiative, risk taking, and innovative behavior. Because we focus on broad and generic executive skills, rather than unique and idiosyncratic qualities of leadership, our lessons are transferable.

These lessons from success challenge the public policy schools' prevailing models of teaching and action. These schools arm the would-be public manager with policy analysis and statistics. But they would be better off promoting the study of the approaches of bureaucratic entrepreneurs. Just as *In Search of Excellence* illuminated important lessons by describing success stories at America's best-run companies, we seek to inspire and enlighten by identifying a wide range of highly successful public sector innovations and the executive practices that made them possible.[5] In short, we provide an operational guide that outlines the conditions under which these entrepreneurs work, how they develop and implement their initiatives, and why they succeed.

Perceptions of Management and Policy Failure

In the introduction to his hopeful book on American government, Steven Kelman documents the declining esteem with which public officials are held by citing a wide range of surveys.[6] Public officials and institutions, he demonstrates, continue to decline in the esteem and trust with which they are held by citizens and even by academics studying them. Public service, once a noble and respected calling, is increasingly viewed with skepticism and cynicism—the inevitable casualty of perceived government failure.

Policy Failure: Is Executive Talent Really Scarce?

Since the mid 1960s, one of the common explanations for policy failure has been a scarcity of executive talent. James Q. Wilson's classic, "The Bureaucracy Problem," forcefully made this argument: " 'Talent Is Scarcer than Money' should be the motto of the Budget Bureau. . . . The supply of able, experienced executives is not increasing nearly as fast as the number of problems being addressed by public policy."[7]

This lack of talent, they argue, is a result of the difficulty of attracting the best people into public service. From an individual's point of view, the opportunity costs in terms of income and reputation of government service are very high, given private market alternatives. Public sector executives' constrained authority to act is another poor incentive to attract talent. Even when talented individuals are recruited, these conditions provide weak encouragement to perform. A recent study of government service outlined the difficulty of attracting high-quality managers to government.[8]

The Deadening Demands of Bureaucratic Routines

Talent is always in short supply. In government today, however, the scarcity of executive talent is rarely the central problem. Indeed, as we will describe in detail, we found many innovative executives at all levels of government. These bureaucratic entrepreneurs practice a wide range of executive skills. Aggressive and risk-taking, they are continually adapting to the changing environment to meet the challenges posed by increasing public demands.

Rather the problem is that executive talent is often suppressed and discouraged in the public sector. There are analytical requirements in the public sector. Public agencies are urged to examine policy proposals in terms of alternatives. Analysis is undertaken to evaluate the relative trade-off among alternative options for achieving desired goals at least cost. The analytical process may provide important insights for improving the relative payoffs from any given investment. But it also can easily lead to the "paralysis of analysis." Projecting future impacts is time-consuming because it requires data collection and modeling to try to anticipate all the direct and indirect effects of various options. Even when it is systematically done, rarely are the data or the analyst's ability to anticipate all relevant fields conditions good enough to project with high accuracy.

Similarly, bureaucratic routines, with their formal rules and procedures, developed to ensure accountability, also suppress the legitimate exercise of executive initiative. Although these procedures and the legislative and budgetary oversight that gives rise to them were appropriately developed to maintain democratic accountability over executives, they often have perverse effects. Nevertheless, the absence of adequate accountability mechanisms compromises democratic values and can easily result in waste and fraud. Corruption and waste of public resources are simply the flip side of insufficient oversight.

The public sector, however, is not alone in facing the dilemma of innovation versus accountability. Even private sector companies suffer from the discouraging effects of oversight on innovation. Chapter Two analyzes the development of personal computers at Xerox and IBM. Xerox created the world's first commercial PC long before its competitors. But the company failed to bring its innovation to market because executives were unable to moderate their crippling oversight mechanisms or to work around them. By contrast, though IBM entered the PC market much later than its competitors, such as Apple, it was able to do so rapidly and to dominate the market in the 1980s. This was the direct result of its executives' abilities to work around the company's famed oversight and testing mechanisms. (But in the late 1980s and 1990s, IBM's top executives paid a heavy price for ignoring the lessons of their hugely successful IBM PC end run: these lessons were to introduce and protect new ideas by using decentralized units within this mammoth and bureaucratically centralized corporation; to avoid being dominated by an emphasis on mainframes and hardware, especially when the industry is moving towards mini and microcomputers and software; and to prevent allowing new ideas from being delayed and diverted by the company's thorough but slow testing procedures. During this later period, IBM's reversion to an emphasis on mainframes, slow testing and oversight, and corporate centralization probably contributed greatly to its market share declining in every facet of the business, its large financial losses, and the necessity of dismissing many employees. By contrast, competitors such as Microsoft, Asian computer manufacturers, and the so-called "IBM clones" here and abroad, had the opposite experiences as they pursued the very corporate strategies that IBM had used to develop its PC in the early 1980s.)

The Scarcity of Political Incentives for Executives

Reinforcing the discouraging effect of bureaucratic demands on public executives is the absence of sufficient political incentives for executives to be aggressive and creative about policy implementation. Most political incentives run in the wrong direction, and the few positive incentives are weak. The electoral imperative is the strongest disincentive. In any organization in which officials are elected, the first priority is to ensure reelection. Thus, a primary motivator of elected public officials and their staffs is to take actions that will support a reelection bid. This severely constrains their choices, particularly in light of the decline of political parties—the traditional vehicles upon which they ran.

The electoral imperative creates a short-run orientation and pressure for fast action. The constraint becomes the next election, typically in less than four years (less than two years for congressional representatives and many state legislators). All this precludes working on implementation or even developing an interest in it. Instead, to capture public attention, leaders opt for the dramatic—not necessarily a dramatic achievement; a dramatic disclosure or proposal might provide the appropriate political impact. In contrast, implementation of an existing proposal, even if potentially effective, rarely is dramatic or exciting and often it is downright dull. Perhaps most fatal is the indifference of the media to matters of management. Thus, public officials who are so dependent on the media for shaping their images, are seldom rewarded for this kind of investment of time. The media also make their reputations on seizing the novel idea or dramatic presentation. Boat rockers are even discouraged in the private sector, as we will show in Chapter Two in the Xerox and IBM cases. This attitude thwarted innovation at the former but not at the latter.

Creative Subversion: The Dilemmas of Innovation and Accountability

We found that creative subversion is a common approach used by innovative executives facing bureaucratic demands. Bureaucratic entrepreneurs have a bias toward action. Confronted by serious social problems and often saddled with vague and diffuse legislative mandates, they move rapidly to create or redefine new and personal missions for their agencies. They emphasize rapid and visible outputs rather than deliberate prior analysis of options. They pick up familiar approaches from other settings and implement them in a "ready, fire, aim" manner. Sometimes they even move forward before obtaining full budgetary authorization.[9]

All this often produces innovative programs. These bureaucratic entrepreneurs avoid the paralysis of analysis. But there is a real difference between getting things done and choosing the right things to do. Their entrepreneurial strategies can have important costs. This points to the dilemmas of accountability and innovation. The regulations they try to move around tend to yield accountability but discourage innovation. Risk taking, ready-fire-aim strategies can produce innovation. But they may also leave their agencies and their executives open to the risk of poor policy choices and ill-considered programs.

These are the dilemmas posed by over- and underregulation: overregulation creates a drag on action and the free exercise of executive talent; underregulation can lead to waste, fraud, or the subversion of legitimate organizational goals. In Chapter Two, we will analyze cases that illustrate these dilemmas.

Beyond Leadership: An Environment that Balances Innovation and Accountability

Innovation is often dependent on creative subversion of bureaucratic constraints, but inadequate oversight poses risks for abuse. A balance between innovation and accountability must be maintained. Chapters Seven and Eight describe the means for developing innovation while preserving democratic values. We suggest that two central management roles are necessary to ensure this balance: the program executive and the chief executive. The program executive is vital to create a program and get it implemented. This person cannot be too self-questioning about the program, lest it lead to inaction. But the chief executive is also necessary to undertake analysis and to determine whether a program should be implemented at all. Both management approaches are needed in any administration. We suggest a balanced *system* that encompasses both.

It should be clear that this book is about more than just leadership. We describe in Chapter Nine a system and an environment. The development of the kind of environment that makes innovation possible is even more important than leadership—one that encourages innovation by enabling talented executives to exercise their creative abilities. It is an environment that nurtures innovation while providing the guidance of oversight and accountability. The incentive structure in public sector organizations must be changed. Too often it discourages executives' innovative behavior in the name of necessary oversight. Yet a balanced system must be maintained. So we also seek to develop an environment that ensures that democratic accountability and oversight are maintained while innovation is being pursued.

In Chapter Nine we also examine the implications of our findings for the training of future public managers. We caution against training or experience that is too closely tied to a particular policy area or academic discipline. Innovation thrives on having a broad inventory of approaches and experiences to apply in different settings and contexts. Narrow technical or policy training runs the risk of reducing environments from which useful inspiration can be sought. The experiences of Jackson, Schall, Chase, and Ruckelshaus show the power of being an outsider to their agency's policy area. It helped give them the license and freedom to create new visions for their agencies.

Innovations are often the products of outsiders to a

field. There are many cases of this in science. Major breakthroughs in molecular biology came from the insights of physicists and chemists. Kidney dialysis was a technique first scoffed at by kidney specialists and then developed by a cardiologist. Most of the scientists and doctors who played key roles in conquering TB were in the field of neither TB nor even infectious diseases. Chapter Three provides further elaboration of these examples from the sciences.

Innovation often depends on fundamental change in institutional values. But change can be threatening in organizations because it involves risks for members at every level. Most organizations are imbued with values in which its members can become highly invested because of the psychic rewards and the security that they provide. These values are part of the organizational culture, which establishes the norms of behavior that are expected and the rewards that conformity can confer.

An organizational culture can be valuable in supporting a manager's mission. But as we argue in Chapter Six, efforts to change an organization's mission often encounter strong resistance from prevailing cultures. Launching new enterprises can be significantly strengthened by a concurrent development of a culture that supports the new mission. Managing the organizational culture can therefore be a critical tool for change for a bureaucratic entrepreneur. Indeed, developing an environment that provides incentives for managerial discretion and innovation while holding managers firmly accountable for achieving well-defined organizational goals is an important prerequisite for creating a balanced system.

Bureaucratic Entrepreneurs

Creating an environment that promotes and rewards innovation and building a supportive organizational culture are important in opening up the options and reinforcing the initiative of the innovator. But real initiative derives from focused management and executive action. Here we highlight the success stories of a few of the highly successful managers in our sample. The message is simple: success is not hard to find; it is achievable. All our managers depended on an innovative policy or management idea. But each innovation represented the use of a known intervention in a new way or in a new setting. In none of the cases did any initiative spring full blown as if from blueprints. Indeed, all were shaped through learning about what works in the implementation process.

Perhaps most important, the success of each depended on the skillful shepherding of an entrepreneurial manager— a bureaucratic entrepreneur. First, each developed a new mission for the enterprise. Each took risks and had an opportunistic bias toward action. Though facing substantial bureaucratic and political obstacles, each consciously underestimated them.

Steven Swanger, Director of Tenant Services, Cambridge Public Housing Authority

Steven Swanger was hired by the housing authority in Cambridge, Massachusetts, to build and direct a social service function that had suffered from a historic lack of goals, accountability, and professionalism. Evidence of the obstacles he faced could be inferred from the fact that he was the seventh director in four years! Nevertheless, he made two early and important decisions: first, to redefine the role of social services in a housing organization, and second, to concentrate his efforts on teens. He shaped an after-school unemployment prevention program for low-income teens called the Work Force.

After trying several programmatic efforts, Swanger succeeded in enrolling large numbers of teens in a counseling program that uses vocational training as a vehicle to build self-esteem. Following a progressive sequence (of twelve weeks each) of highly structured, paid classroom and try-out employment experiences, the Work Force starts with thirteen-year-olds to teach employment-related norms, values, and skills. Over time, youths choose placements where they learn to use newly acquired skills in actual job settings. Integrating the program with school performance, school liaisons monitor school attendance and grades and provide teens with access to relevant educational services as they are needed.

Especially innovative were the location of the program on-site in the housing project where the youngsters live and its systematic linkage and involvement with schools, families, and the worksite. This presence in the living environment provides accessibility and credibility in the community.

Swanger has succeeded in attracting large numbers of youths and participating employers. Completion rates are high, and self-esteem among participants has improved. Providers view the program as a valued resource. All this was achieved without historic precedent within the authority and despite a relatively unsympathetic attitude toward preventive youth programs on the part of both traditional housing administrators and state funders. Furthermore, employers were recruited for what is generally viewed as an undesirable population, and cooperation and support were wrested from a traditionally unresponsive urban school system.

Barbara Levin, Medical Director,
Monroe County Maternity Center

As a young rural public health officer in Tennessee, Dr. Barbara Levin recognized the problems associated with a shortage of physicians in the Appalachian foothills of the eastern part of the state. Meeting the needs of a low-income population in a medically underserved county posed special challenges for her. Dr. Levin developed a highly innovative response. The Monroe County Maternity Center, Inc., is a freestanding birth center that relies on certified nurse-midwives to provide prenatal care and full obstetrical services to women with normal deliveries. It is the first fully public birthing center in the nation that is not attached to a major hospital. Compensating for the physician shortage, certified nurse-midwives rather than physicians form the core of the staff and use a family-oriented model of childbirth and delivery rather than a technology-based medical model. Care is comprehensive and has extended to general gynecological care.

A crisis generated the program idea. Five of the seven available family practitioners in Monroe County had stopped providing obstetrical care. The only alternative was for women to travel far away to Knoxville hospitals. The risk was that low-income women would forgo necessary prenatal visits, using the hospitals in Knoxville only for delivery. These incentives imposed significant health risks for women and babies. Further, even if rural women were willing to travel to distant urban hospitals, high-tech hospital care is often ill suited to the provision of comprehensive primary care to expectant or recently delivered mothers and is costly and unnecessary for the large majority of women with normal deliveries.

The center's initial objective was to serve indigent women whose care was financed by Medicaid. It has evolved into a women's community resource and now boasts that 45 percent of its users have third-party insurance—a population with alternative options. It has clearly met the market test. Indeed, the center has become an important community symbol and has caught the imagination of various constituencies, including state health administrators and women in the community. Further, the health outcomes at the center have been excellent by standard measures.

Dr. Levin generated the idea—an adaptation of an existing model—to solve a critical problem. The public health service that she developed, marketed, and directs provides quality care to a wide public at low cost. In a rural setting rife with political, cultural, and philosophical obstacles, she succeeded in generating gubernatorial support as well as enlisting the medical establishment even though she eschewed a traditional medical model. She succeeded in establishing a symbol of women's empowerment in a community unsympathetic to women's rights. Indeed, Dr. Levin sold an innovative model of service delivery that relied on a relatively unconventional set of social values.

Ed Tetelman, Director,
Office of Legal and Regulatory Affairs,
New Jersey Department of Human Services:
School-Based Youth Services Program

A former advocate from a legal services background, Ed Tetelman was brought to the New Jersey Department of Human Services by its commissioner, Drew Altman. Developing a mission consistent with the department's commitment to empower families to meet their full potential, Tetelman developed a program to use schoolkids to reach families. Tetelman recognized that outcomes for youths—school attendance, graduation, employment preparation, advanced education, and physical and mental health (including drug use)—depend on the integration of numerous services. The School-Based Youth Services (SBYS) program provided access to comprehensive services at or near a secondary school. Undertaking a top-down program development under the governor's auspices, Tetelman adapted and expanded a school-based health clinic model to package a comprehensive set of health and social services to support the social, health, and educational needs of high school students. Using a "kid-centered orientation," Tetelman succeeded in marketing his program statewide and in developing a productive and cooperative relationship among historic adversaries—the departments of health, labor, and education.

Each site around the state offers a core of services. Though not new, the services were often inaccessible to teenagers, and school personnel were not always well informed about services to which students could be referred. School-based "one-stop" services provide easy access, integration, and a comprehensive range of core services. Because community resources and needs vary around the state, local districts were required to design their own programs and to demonstrate through signed agreements that local school districts supported the application.

The program is already helping one of every three teens in the schools served by the program. It provides a supportive, nonthreatening, fully accessible environment with caring adults while building productive relationships between otherwise noncooperating institutions. As a result, services are comprehensive, eligibility is universal, and the ability to package services for the needs of individual youths is maximized.

Tetelman faced significant obstacles due to recalcitrant and parochial interests at some state agencies. Further, because participation was to be generated by local applications, which depended on coordinating services locally, skilled and effective marketing was necessary to sell local districts on the benefits of participation. Success of the high school–based programs has subsequently generated expansion into middle schools.

These cases and the dozens of others described in the chapters that follow point up the rich possibilities for creative and effective public enterprises. They inspire and encourage, and they also teach critical lessons for anyone charged with preparing the managers of the future and for all who aspire to improve public performance. It is principally toward these goals that our research and findings are directed.

The Design of Our Study: The Cases

The model we will develop in the chapters that follow is based on an analysis of a diverse group of more than thirty highly successful public programs and agencies since the 1970s. All are cases considered highly innovative by academics and policy and management elites.

One group of cases was selected from among the winners and finalists of the prestigious Innovations in State and Local Government award funded by the Ford Foundation and administered by Harvard University's John F. Kennedy School of Government. Extensive and rigorous evaluation accompany the selection process, including multiple assessments by diverse evaluators.[10] We had access to both applications and the evaluators' site visit reports. We have also been able to conduct intensive follow-up interviews with many winners.

Other cases, well known in the public management literature, are frequently used as models for teaching in the field. Having been subjected to intense scrutiny in academic and policy circles, they have stood the test of time and rigorous analysis. Several contrasting cases are used as well. In Chapter Seven, for example, where we explore the costs and risks of innovation in a democratic society, we introduce several cases of well-known public failure. These cases (and others) were selected for their illustrative and comparative value.

We present an unusually broad range of cases, across two decades and three levels of government, in a wide range of functional areas, including the application of new technologies, capital improvements, social services, criminal justice, health care, revenue collection, and environmental policy.

The Approach

Our objective in selecting cases for analysis was to focus exclusively on successes. We might have also studied failed attempts, examples of which abound in the literature and in daily experience. We sought instead to seek insights into *what works*. First, we wanted to see whether significant examples of successful public enterprises could be amassed. Then we sought to draw both inspiration and useful lessons from them. Research on the impediments to success is often highly illuminating. The rich literature on implementation has provided an important body of knowledge for theory and practice.[11] But these studies tell us primarily what *not* to do. Our research was motivated more by the desire to learn what to do. From this broad range of successful government enterprises we sought to build an impressionistic model of the characteristics of innovative policies and the conditions under which they could be generated.

Meeting the Challenge: Answering the Critics of Government Performance

Recent calls for rethinking the design and functioning of government institutions have been greeted with considerable enthusiasm.[12] Capturing the imagination of both popular and academic audiences, these calls for change have lauded the values of the market for reinvigorating public enterprise. They berate public bureaucracies: They no longer meet the changing needs of citizens; they are slow, wasteful, and unresponsive; they are hamstrung by constraints that make them ill suited to quick change, choice, quality, and efficiency. To meet citizens' needs for better and cheaper services from government, public organizations must be driven by new principles, most of which come from the private sector: competition, customer service, decentralization, mission, and prevention.

Some of these popular critiques share similar goals with our book in working for the improvement of government through innovation. David Osborne and Ted Gaebler's concept of "catalytic government" is similar to our emphasis on working with the private sector and identifying interest convergence.[13] We share an attention to circumventing the maze of government rules and regulations hindering innovation and recognize the value in many of the popularly touted characterizations of effective entrepreneurship: innovative, market-driven, close to customers.[14] What has been lacking in this literature of renewal has been a usable road map for enterprising managers to accomplish these goals.

Though Osborne and others sketch a useful portrait of a transformed public sector, they do not provide the route or suggest the managerial skills that will be necessary to produce it. This book, by contrast, reaches beyond the envisioned endpoint to explain how it can be realized by focusing on executives, the people who are going to carry out the strategies to improve government.

The problem is that these innovations do not appear on their own. Though many of the successful government innovations we have studied possess the characteristics that market enthusiasts recommend, a more fundamental insight is that they spring from effective management. The most brilliant and innovative idea is simply that—an idea. Care and concern for line decisions drives government success. Not only is the devil in the details, but the good is in the particulars. Innovation derives from attention to implementation. We show that this is where most innovation develops.

We are more realistic about the obstacles to public sector innovation. Government agencies often resist change. But executives can surmount this. To do so, they must understand, first, how these changes are brought about, by what process "entrepreneurial government" is realized, and, second, what managers do to effect change. Recognizing what success would look like is important. But understanding the means by which it can be realized, and the role and style of managers capable of implementing change, is perhaps more important.

We will spell out the strategies and tactics that executives employ. The strategic aspects of successful innovation are detailed in Chapters Three through Six. We also provide an operational guide for public officials and others aspiring to improve public performance. In Chapter Nine, we suggest ways to train executives to be receptive to these strategies and more likely to know how to use them. Students of public policy, whose task will be to devise strategies for carrying out programs and not merely to sit by, helpless to respond, have much to learn from successful executives. However, our educational institutions must alter their prevailing models to shift the focus of their interest from policy analysis to management.

Decisions not only must be made at the top but they also must be implemented along the line as well. We must get beyond point decisions to line decisions. Recommendations for reform that emphasize steering leave the rowing—the line decisions—mostly unaddressed. We emphasize the rowing, or line decisions, at the implementation stage, where it is most crucial: that is where policies fail or succeed.

Finally, entrepreneurial government is an important objective. But what are its costs? Critics of government performance follow the more conventional rebellion against oversight and accountability mechanisms as obstacles. They do not appreciate their necessity for democratic and accountable government. Entrepreneurial government imposes potential costs as it increases managerial discretion and initiative.

In Chapter Seven, we realistically address these "tragic" dilemmas between innovation and accountability and between action and oversight. Reinventing government is not the only option left. Success is achievable if we cultivate our public executive talent and arm managers with the appropriate strategies. These executives nevertheless need some oversight and accountability, but not too much—there must be a balance. Chapters Seven through Nine suggest how to avoid the extremes of overregulation and underregulation that plague American public policy.

Notes

1. For purposes of clarity, from time to time, we will employ the conventional distinction between policy choice and management. In the argument that we will develop over the next five chapters, however, we will show that such a clear distinction is misleading. Indeed, a central argument in Chapters Three, Four, and Five is that policy innovation often evolves in the implementation stage when a good idea generates a practical test in the field through implementation and that lessons learned at that stage help refine and develop the ultimate policy innovation.
2. Despite some controversy about its level of success, the most systematic evaluation supports the conclusions that ET Choices has been successful and that it introduced real innovation in work-welfare programming and management. See Demetra S. Nightingale, Douglas Wissoher, Lyn C. Burbridge, D. Lee Bawden, and Neal Jeffries, "Evaluation of the Massachusetts Employment and Training (ET) Choices Program" (Washington, D.C.: Urban Institute Press, Urban Institute report 91-1, 1991); Robert D. Behn, *Leadership Counts: Lessons for Public Managers from the Massachusetts Welfare, Training and Employment Program* (Cambridge, Mass.: Harvard University Press, 1992).
3. Managers with a bias for action often, according to Thomas Peters and Robert Waterman, *In Search of Ex-*

cellence (New York: HarperCollins, 1982), pp. 119–123, 155, take a "ready, fire, aim" approach. They do not take the time to plan and prepare for an extensive attack with a few big shots. Rather, with their rough knowledge of the terrain (often gained by wandering around), managers fire quickly in the general area of the target. Based on that shot's results, they ready the organization for the next round (by digesting the new information, modifying the sight, or getting a different gun), aim, and fire again. This produces more information and keeps repeating the process.

4. Robert D. Behn, "Ira Jackson and the Massachusetts Department of Revenue," The Duke University Policy Studies Institute, 1986.
5. Peters and Waterman, *In Search of Excellence.*
6. Steven Kelman, *Making Public Policy: A Hopeful View of American Government* (New York: Basic Books, 1987).
7. James Q. Wilson, "The Bureaucracy Problem," *Public Interest,* Winter, 1967, p. 7.
8. National Commission on Public Service (Volker Commission), *Rebuilding the Public Service: Task Force Reports* (Washington, D.C.: National Commission on Public Service, 1989). See also Frank J. Thompson, ed., *Revitalizing State and Local Public Service: Strengthening Performance, Accountability, and Citizen Confidence* (San Francisco: Jossey-Bass, 1993).
9. Our analysis in Chapter Two of the private sector cases of the IBM and Xerox PCs also shows that creative subversion is a common reaction to oversight mechanism in the private sector.

10. From hundreds of preliminary applicants, seventy-five semifinalists are selected. After additional site visits by academics and other specialists, twenty-five finalists are selected by program staff and are subjected to a blue-ribbon evaluation review. From these, the judges select ten winners.
11. For example, see Jeffrey Pressman and Aaron Wildavsky, *Implementation* (Berkeley: University of California Press, 1973); Eugene Bardach, *The Implementation Game: What Happens After a Bill Becomes Law* (Cambridge, Mass.: MIT Press, 1977); Erwin Hargrove, *The Missing Link: The Study of the Implementation of Social Policy* (Washington, D.C.: Urban Institute, 1975); Martha Derthick, *New Towns in Town: Why a Federal Program Failed* (Washington, D.C.: Brookings Institution, 1977); and Edward Banfield, *Political Influence* (New York: Free Press, 1959).
12. Note especially the media attention generated by David Osborne and Ted Gaebler, *Reinventing Government: How the Entrepreneurial Spirit Is Transforming the Public Sector* (Reading, Mass.: Addison-Wesley, 1992). Other examples include John E. Chubb and Terry M. Moe, *Politics, Markets, and America's Schools* (Washington, D.C.: Brookings Institution, 1990); E. S. Savas, *Privatizing the Public Sector* (Chatham, N.J.: Chatham House, 1982); and Jacob B. Ukeles, *Doing More with Less: Turning Management Around* (New York: American Management Association, 1982).
13. Catalytic government, according to Osborne and Gaebler, is policy-making process that defines problems and then assembles resources for other institutions

to use in addressing these problems. The government does not physically take part in the delivery of services. It depends on a third party (economic and social institutions) to deliver the services that carry out public objectives. See Osborne and Gaebler, *Reinventing Government,* 1992, pp. 25–48.
14. We differ on how much to glorify private markets. After all, in America, being a private organization doesn't ensure success. Recent cases of inefficiencies and mismanagement in dozens of key private industries demonstrate that even freedom from many of the constraints facing public organizations cannot ensure success. Even though they possess the managerial discretion and positive incentives for success, private organizations can still exhibit unproductive characteristics.

2

Management Matters
It's Where Policy Succeeds and Fails

Policy choices grab all the attention. But the less glamorous job of management matters because that is often where policy fails *and* succeeds. An initial policy choice is clearly fundamental. Imbued with substantive and symbolic meaning, policy choices define a course and carry with them commitments and goals. Policy is connected in our minds with the most elevated concerns of government: protecting the national security, providing health care for all who need it, preserving clean air and water.

Though initial policy choice is fundamental, it is just the beginning. The less glamorous job of management receives considerably less attention. Government management evokes contradictory images—bean counters with green eyeshades, or worse, incompetent or corrupt bureaucrats. Nevertheless, management often matters more than the policy choices it is designed to bring about. Indeed, outcomes define policy success. And even bold and innovative policy options—perhaps especially these—depend on successful management for their ultimate impact. Having a goal and a vehicle designed to achieve it is not the same thing as creating and sustaining the actual apparatus, both human and technical, to launch, steer, and see it through. As the savings and loan debacle and several other scandals in recent years have demonstrated, performance and ultimate success depend on the successful implementation of an initial policy choice—in short, on sound management. Successful policy requires more than a single or fundamental choice. It requires line decisions as well as point decisions. Good initial point decisions are necessary for successful outcomes, but they are not sufficient. They depend on line decisions—complex processes of assemblage, coordination, and bargaining among many independent actors that take place after the initial point decision. These line decisions are the multiple and critical implementation steps that give life to the larger ideas generated by a policy decision.

Moving Beyond Clever Policy Choices: Gordon Chase and New York's Health Services Administration

Gordon Chase became New York's health services commissioner under Mayor Lindsay.[1] Among the policy problems he tackled in his four years was lead paint poisoning. A serious and costly public health crisis, lead paint poisoning resulted in kidney failure, brain damage, and death among potentially thousands of children. The number of children at risk when Chase assumed office was thought to be great. His bright idea to develop a policy to treat and prevent lead paint poisoning in the city was an ambitious and bold policy choice.

But the assertion of the policy could not ensure the outcome. Indeed, the real brilliance of Gordon Chase, as we detail in Chapters Four and Five, was his ability to bring together rapidly the means, resources, organizational relationships, and cooperation necessary to launch and sustain a citywide effort: first to test each at-risk child, then to treat all children found to require it, and finally to inspect and remove lead paint from their homes.

Turning Bright Ideas into Real Results

In Chapter One, we argued that successful innovation was possible. In this chapter, we will explain why there isn't more of it. The first reason is that management matters. Good ideas and bold policy choices are not enough. Most policy makers and analysts give insufficient attention to the less glamorous task of management. Conservatives are fond of criticizing liberals for failing to worry about implementation. But it has been a problem for conservatives as well.

A second reason why innovation is less prevalent in government than it might be is that management is hard to carry out successfully. This is especially true in our political system, with its fragmentation of power and multiple levels of government. American governmental structures and the numerous and conflicting demands on public agencies are significant impediments to the free exercise of managerial authority.

Third, although there are many talented executives who effectively manage in the public sector, their talent is often discouraged and suppressed by the deadening demands of bureaucratic routines.

Fourth, reinforcing the discouraging effect of these demands is the absence of sufficient political incentives for executives to be aggressive and creative about policy implementation. Most political incentives for executives to become active in implementation run in the wrong direction, and the few positive incentives are weak. The electoral imperative is the strongest disincentive.

Management of policy is hardly glamorous when compared with generating the big idea. Indeed, management and implementation are often treated as afterthoughts. Their importance is largely misunderstood by the public and even by public policy schools. Policy analysis is the preferred approach to help make point decisions. It has an accepted methodology and an academic and organizational constituency.

Managing public policy requires a very different set of skills, the application of which is highly contextual and variable. It has neither a generally accepted methodology nor a solid constituency.[2] A policy decision is completed when it is made. But management is continual, fluid, and adaptive to new field circumstances. Rather than involving one central decision, management involves a process of continual decision making dependent on a high level of interaction that is constrained by both organizational resources and situational factors.

Public Sector Management: The Heavy Responsibility of Accountability and Participation

Public sector organizations are committed to participation and accountability. Thus they labor under heavy responsibilities and multiple goals. Accountability to the public results in bureaucratic routines developed to ensure continual oversight and protection against fraud, abuse, and waste. Struggling to meet the public's demand for access while ensuring accountability and equity, public organizations often founder. Performance measurement may be easy when specific service delivery goals are defined in the private sector. But it is far more elusive when public entities are held concomitantly to other goals desired by a free society.

Even the most seemingly routine government activities are not immune to these difficulties. Few people would dispute the mandate of the New York City Department of Sanitation: to collect the garbage and clean the streets. Nevertheless, the department is seldom judged simply on the efficiency of its service delivery (for example, how many tons of garbage it picks up given the resources it allocates to the task). Citizens are also interested in the comparative levels of service it provides to different neighborhoods (the relative frequency of pickup in different neighborhoods) and the cleanliness of streets it achieves in areas with very different initial conditions. This represents a concern about equity.

Further, citizens demand opportunities to lobby sanitation officials for what they want. They demand access to and participation in the decision-making process. As a result, managers who make decisions to change routes or pickup schedules to achieve greater operating efficiencies may also encounter strong community resistance.[3] The most resource-efficient decisions may not necessarily be the most politically popular because they compromise other values. Thus responding to these other legitimate concerns comes at the expense of operational efficiency. This leads to higher costs per ton of garbage hauled. In what would seem to be a simple case, we see that there are continual trade-offs between efficient performance—service delivery—and access, accountability, and equity.

Entrepreneurial Executives and Creative Subversion

Success in this setting often depends on mastering and, perhaps, circumventing what appear as impediments to action. Ignoring the rules, short-circuiting the process, or simply cutting corners to keep an agenda from becoming derailed comes to be seen as the best way—perhaps the only way—to overcome these impediments. Entrepreneurs in government are often successful innovators because they are creative in getting around the constraints that dilute their managerial authority. These constraints suppress and subvert the legitimate exercise of executive initiative.

Creative subversion is often the key to success for executives, but it can also entail serious risks. Ignoring or violating bureaucratic rules can encourage organizational anarchy or worse. It can result in fraud and abuse—the very ills that routines and rules are designed to prevent. Meeting organizational obstacles and bureaucratic logic with aggressive disregard for the rules has significant potential costs even as it can create new opportunities for effective managerial initiatives. How needed oversight and accountability in government can be reconciled with the need for creative initiative and innovation will be the subject of Chapters Seven and Eight.

The rest of this chapter explores why management matters and where public policy succeeds and fails. We explain why it is so hard to get things done in government and why it is so easy to fail. We explore the role of management in policy success through a wide range of cases. This reveals the vulnerability of policy outcomes to the inadequate attention focused on the line decisions that follow on the heels of a policy choice.

Further, we explore why failure is so common at the level of line decisions. We also examine how private sector organizations compare to public organizations in their attention to and success at managing the line decisions. We find that in both the public sector and the private sector, policy outcomes are largely the result of managerial skill and not simply the wisdom of a particular policy idea. But bureaucratic routines—rules and procedures devised to ensure accountability—suppress and subvert the legitimate exercise of executive initiative. This is reinforced by discouraging political disincentives for executives' initiatives and creativity. Executive talent is scarce enough, but what we observe in government today more often is that executive talent is suppressed and discouraged. The absence of sufficient political incentives reinforces the demands of bureaucratic routines.

The response to these constraints is that managerial success has come increasingly to rely on subverting organizational rules and culture. These behaviors pose serious risks and challenges for how needed oversight and accountability in government can be reconciled with the need for creative initiative and innovation.

Finally, we explore models of executive success—especially those undertaken by bureaucratic entrepreneurs—to understand the virtues and limits of their strategies. We conclude with some concrete lessons and caveats for aspiring executives.

Point and Line: The Messy, Complicated World Beyond Ideas and Choice

When politicians and the electorate say that they are interested in policy, they usually mean that they are interested in policy *choices:* the choice among alternatives, among several courses of action. But as Martin Shapiro and James Q. Wilson have each suggested, policy making involves both point and line. Wilson put it this way: "Point decisions are problems of choice, and line decisions are problems of management. . . . A point decision is one that involves a self-effectuating choice among competing alternatives; a line decision is one that requires the coordination by plan of the actions of many people extending over a substantial period of time."[4]

Point decisions are shaped by our larger and more influential *ideas:* "Military intervention will provide better outcomes in returning the hostages from Iran than diplomatic means." Line decisions, by contrast, are mostly shaped by organizational or situational resources and how they are assembled: "Helicopters are to be preferred to tanks, and secrecy and speed are to be preferred to experience and practice."

Assemblage is the essence of line decisions and is the essential difficulty. It is the process of following the formulation and initial adoption of a policy mandate. That mandate can come from the executive or the legislature. It is, in Eugene Bardach's phrase, the process of implementation: what happens after a bill becomes law.[5] Jeffrey Pressman and Aaron Wildavsky called it the "process of interaction between the setting of goals and actions geared to achieving them."[6] It is the process by which desired policy results are obtained. And that process is one of program assembly; it is interactive.

For purposes of clarity, we make the distinction here between a point decision (a policy goal) and line decisions (the means to realize a policy). In the following chapters, we elaborate further on the distinctions between these two functions. We show that in practice, policy choices are actively shaped and defined through the management process. Thus the boundaries between point and line decisions are not as clear in practice as we suggest here. The distinction is therefore more analytical than real, but it allows us to grasp the meaning and significance of the differences between the two activities and their relative contributions to achieving public outcomes.

Point and Line Decisions:
Bold Choices Are Not Enough

Many recent policy failures at all levels of government result from inadequate consideration of management decisions. The Reagan administration was a succession of bold point decisions: tax reduction to stimulate investment, deregulation to increase competition. But in certain instances—some quite conspicuous—insufficient attention was given to the line decisions necessary for success. Management mattered for the Bush administration as well. It faced important tests of its policies on the basis of how well it dealt with line decisions. A war on drugs is no easier to implement than a war on poverty. Choosing the right thing to do is not the same as getting things done. (And liberals are just as likely as conservatives to fail to understand this.)

The savings and loan (S&L) debacle of the Reagan administration resulted not so much from poor policy choices as from flawed management of the deregulation process. In the mid 1980s, savings and loan institutions were deregulated to improve their competitive position, as we explain in Chapter Seven. They had been facing deteriorating fiscal prospects for several years as the regulatory constraints under which they operated prevented them from responding properly to changing market conditions. Loosening those constraints through deregulation freed them to enter new markets and make new types of loans in new areas.

These new activities, however, required more, not less, regulatory oversight. The Reagan administration failed to distinguish between, on the one hand, the legitimate regulatory target of less government intervention in setting interest rates or dictating allowable loans and, on the other, more oversight of accounting practices and possible fraud. The latter—management of deregulation—was in fact necessary to make deregulation work effectively. Therefore, this was a time when more financial regulatory oversight was needed as the S&Ls experimented with new financial instruments and riskier loans.

But the Reagan deregulators allowed less oversight for two reasons. First, as we noted, they failed to make the distinction between these two very different targets. Second, as part of their push for less government and smaller budgets, they cut the number of bank examiners. This inadequate accountability and oversight led to the scandals and a more than $200 billion public bailout. Conservatives unwisely assumed that degregulation was a self-effectuating policy choice the management of which would be assumed by the market.[7]

This and other deregulatory and privatization experiences suggest that even relatively simple policy choices require attention to management. The costs of acting as if bold policy choices were sufficient can be great. Indeed, the even broader general privatization of government functions was a key point decision of the Reagan and Bush administrations. This was carried out by contracting out jobs to private companies ranging from managing parts of government laboratories to supervising the cleanup of toxic waste sites.

This privatization through contracting out represented

both a central policy decision and a philosophical tenet of the Reagan and Bush administrations: that the private sector can perform government's work better and cheaper. The essence of this concept—that the market would carry out these functions—seemed to obviate the need for management: the market would do it, as if by some invisible hand. Whether this represents a wholesale rejection of the role that management plays in policy success or simply a misguided view of the operation of specific markets is debatable. Nevertheless, the result was the same: the systematic mistrust and deemphasis of regulation and oversight of even privatized public activities. But management was needed, at least in the form of financial oversight and audit.

Indeed, in the final month of the Bush administration, its own Office of Management and the Budget (OMB) issued a report critical of the federal government's failure to manage the privatization of federal government functions over the previous dozen years. The report, commissioned by OMB director Richard Darman, acknowledged that private contractors and consultants wasted very large sums because federal agencies failed to oversee how they carry out their contracts. This "basic management problem was wasting billions of dollars, though the exact amount is not known."[8] This was the result of both the willingness of federal agencies to contract out many functions and their failure to impose appropriate oversight of those contracts.

These outcomes, the report concluded, were, first, the result of acts of omission—failure to appreciate the necessity of this oversight, perhaps because of the incorrect assumption that a market does not need management mechanisms. Second, oversight was diminished because both administrations, perversely, sought cost savings through the reduction of federal staff charged with managing contract compliance and oversight. These are the very functions critical to ensuring accountability and controlling costs, as private vendors take on the provision of public services.[9] Thus, again, more oversight was needed. But less was provided, and much less effective deregulation and privatization occurred, with significant waste.

These cases demonstrate that management is the step where policies can trip and fail. And other experiences in deregulation show the centrality of management: when it is done well, it produces success. Indeed, the entire economic deregulation movement was originally conceived of and executed with significant concern for the necessity of oversight and management of the deregulation process—with a very light hand and specifically targeted—to make it work effectively.

For example, the deregulation of airlines (the first industry to be deregulated) was neither conceived of nor achieved simply by the force of a good idea left to the mechanisms of the marketplace. The implementers who carried out this policy, in this case market-oriented economists in the Carter administration, had to create a thorough and detailed management strategy for the transitional period between regulation and deregulation. Then they had to execute it carefully. Fare structure and the granting of new routes, for instance, were proper deregulatory targets. But regulation and oversight of airplane safety had to be retained because the market could not be relied on to provide sufficient safety on its own.

Thus the architect of airline deregulation, economist and Civil Aeronautics Board (CAB) chairman Alfred Kahn, managed accordingly. Even before economic deregulation went into effect, he wrote to the Federal Aviation Administration (FAA) to say, in effect, that now that we at the CAB are going out of the business of regulating fares and routes, there will be many new entrants into the market. Therefore, the FAA will have greater—not fewer—regulatory oversight duties to perform with respect to safety. This is because the market, in the form of individual airlines, could not be relied on to enforce safety at the level that the public interest required.[10]

This is analogous to S&L deregulation, where the freeing of interest rates was appropriate but oversight to prevent potential fraud should have been retained. Airline deregulation was both safe and very successful in its early period; S&L deregulation was plagued by fraud. The unsuccessful result set off a deregulatory backlash.

Later airline deregulation faltered because it lacked the earlier commitment to oversight and management of the deregulation process central to success. The original airline deregulators understood that oversight was necessary to maintain the competitive context that would allow economic deregulation to work. The potential problems they were concerned about included predatory pricing and airline mergers, which could have an anticompetitive effect. The latter, for example, could create regional monopolies so powerful that they would overwhelm or discourage potential entrants by their sheer size rather than their competitive efficiency.[11]

This is what happened because the Reagan administration thought that deregulation did not have to be managed and that the market would carry it out. The result was the complete abandonment of antitrust policy in general and for airlines. The Reagan Justice Department allowed all airline mergers. Thus the competitive context necessary for deregulation to work was not maintained.[12]

Recent administrations have made many bold policy choices. But realizing the desired result of a single point decision involves many complicated line decisions. Yet producing the desired result depends on more than good line decisions; it depends on an appropriate underlying causal link between an intervention and an expected outcome. If that relationship does not hold, even close attention to managing the line decisions will not produce the desired result.

Deinstitutionalization: The Failure of Line Decisions Plagues Liberals As Well

Management matters just as much for the ultimate success of liberals' bright ideas. In the 1960s, after years of dismal results and high costs at state mental institutions, the bold concept of deinstitutionalization was seized on. After several years of difficult legislative politics in California, a decisive point decision was reached in 1965: deinstitutionalization was formally adopted by the state legislature as a mandatory policy. Eschewing a policy that in effect warehoused patients in impersonal and remote state institutions, deinstitutionalization sought to protect the civil liberties of the mentally ill and accelerate their integration into community settings with supportive community treatment.[13]

The success of this point decision, or policy choice, depended on development and expansion of community treatment services. Outpatient mental health services were to be combined with community resources and support services to assist patients' integration into society. The policy therefore depended on a complicated set of line decisions that included the design, funding, and coordination of services and social supports at the community level. In reality, these services were inadequate, underfunded, and poorly coordinated with necessary social supports. Outpatient services reach only a fraction of the people released from state institutions in California and elsewhere.[14] Indeed, this is often cited as a major contributing factor to the homelessness problem. Many studies show that a good deal of homelessness is less a function of a housing shortage than a shortage of community outpatient facilities for deinstitutionalized patients. Without these facilities, patients are unable to develop access to the housing resources that are available.[15]

Deinstitutionalization has been judged a failed policy idea around the country. However, it had little opportunity to succeed. Failure to attend to the critical line decisions—to invest sufficiently in policy implementation and management—ensured failure. And the consequences of this failure have created a major source of our homelessness problem.

The Iranian Hostage Rescue: Bold Point Decision, Failed Line Decisions

The United States' unsuccessful 1980 hostage rescue mission in Iran illustrates both that this assemblage process of line decisions is central to obtaining desired policy results and that insufficient attention to it can doom a policy. The policy choice of pursuing military rather than diplomatic means to rescue U.S. hostages in Iran was made in absolute secrecy; men and equipment had to be moved into Iran, and hostages had to be rescued and returned. But it involved many line decisions, some of which were poor ones, and this led to a failed policy.

Men and equipment were moved to bases in Egypt and the carrier *Nimitz* in the Persian Gulf. The need for secrecy meant that the plan was rehearsed with full personnel only twice. On the appointed night, eight helicopters left the *Nimitz* for a five hundred–mile flight into the Iranian desert. There they met six C-130 transport planes for refueling, picked up assault teams, and flew to Tehran. Eight miles into Iran, motor failure forced a helicopter to be abandoned. Four hundred miles farther, in a dust storm, another helicopter malfunctioned and returned to the *Nimitz* at the pilot's discretion, though he did not know of the earlier loss. At the desert rendezvous, a third helicopter failed, reducing the force to five. Two mission commanders, with presidential approval, decided to abort the mission. As one helicopter turned around, it struck a C-130. Both burst into flames, killing eight crewmen.[16]

The hostages were not returned and were instead dispersed throughout Iran, and the United States continued to look impotent. The fault lay clearly in the implementation stage, in insufficient attention to line decisions: the failure to assign more backup helicopters given the high malfunction rate to be expected in desert conditions. Thus when the absolutely predictable occurred, the mission had to be aborted. The hostage rescue mission experience dramatizes that bold initial policy choices are not enough to ensure results.

Line Decisions: Bargaining, Coordinating, and Lots of Delay

A point decision tends to be simple; it involves choice at a *single point*. A line decision is a process and tends to be more complicated. It involves a *complicated line* of many decisions about many elements. It involves a good deal of bargaining among many actors. A great deal of effort goes into controlling and coordinating these various actors and the various elements of the program. All this adds up to what Pressman and Wildavsky call the "complexity of joint action."[17] That is, line decisions are a process born of many actors' perspectives and the multiple clearances that so characterize our fragmented political system. It is a process that is often characterized by gamesmanship and hence delay. Indeed, its dynamics are often negative: the longer the players interact, the worse the prospects for agreement and program success.

Take the now classic case of the performance of the Economic Development Administration (EDA) in the mid 1960s. The EDA developed a special demonstration project in Oakland, California, to show that public works and building loans could provide incentives for employers to hire minorities. The EDA made special efforts to avoid the implementation obstacles known to have hampered other programs, such as "institutional fragmentation, multiple and confusing goals, and inadequate funding."[18]

The EDA sought to follow a simple and straightforward course, coupled with ample funding. But the program in Oakland in practice was complex and convoluted. Even after several years, it resulted in few new jobs, without even a third of the $23 million earmarked for Oakland actually being spent. Implementation ultimately took five years.

The delay resulted from interdependencies evolving between actors over time. With multiple actors and diverse perspectives, the seventy clearance points that the project involved—a not unusual number, given that federal, state, and local actors were involved, plus a couple of federal agencies and several private companies—produced a quagmire. Pressman and Wildavsky calculated that if one-third of the clearance points faced minimal delay (which they arbitrarily but not unrealistically assigned the value of one week), one-third faced minor delay (three weeks), and one-third faced a moderate delay (six weeks), it would take 233⅓ weeks to implement the project. That is four and a half years, which is not far off the mark.[19]

Conservatives Need to Worry About Management: A War on Drugs Is No Easier to Implement Than a War on Poverty

The lessons of some recent conservative administrations—Ford, Reagan, Bush—provide additional support for the view that management is where policy most often fails and that line decisions are pivotal. Even conservative administrations need to be concerned with managerial and line decisions. For example, privatization of many HUD activities had to be accompanied by implementation and management: oversight and control. Many policy failures of recent conservative administrations, like those of earlier liberal regimes, can be explained by problems at the implementation stage. Good ideas were not enough to ensure innovative policy outcomes in the 1960s, when liberal ideas dominated, or in the 1980s, when conservative ideas dominated.

Conservative Bright Ideas Are No More Self-Executing Than Liberal Ones

All administrations, regardless of ideology, need to give more attention to managerial tasks than they have. When government is most activist, policy success will be determined principally by the quality of line decisions. Its leaders must therefore tend the program assembly process. And recent conservative administrations have been unusually activist in many areas. For example, liberals had a war on poverty; conservatives waged war on crime and drugs. However, the program assembly process was no easier for conservatives than it was for liberals.

The Reagan administration's war on drugs, for instance, was plagued by the typical implementation problems of poor interagency coordination, despite the seeming societywide agreement on its goals. The administration sought to end the historically poor coordination between the various agencies involved in stopping the flow of illegal drugs into the United States by creating the National Narcotic Border Interdiction System (NNBIS) in 1983. Fourteen months later, the head of the federal Drug Enforcement Agency criticized it for having accomplished little while taking credit for other agencies' successes. At the same time, a General Accounting Office report called the NNBIS's involvement "quite limited" in the eleven drug seizure cases that it analyzed. And in a particular instance of this larger coordination problem, the U.S. Customs Service (which is part of the Treasury Department) relinquished to the Defense Department its responsibility for detecting smugglers. It did so to concentrate on its task of intercepting smugglers, but some members of Congress criticized the Customs Service for "walking away from the problem" when it knew that "Defense is not going to do it."[20]

A similar pattern occurred in the war on crime. In October 1982, the Reagan administration announced the goal of "crippling the power of the 'mob'" by creating twelve special narcotics task forces. But this required an extensive and complicated program assembly. Six months after having persuaded Congress to provide an extra $127.5 million for the fiscal year, less than $7 million had been spent, and only 550 of the 1,600 planned lawyers and staff were assigned to the task force. In addition, the Department of Justice, the lead agency, had difficulty allocating resources among the six participating federal agencies, and disagreements surfaced over the appropriate chain of command and the task force locations. As the FBI's assistant director said of these program assembly problems, "This is not like a rabbit that you can set on the ground and watch it hop off. It takes time to build and make it run."[21]

Insufficient Attention to Management

Most actors tend to neglect the importance of management. Intellectuals of all political stripes often rely too heavily on brilliant "new concepts" and neglect the central significance of implementation. Too often they seem to trust some invisible force and the mere fact of wielding authority to bring these concepts to reality. This neglect is not confined to intellectuals, however. Even top executives, regardless of how much experience they have had at the front line, tend to ignore management. Executives at the top always face the dilemma of whether to spend their time and political capital on being good managers and administrators or being leaders who capture public attention with new initiatives to set the tone for the nation or their city. Most choose to neglect the management stage. Political dynamics usually leads them away from shepherding innovative ideas to implementation.

Since the 1960s, we have become familiar with these flaws in liberal administrations. But even in conservative administrations, the brightest staff people seem likely to assume that having both good ideas and power is enough to achieve good policies. Deregulation of the S&Ls and the wars on drugs and crime were complicated and controversial policies and would have been difficult to carry out even if management had been given appropriate attention. But even modest programs of conservative Republican administrations, such as the swine flu vaccination program and the Community Development Block Grant program, also had management difficulties because top executives neglected the importance of implementation.

The Swine Flu Debacle:
Discovery Is Not the Cure

The swine flu vaccine program during the Ford administration is a classic illustration of top policy makers' failing to recognize the importance of management. In response to four cases of swine flu at Fort Dix, New Jersey, in January 1976, one of which resulted in death, the National Influenza Immunization Program attempted to vaccinate the entire U.S. population against a new flu virus by December 1976. The mass immunization was designed to prevent a recurrence of a 1918-type pandemic in which 500,000 deaths resulted from a similar flu. Federal public health officials also were strongly attracted to the opportunity for public education on the "virtues of preventive medicine." The program was to cost $135 million, mostly for federal purchase of vaccines, to be distributed by the states and administered by public health agencies and private physicians. In February 1976, agreement and coordination seemed assured among the federal agencies—the Center for Disease Control (CDC), the Bureau of Biologics, and the National Institutes of Health—and the nation's four vaccine manufacturers. But no one at the CDC, Department of Health, Education, and Welfare, or the White House took steps to anticipate potential implementation difficulties, which in fact were rather predictable.

The program's initiation was delayed from September

1 to October 1, 1976, for several reasons: the manufacturers and their insurers' refusal to accept liability and the subsequent need for special legislation; Parke-Davis's June 1976 discovery that they had prepared two million dosages using the wrong virus; production delays that made only 40 million of the 160 million dosages requested available by October; and disputes concerning dosages for children.

In October, local suspensions of the program occurred in nine states following deaths coincident with vaccination. But in each state the program was resumed within a few days, and then President Gerald Ford and his family received shots before television cameras. However, the national program was suspended in December 1976 after an association was found between the vaccine and higher rates of potentially fatal Guillain-Barre syndrome.

At that time, only 20 percent of the general population—significantly less in the black population—had received the inoculation. Incidence of measles had increased 64 percent over 1975, possibly due to the diversion of resources. Over 100 damage claims totaling $11 million had been filed against the government. Public acceptance of new initiatives in preventive medicine probably was *diminished* by the lost credibility of the CDC, previously a highly respected agency. The swine flu never appeared in human-to-human transmissions.[22]

These policy makers acted as if implementation of the program would follow easily and automatically from their point decisions. They made several erroneous assumptions and flawed management decisions: the program's planners operated without what we call a "dirty mind"—the ability to anticipate and predict implementation difficulties and to be attuned to conflicting interests and their likelihood of delaying, even outright resisting, implementation. They also designed the program on too grand a scale, assumed that participants would readily agree with the program, misjudged the participants' interests, failed to anticipate production problems, and failed to realize the potential impact of media coverage and high-profile accidents. These miscalculations undermined the immunization program from its very inception. They are a striking illustration of the danger of insufficient attention to management.

The Scarcity of Political Incentives for Executives

In addition to the inherent institutional constraints that public sector organizations place on enterprising managers are political disincentives for executives to be aggressive and creative about policy implementation. Most political incentives run in the wrong direction, and the few positive incentives are weak. The electoral imperative is the strongest disincentive. In any organization in which officials are elected, the first priority is to ensure reelection. Thus a primary motivator of elected public officials and their staffs is to take actions that will support a reelection bid. This severely constrains their choices, particularly in light of the decline of their traditional vehicles, political parties.

The electoral imperative creates a short-run orientation and pressure for fast action. The constraint is the next election, typically in less than four years (less than two years for congressional representatives and many state legislators). All this precludes working on implementation or even developing an interest in it. To capture public attention, leaders opt for the dramatic. It need not be a dramatic achievement; a dramatic disclosure or proposal might provide the appropriate political impact. In contrast, implementation of an existing proposal rarely is exciting and often is dull. Moreover, the media are seldom attracted to this kind of investment of time. They too make their reputation on seizing the novel or dramatic idea.

These pressures also create incentives for symbolic politics rather than substantive activity. To convey a symbol—or an effort, a position, or a commitment—it may often be sufficient for the official to take a stand, make a proposal, or initiate a program, thereby meeting the electoral imperative without actually having to lead the implementation effort. In the extreme, many officials "proclaim and abandon": they are more interested in obtaining a podium for policymaking than in actually implementing policy.

This pattern is striking and comprehensible when we look at legislators because we expect them to legislate rather than oversee implementation. But unfortunately, executives whom we expect to provide leadership in the management of policy implementation are also very vulnerable. Any executive is always confronted with choices about the allocation of scarce executive political capital and time. Should the executive spend scarce resources on being a leader who captures public attention—especially with new initiatives—and sets the tone for the nation or state or on undertaking the more prosaic activities of getting things done in government organizations?

Since Franklin D. Roosevelt, most executives have focused on the former. Implementing programs is much riskier than promulgating initiatives and aspirations. Even when the choice is to implement, there is the matter of executive control: getting one's subordinates to do one's will. And even when executives have a great deal of formal authority, this is not automatically translated into formal power and influence. They are surrounded by other institutions and actors who hold significant pieces of independent power. In almost all instances, they must persuade rather than command.

And what rewards accrue to aggressive and innovative policy implementation? Most rewards come to individuals who are driven by a strong sense of mission and social values. For them, the motivation for public service and for efforts to get things done in government derives from a sense of professional identity and mission. But they are not likely to get external rewards from an ungrateful political elite or an uninterested public. Indeed, the personal costs of behaving like a bureaucratic entrepreneur can be great. Innovation and change threaten the existing order and "rock the boat" in conventional agencies. Thus political disincentives are also a product of the fact that in conventional agencies, innovators tend to be viewed as boat rockers. It is probably not an accident that following their successes, several of the most innovative executives in our study—including Ira Jackson, Chuck Atkins, Thomas Glynn, Ellen Schall, and William Ruckelshaus—were not rewarded with another public sector appointment and next served somewhat involuntarily outside government. And interviews with several of the Innovations award winners revealed that their recognition threatened established interests and, perversely, often made their situations more difficult. That type of disincentive is not lost on aspiring executives.

Private Organizations: Paying Attention to Line

This book primarily examines the constraints on public executives and their pursuit of innovation. But a look at two large private organizations and how they have faced the dual challenges of policy and management, of point and line, illustrates both the potential payoffs and the opportunities forgone from failure to attend to the line. The contrasting stories of how Xerox invented and ultimately lost the opportunity to bring the first personal computer to mass market and how IBM came from behind to dominate the PC market support our central finding that management matters. Even without the special constraints that public executives face, bureaucratic constraints in all large organizations provide formidable obstacles to innovation. Management strategies to cope with them are a universal necessity.

Bright Ideas Are Not Self-Executing in the Private Sector

An excellent idea or an innovative product does not guarantee success. Management matters just as much in the private sector. Private enterprise suffers less from oversight mechanisms than the public sector. Private sector top executives exercise greater authority and control over their organizations. However, having discretion does not ensure its appropriate use. Without effective executives, even brilliant ideas will not become successful policies or products. But with effective chief executives, even less than completely original ideas can become very successful.

Inventing the First PC at Xerox

The Xerox Corporation invented and successfully marketed xerographic photocopying in the late 1950s. As a result, it experienced unparalleled growth, dominating the industry for more than a decade. Its success depended on technological innovation and the monopoly position it enjoyed through the patent on xerography, which would expire in the mid 1970s. Thus by 1970, the company's president, Peter McCoulough, understood the need to redefine the corporate mission to meet changing market needs and thus allow Xerox to maintain increasing levels of growth and technological innovation.[23]

McCoulough identified the need for Xerox to develop an architecture of information. When almost no one was speaking this language, he described knowledge as "an industry in its own right." His first action geared to achieving this objective was directing the creation of a generously funded independent unit—a computer research center, the Palo Alto Research Center (PARC), in Palo Alto, California. Its goal was to discover how to strengthen the company's role in digital technology, computers, and information processing. In less than four years, this independent unit, composed of a brilliant group of scientists who had been assembled and isolated from the normal corporate environment, developed the first personal computer, the Alto PC. Forty more were built within a year.

The brilliant idea was the concept of personal computing. Revolutionary at the time, personal computing was based on the notion that a single machine could serve a wide range of needs for a single user and that these machines could be linked to networks to share resources and knowledge. Thus in a very short time, Xerox's chief executive articulated a new mission and created a vehicle to develop new products for that mission. Further, that vehicle actually produced the innovation, featuring such advanced items as the first handheld mouse, the first word processing program, and the first laser printer.

Balancing Innovation and Accountability

The Alto PC, however, never came to market. Despite the new mission and even the product innovation, a failure to attend to the process of program assembly resulted in an egregious squandering of market potential. Xerox failed because of poor management—especially at the top—and because of excessive and poorly managed analysis and oversight: the top executives failed to balance tensions between innovation and accountability. The chief executive identified a new corporate mission and created an institutional setting for innovation, but he failed to communicate the importance of his vision throughout the organization. Indeed, the top executive failed to champion the PARC effort or to reward other critical organization players for supporting it. Instead, financial control dominated his thinking, and that succeeded in resisting and ultimately derailing new product innovation.

Crisis at Xerox: The Opportunity Not Taken

Executives rarely get advance notice of crises, but the Xerox executives did. They knew that the patent that was the basis of their monopoly on xerography would expire in the mid 1970s. The imminence of this crisis could have given the top executives the freedom to innovate and take risks. Crises often quiet natural opposition and stimulate political and organizational support for innovation. The top executives failed to take advantage of this potential openness to change to push recalcitrant divisions and financial control overseers toward innovation, especially with PARC and the Alto PC.

Poor Management at the Program Level

The top executives were not the only poor managers at Xerox. Executives at the program level conceived of and developed the Alto PC. But these executives were poor program advocates and managers. They acted as if their idea was so clever that it would sell itself to Xerox's top executives and to the public. Executives failed both at implementation and at managing organizational culture. Managers throughout the innovation process failed to manage the sales and marketing of their product to critical internal corporate constituents.

Moving new projects "off campus"—setting up independent units away from central headquarters—is often used to stimulate innovation. But one of PARC's many management errors was allowing its physical isolation to become a serious liability both with central headquarters and with other development units.

IBM's PC: "Old Stuff" Yields Innovation with Effective Top Executives

In striking contrast to Xerox, IBM had neither a brilliant idea nor an innovative product. But it had effective management, both at the top and at the program level. The personal computer had become a viable technology; Apple had been producing one since 1976, and by 1980 it had a huge market share.[24] IBM continued to see its core business as the mainframe computer, sold through a highly skilled direct sales force to corporate customers. It had simply relinquished any role in the growing PC market.

IBM's New Mission: Crisis as Opportunity

In 1980, Bill Lowe was director of IBM's Independent Business Unit (IBU) at Boca Raton, Florida, which had been developed to experiment with low-cost computers. He argued to the corporate management committee that the crisis IBM faced in the PC market should be viewed as an opportunity. With existing technology, IBM could be a successful player in the PC market. He cautioned, however, that existing IBM culture was potentially fatal to the new effort because it relied on a very different set of business assumptions based on its mainframe business. "The only way we can get into the personal computer business is to go out and buy part of a computer company, or buy both the CPU [central processing unit] and software from people like Apple or Atari—because we can't do this within the culture of IBM."[25]

Radical Departures from Traditional Corporate Strategy

Lowe had one month to prepare a design proposal. He developed a plan that deviated radically from the traditional IBM philosophy and practices for design and sales.

First, rather than creating a technologically innovative machine subject to IBM's slow and thorough testing procedures, the goal would be to produce a reliable one using off-the-shelf components, from outside vendors, that had already been tested and had already survived in the market.

Second, rather than being tied to IBM software and peripherals, the new machine would have an "open architecture" allowing non-IBM products to be used with it. Revolutionary for the company and for the industry more generally, this innovation would allow faster initial development through the use of outside hardware and software vendors.[26]

Finally, contrary to IBM tradition, the machine would be sold through outside retailers (Computerland and Sears) rather than through IBM's vaunted sales force. This bypassed IBM's corporate marketing and service units but gave the PC quicker access to retail markets.

IBM recouped its initial market forfeiture and produced a machine that became the industry standard. Its market entry was responsible for revolutionizing the way people conducted business throughout the world. By 1984, it had already achieved a 63 percent market share, having displaced Apple in a mere two years! The PC became the most successful project in the corporation's history. Success was not, however, simply the result of IBM's mystique or its market power, as some observers have suggested.[27] Indeed, when contrasted with the Xerox case, it illustrates starkly the lesson that management can make all the difference.

Attention to Line Decisions at IBM

How did IBM succeed so brilliantly despite its lack of product innovation while Xerox failed so egregiously? Like Xerox's McCoulough, IBM's chairman, Frank Cary, understood the need for an independent business unit, but his management strategies went further. First, he took a great risk with radical new strategies. Although protection of these concepts from traditional corporate policy was critical, a number of other line decisions guaranteed success: openness to seeing crisis as opportunity; a desire to create and foster innovation through the IBU; and most important, the inclination and ability to protect Boca Raton from the oversight divisions within the company and from competition from the sales, marketing, and mainframe divisions.

Though potentially isolated in Boca Raton, IBM program managers integrated development, manufacturing, and finance in the early stages of the business concept. Further, unlike managers at Xerox, Boca Raton managers invested significant energy in internal marketing and communication, explaining the project throughout the company to top management. Understanding the dangers of being seen as mavericks, they demonstrated loyalty and acted like team players. Their subordinates viewed them as charismatic leaders. (Recent downturns in IBM's dominance seem to confirm our analyses of both the IBM and Xerox cases. This decline coincides with both IBM's moving away from its successful efforts to encourage independence and innovation through the use of IBUs and the reemergence of its dominant mainframe orientation. Facing the 1990s with the corporate strategy of continued dependence on its traditional core business of the mainframe and reasserting a thorough but time-consuming process of review for new ideas and projects, IBM tended to stifle innovation and responsiveness to new market opportunities. IBM did not pursue a decentralized strategy that would encourage competition with the existing corporate divisions—a strategy that led to the success of IBM competitors during this period. IBM's enduring attachment to outmoded values ultimately seems to have contributed to its decline.)

Executives and Line Decisions

These cases point to the critical attention executives must pay to ensure that the multifaceted and continuous process that accompanies a policy decision is meticulously managed. Whether it be managing the organizational culture, designing the organizational structure to support the enterprise, or simply assembling the necessary elements and supports to launch the venture, most of the essential difficult work comes after rather than before policy choices are made. The rest of this chapter will explore why it is so difficult to attend to these decisions in the public sector and some of the approaches taken by successful entrepreneurs.

Public Organizations: Multiple, Unique, and Conflicting Goals

Critics of the public sector are fond of pointing to the example of private sector organizations to highlight the disparity between public performance and what is typically expected under private auspices. Dissatisfaction with public outcomes is so great that attraction to an expanded role for the private sector in traditionally public domains is proliferating in both popular and academic circles.[28] The Reagan administration elevated the virtues of the private market and privatization in the United States, and now the failures of state planning around the world continue to fuel the debate.

The attraction of privatization often emanates from a rather simple and incomplete analysis of the relative merits of private provision. But recent debate fails to consider the various constraints and incentives that affect public sector organizations. First, public managers face more complicated mandates and goals that are defined for them by others. Second, these goals are often contradictory and not necessarily as simple as efficiency and profit maximization, meaning success and performance are defined differently in the public sector and in the private sector. Third, public managers have less opportunity to exercise personal discretion in the use and allocation of resources.[29]

Private organizations can face similar managment challenges, and public executives may have important lessons to learn from them. We have included several private sector cases in this book, largely for illustrative purposes. However, executives in public enterprises will always differ fundamentally in their ability to mobilize resources, in their options to provide incentives for productivity and innovation, and in their ability to demonstrate and be rewarded for their accomplishments. Thus the role of public managers and the context in which they must seek to realize their goals pose a more daunting challenge than is faced in the private sector. It is in this differing context that their real opportunities and limitations must be understood. Private sector solutions should not be imposed uncritically, especially because they cannot resolve the fundamental conflict of values inherent to public purpose; we turn to these next. The discussion here is intended to identify why public organizations face different challenges from private firms and why public management will always be more problematic. Public sector success can be achieved and increased. But it will not come from the simple application of private sector techniques in public settings.

Goals of Public Sector Organizations

Public organizations have diverse and multiple goals, defined for them by external elements; private firms have far fewer and can define their goals themselves. Measurable indicators of private performance such as profitability, market share, and earnings are often discrete; public enterprises, by contrast, are judged by many more and often conflicting standards.

Take the example of private versus public education.

Public schools have very different goals. They seek to socialize and educate all children, regardless of skill level or ability to pay. By law, public schools may be directed to provide special services to meet the needs of the educationally disadvantaged or mentally or physically disabled students. Further, parental access to the decision-making process is a critical requirement of public education. Equity for diverse users and accountability for behavior are basic. Public school executives are by necessity involved in a complicated series of bargaining and coordinating tasks among critical actors: teachers' unions, parents' and citizens' organizations, elected officials, social service providers, even the media.

Most of the rules, regulations, and procedures that come to be seen as impediments to efficient operation and constrain executives managing public schools are intended to ensure access, participation equity, and accountability. Public organizations often achieve these important public values only by sacrificing efficiency.[30] Multiple checks on managerial authority ensure accountability, but they also dissipate executive authority and operate as a brake on executive initiative.

The price public organizations must pay to achieve these important but frequently overlooked public values is the sacrifice of efficiency. Indeed, subject to the demands of the political process, managers are more often "constraint driven" than they are "task driven." Whereas private enterprises develop decision rules that focus on the bottom line (profits), public organizations more often develop rules that are top-line focused (constraints). Multiple checks on managerial authority through regulation and process is one way to ensure accountability. But it also operates to dissipate authority. Whereas multiple decision points allow consecutive review, they also allow endless opportunities to say no. This ultimately operates as a brake on affirmative executive initiative.

Public goals create constraints that compromise efficiency and constrain executive initiative. But in a democratic society they must also be understood as furthering important public values. In general, then, they are costs that may be willingly incurred. Nevertheless, the line problem derives from them, and they account for why it is so hard to get anything done.

Defining Success: Easier in the Private Sector

The field of education illustrates the different constraints and incentives in the public and private sectors. When critics argue that education should be privatized (even if its redistributional elements are retained through the use of vouchers), they generally point to school performance measures between public and private institutions. These measures are discrete, limited, and only narrowly reflective of the returns from education (such as scores on standardized tests and graduation and dropout rates).

This creates incentives for private schools to cream and to invest where the value added is maximized. State requirements may constrain some of their curricular choices, but private schools are generally free to invest where they think the payoff may be greatest. They can allocate resources however they see fit. They can freely select their students, teachers, and administrators. Private schools can thus shape their educational programs in ways that maximize their performance outcomes.

Public schools are often judged by the reading and computational scores of their students, but, as we have seen, there are many other standards and goals by which they are ultimately held accountable. Public schools are at a disadvantage in such comparisons because the larger social goals involved often result in lower standardized test scores. The performance of private schools, by contrast, is not judged on the basis of the more difficult and more subjective areas of equity and accountability. And many other constraints hamper innovation and managerial efficiency.[31] Defining success and measuring performance are generally much easier in the private sector, and the public sector often suffers in simplistic comparisons.

Executive Discretion and Resource Use: Constraints on the Public Sector

Public sector organizations face a different set of incentives in using resources and taking risks. Whatever product or production improvements private sector executives can achieve are directly internalized by the organization for its own use, to reward, expand, and improve. Incentives and motivations for executive behavior are clear, and the rewards are tangible. Since an acceptable rate of success may only be one in five, a considerable amount of failure can be tolerated.

These conditions do not prevail in the public sector. Because public executives are most often prevented from maintaining or acquiring control over any resources they may generate, they cannot benefit directly from the tangible rewards of marketing successful "products." Fear of public scandal and of accusations of corruption, mismanagement, and incompetence so dominates the consciousness of public officials that the necessary willingness to accept some failure, which is a precondition for innovation, is lacking.[32] Although the image of the public executive as totally risk-averse and obsessed with damage control is clearly a caricature, that is the direction of the incentives. Public executives are punished for failure and seldom see the direct rewards from innovation or from saving resources. Given the institutional biases, few are willing to risk their reputations and careers.

To use the example of education, a private school can have a relatively consistent set of decision rules including everything from hiring and firing to purchasing inputs and making investments in new technology to choice of students accepted. Private schools can take advantage of these opportunities in ways that public schools cannot. Public schools are rarely able to select their students. They often cannot hire and fire independently, and they cannot alter the allocation of inputs and resources as they see fit.

The Public Sector: Inverted Incentives on Resources and Risk

Public sector organizations suffer from an inherent and seemingly perverse set of incentives that discourage resource-sparing behavior and the risk taking necessary for innovative initiatives. Both incentives are absent due to the lack of competitive pressures that ultimately reward such behavior in the private market. A better example than public education, perhaps, of the perverse effect of constraints on public executives can be seen in the case of Sandra Steiner Lowe.

Lowe, an executive in the Fairfax County (Virginia) Department of Community Affairs, faced a previously undocumented problem: in a relatively affluent community were a large number of indigent children of working-poor families without medical or dental coverage. Were she a private executive discovering an unsatisfied demand for services, her incentives would be clear. She would develop a service package based on careful market analysis that reflected market demand. She could expect the package, if appropriately designed, priced, and marketed, to generate increased revenues for her organization, which she could use to expand her operation and reward innovative executives as well as to increase the company's profits, operating income, and investment capital.

As a public sector executive, however, any cost savings resulting from innovation by Lowe will not accrue to her agency. If she successfully develops, finances, and provides comprehensive, case-managed health and dental services to the county's unserved children, significant public savings will indeed result. But these savings cannot be captured by the Department of Community Affairs' budget, nor can they be paid out to hardworking agency employees in the form of rewards or bonuses.

Indeed, these savings are unlikely to result in even a modest improvement in the working environment of the agency. Reduced public expenditures resulting from Lowe's program will revert to the general fund. And if savings accrue due to increased efficiency, any surpluses generated may even serve to *reduce* budget allocations in future years, as the need for larger resources to finance existing services will seem unjustified.

When critics argue that it is impossible to get anything done in government, they are generally venting frustration with the perceived competence and speed with which line decisions are made. But as we have argued, executives seeking to carry out programmatic mandates or even simple government service functions often fail because of inherent institutional obstacles.

Making the Line Problem Even Worse: Our Political System's Fragmented Power Structure

Suspicious of highly concentrated power and protective of minority rights, the U.S. political system divides power and authority among the three branches of government and three levels of governing. In U.S. political institutions, decision making is highly decentralized, subject to review at many levels. Fragmentation of power is the characteristic of the U.S. political system that is central to the difficulties of adopting and implementing effective policies for social intervention. Public power has been further fragmented because of the influence of American political culture's participatory ethos: the belief that public decisions, whenever feasible, should be based on the widest possible participation of the governed and not left to a governing elite.[33]

Interest group politics further fragments power. It is dispersed not only among thousands of different units in the largest government in the world but also among countless private actors who try to influence the manner in which the government functions. Not only do economic, social, professional, and religious elites; commercial, industrial, and trade organizations; and political parties, political action groups, and organized citizen constituencies have influence in nongovernmental spheres of activity, but they also have influence on governmental structures and decisions.

Institutional and individual actors in the political system more often than not come into conflict. Many times there is no clear path to implement what has been designed by and passed by a legislature because it has vague mandates and sometimes even benign booby traps. Unfortunately, this fragmentation and conflict produce these diffuse mandates because legislative consensus is difficult to achieve without them.

In recent decades, implementation has become the single most problematic aspect of policy making. It is the stage at which most domestic policies have foundered. This has been increasingly true as the problem of institutional incapacity in American politics has grown. Anthony King concluded his trailblazing *The New American Political System* by describing a pattern of increasingly fragmented and atomized political institutions. With this paucity of materials out of which coalitions might be built, "building coalitions in the United States today is like trying to build coalitions out of sand."[34] When the implementation of programs depends on so many different actors, there are numerous possibilities for disagreement, delay, and resistance. Implementation is sure to be difficult when democratic, individualistic, and participatory values have become so predominant in our political culture. This means that the ability to assemble power and achieve coordination within governmental institutions is increasingly problematic. The greater demands made of government to address even more complex problems have made the process even more difficult and the outcome even more uncertain. Each time a policy is actually approved and set for implementation, the chances of failure, delay, and goal alteration and attenuation increase significantly. Thus the legislative successes of yesterday tend to become the implementation problems of today.

Even in the Reagan years, when a conservative agenda was established and preached, government size and scope increased. Policy space has become much more dense as the number of large programs and agencies has increased. At the same time, political power has become more fragmented as informal coordinating mechanisms like political parties have declined.[35] Without strong political parties, agreement among political factions is harder to achieve.[36] With so many additional actors striving toward rights-based ideologies and programs, it is no wonder that managers face extremely difficult conditions when implementing new policies.[37] This is why management matters so much in the success or failure of a program.

The Dilemmas of Innovation and Accountability

Management is difficult in the public sector. All the incentives run in the wrong direction. Bureaucratic entrepreneurs face a fragmented political system that resists providing a clear mandate for action. Public organizations face multiple and conflicting demands and goals. Rewards for success are limited by bureaucratic rules. And political pressures push executives in directions that compete with the requirements for sound managerial practice. Indeed, it's surprising how much success we actually find in public enterprises.

Success, we have argued, does not come simply from choosing the right things to do. Policy choices are important, but the more difficult activities that accompany the fluid and adaptive process of managing are often the most critical determinants of policy outcomes. Yet they enjoy none of the public praise and recognition that accompany policy choices. Nevertheless, policy making has two parts, often inextricably bound and not necessarily sequential: policy choice and policy implementation. Because few public policy decisions are self-effectuating and most involve difficult problems with multiple and competing constituents, managing the policy implementation process is often the most challenging and difficult activity of government.

Bureaucratic entrepreneurs are innovative public managers and executives who succeed at this level. But because the constraints and impediments they face are frustrating to the free exercise of managerial initiative, they often embrace an uncritical admiration for action. The result has been a sometimes troubling search for strategies designed to "get things done." Though often key to their success, these strategies have a bias toward action that sometimes do not sufficiently consider their costs. A moderate form of the behavior is exhibited by the bureaucratic entrepreneurs in our study. Seeking to be innovative in inhospitable environments, they often used creative subversion to outwit and overcome the perverse rules of bureaucratic logic that impede their initiative.

Creative subversion produces innovative outcomes, but it also has its costs. Thus there is continual tension between choice and action, which pits getting things done against critical democratic values. The absence of adequate accountability mechanisms compromises democratic values and can easily result in waste and fraud. These are the dilemmas of innovation and accountability, the trade-offs between underregulation and overregulation. We address these dilemmas in Chapter Seven.

In Chapters Three through Six, we analyze the first half of this dilemma: how innovation is achieved. We suggest effective executive strategies based on a wide range of success stories. Despite the tensions, we observed considerable success in public enterprises. To achieve it, public managers and executives pursue similar strategies. Private sector managers often face tensions and constraints inherent to large organizations. But in addition to these, the public sector adds unique and different challenges. We recognize how hard it is to be successful in this environment. Yet we also show how personally rewarding and socially important these successes are. The next four chapters provide an exhilarating and hopeful view of public management because they explore the means by which highly productive people achieve solutions to pressing problems. Further, they provide the road map for a new generation of public sector innovators.

Notes

1. Martin A. Levin, Sylvia B. Perlman, and Bonnie Hausman, "Gordon Chase: The Best and the Brightest Doing Good Deeds in New York City," paper presented at the Association for Public Policy Analysis and Management Research Conference, 1986; Burton Rosenthal, *Lead Poisoning* (Cambridge, Mass.: Harvard University, John F. Kennedy School of Government, 1975).
2. Several recent and notable attempts should be recognized. Most identify the critical range of functions necessary to manage public organizations, as in Steven Cohen, *The Effective Public Manager* (San Francisco: Jossey-Bass, 1988), or describe a few unusually effective public executives, as in Eugene Lewis, *Political Entrepreneurship* (Bloomington: Indiana University Press, 1980); others have attempted a theory of the behavior of public executives and of their contributions to public policy, as in Lawrence E. Lynn, Jr., *Managing the Public's Business* (New York: Basic Books, 1981).
3. This example could be even more realistic were we to consider the constraints that municipal labor contracts might place on these simple managerial decisions.

4. James Q. Wilson, "What Is to Be Done?", unpublished paper.
5. Eugene Bardach, *The Implementation Game: What Happens After a Bill Becomes Law* (Cambridge, Mass.: MIT Press, 1977).
6. Jeffrey Pressman and Aaron Wildavsky, *Implementation* (Berkeley: University of California Press, 1984).
7. It should be noted that the S&Ls themselves faced difficult business conditions and competition: In a period of high inflation, the S&Ls had difficulty competing with commercial banks, as we detail in Chapter Seven. This led them to undertake more risky loans and investment than they might in other conditions. These risky decisions, along with some cases of fraud, all occurred in the context of federal deposit insurance provided to the S&Ls. This insulated most from prudent assessment of risk. All these factors contributed to many of the S&Ls collapsing financially. But economic conditions often present such business difficulties. The weak policy link in this case was, however, the absence of sufficient management and oversight of the deregulation process.
8. Keith Schneider, "U.S. Cites Waste in Its Contracts," *New York Times,* December 1, 1992, p. A1.
9. The Defense Audit Contract Agency, a Pentagon division that also audits 99 percent of contracts in civilian agencies, had 5,900 employees in 1992, compared to 7,000 in 1989. Indeed, by 1992, some $160 billion in contracts had not yet been audited, and there was a five-year waiting period for an agency's request for

an audit to be acted on. Congress, for the most part, went along with these cuts. But when the Bush administration proposed further cuts in 1992, Congress balked.
10. Alfred E. Kahn, lecture delivered at the Gordon Public Policy Center, Brandeis University, Waltham, Massachusetts, May 1989.
11. Alfred E. Kahn, "Deregulation: Looking Backward and Looking Forward," *Yale Journal on Regulation* 7 (Spring 1990): 325–354; "I Would Do It Again," *Regulation,* Fall 1988, pp. 22–28.
12. Alfred E. Kahn, *Change, Challenge and Competition: The Report of the National Commission to Ensure a Strong, Competitive Airline Industry* (August 1993); "Surprises of Airline Deregulation," *The American Economic Review, Papers and Proceedings* 78 (May 1988): pp. 316–322.
13. Eugene Bardach, *The Skill Factor in Politics: Mental Health Reform in California* (Berkeley: University of California Press, 1970).
14. Bardach, *Implementation Game.*
15. A report by the New York City commission on the homeless documents the extent or recidivism among those who enter the city's emergency system. A full 50 percent of homeless families presently applying for permanent housing were previously placed by the city in permanent housing. See "The Way Home: New Directors in Social Policy," February 1992, p. 75.
16. Zbigniew Brzezinski, "The Failed Mission," *New York Times,* April 18, 1982, p. 28.; U.S. House of Representatives, Committee on Appropriations, Subcommittee

on Department of Defense, *Hearings on Appropriations, Fiscal Year 1981, Part 4* (Washington, D.C.: U.S. Government Printing Office, 1980), pp. 605–625; Drew Middleton, "Going the Military Route," *New York Times Magazine*, May 17, 1981, pp. 103–112; David C. Martin, "Inside the Rescue Mission," *Newsweek*, July 12, 1982, pp. 18–20.
17. Pressman and Wildavsky, *Implementation*.
18. Ibid.
19. Ibid.
20. "Director of Federal Drug Agency Calls Reagan Program a 'Liability,'" *New York Times*, May 18, 1984, p. 1.
21. Leslie Martland, "President's Anti-Drug Task Forces Are Falling Behind in Organizing," *New York Times*, May 1, 1983, p. 24.
22. Richard Neustadt and Henry Fineberg, *The Epidemic That Never Was: Policymaking and the Swine Flu Affair* (New York: Random House, 1983).
23. Douglas K. Smith and Robert C. Alexander, *Fumbling the Future: How Xerox Invented, Then Ignored the First Personal Computer* (New York: Morrow, 1988).
24. When Bill Lowe, the executive at IBM in charge of developing the PC, went about analyzing the competition, he immediately looked at Apple Computer, which was the number one producer of personal computers in 1980. "Because Apple was for a long while the only company to 'own' this market, it was uniquely positioned to achieve strong growth and high market profit margins." Apple's revenues rose from $800,000 in 1977 to almost $48 million just two years later. Between 1976 and 1986, Apple grew from a minuscule

business started in a garage with $1,300 to a large international corporation with $2 billion in revenues. See James Chposky and Ted Leonis, *Blue Magic: The People, Power, and Politics Behind the IBM Computer* (New York: Facts on File, 1988), pp. 7–8, 12.
25. Chposky and Leonis, *Blue Magic,* p. 9.
26. The software development for the machine started as soon as the primary machine with its open architecture was released—after four months—on a confidential basis to a select cadre of software developers. Thus while the hardware was being fine-tuned and its cosmetics set in place, software development for the machine was starting.
27. Chposky and Leonis, *Blue Magic,* p. 9.
28. Obviously, we distinguish between how services are financed (privately or publicly through taxes) and how they are provided. For example, local governments finance many child welfare services through tax revenue but contract out their provision to nongovernmental social welfare agencies, largely nonprofit agencies. *Private* in this case refers only to the arrangements for production. Although economic theory helps us determine what decisions should be made by government (for example, through what organizational means should government provide education, health care, prisons, or national defense?), it provides little guidance on what arrangement should be made.
29. For a full discussion of these points, see James Q. Wilson, *Bureaucracy* (New York: Basic Books, 1989), pp. 115, 330–332, 349. For a good summary of common

public sector barriers, see David N. Ammons, "Common Barriers to Productivity Improvement in Local Government," *Public Productivity Review,* Winter 1985, pp. 293–310.
30. Ibid., chap. 7.
31. Indeed, a controversial study of American education recently concluded that the institutional constraints on public education are so intractable and inherently limiting that improving education will require altering the arrangements for providing it. See John E. Chubb and Jerry M. Moe, *Politics, Markets, and America's Schools* (Washington, D.C.: Brookings Institution, 1990).
32. Rosabeth Moss Kanter, "The Organizational Climate for Innovation," in Barbara H. Moore, ed., *The Entrepreneur in Local Government* (Washington, D.C.: International City Management Associates, 1983). See also Alan Altshuler and Marc Zegans, "Innovations and Creativity: Comparisons Between Public Management and Private Enterprise," *Cities,* February 1990, pp. 16–24.
33. James Q. Wilson, "American Politics, Then and Now," *Commentary* 62 (1979): pp. 39–46; Theodore Lowi, *The End of Liberalism* (New York: Norton, 1971); Robert Dahl, *Who Governs* (New Haven, Conn.: Yale University Press, 1962).
34. Anthony King (ed.), *The New American Political System* (Washington, D.C.: American Enterprise Institute, 1990), p. 391.
35. Richard Harris and Sidney Milkis (eds.), *Remaking American Politics* (Boulder, Colo.: Westview Press, 1989).

36. Martin Shapiro, in *The New Politics of Policymaking*, ed. Martin A. Levin and Marc Landy (Baltimore: Johns Hopkins University Press, 1993).
37. See Robert Kagan, "Adversarial Legalism and American Government," and Shep Melnick, "Separation of Powers and the Strategy of Rights," in *New Politics*, ed. Levin and Landy.

| 3 |

Using Old Stuff in New Ways
The Sources of Innovation

Learning from success requires determining the sources of inspiration for innovation as well as its character. When we consider the formidable constraints that public managers face and the difficulty of asserting control over bureaucratic requirements, it is a wonder that any successful initiatives emerge in government organizations. One assumption might be that innovative activities that we and others have identified are unique instances where brilliant ideas or highly unusual discoveries drive success.[1]

If innovation and programmatic success depend on the inspiration of a genius, improving the performance of the public sector would lie in identifying and recruiting such individuals. This would make the prospects for wide-scale improvement rather dim. If, however, successful innovation does not require the rare skills of an inventor, the intellect of a genius, or a thunderbolt of inspiration, ordinary managers can learn how to succeed. This chapter explores the sources of innovation for a large number of initiatives. The lessons they teach suggest some basic approaches that others can learn.

> Evolution does not produce innovations from scratch. It works on what already exists, either transforming a system to give it new function or combining several systems to produce a more complex one. . . . This process resembles . . . tinkering, *bricolage* we say in French. . . . The tinkerer manages with odds and ends. Often without even knowing what he is going to produce, he uses whatever he finds around him, old cardboards, pieces of string, fragments of wood or metal, to make some kind of workable object.[2]

The innovative manager, we found, resembles François Jacob's brilliant evocation of the evolutionary tinkerer. Innovative programs are based on old stuff being used in new ways that develop through evolutionary tinkering. They are imperfect combinations of bits and pieces. Their character—what makes them innovative—very often emerges over time through trial and error. The source of innovation is often not new at all; indeed, it is frequently the novel combination of familiar elements.

Managers innovate through a process of wandering around, informally listening and looking. They pick up old stuff, chosen through the adaptive, trial-and-error process of "ready, fire, aim."[3] New plans change and adapt in response to assessments of actual field performance. This is both how successful practitioners behave to develop innovative initiatives and how they ought to behave. It is more effective and more realistic, especially in light of the bounded rationality and general cognitive limits encountered by more comprehensive approaches.[4]

Chapters Three through Six are organized around closely related themes. In Chapter Three, we analyze the *character* of innovation in the public sector—its nature and its sources. We then examine in Chapter Four the *process* of innovation—how to get there. Chapter Five investigates the *management style* of innovators. Chapter Six shows how to manage the *organizational culture* necessary to support innovative vision. Our emphasis is on the approaches used to bring these initiatives to fruition.

The cases that we analyze in these chapters suggest that the development of innovation is evolutionary, not the neat and orderly process prescribed by the policy analysis model. Indeed, rather than emerging from the rational analysis of alternative choices, most innovative initiatives are developed through experiential learning from experimentation at the implementation stage. Evolutionary tinkering is the essence of the management process that leads to innovation. These findings have important implications for how public managers ought to behave and what students of public management ought to be taught. (We discuss these lessons in Chapter Nine.)

Formal Policy Analysis or Experimental Field-Based Development

Policy analysis is the dominant paradigm for making policy choices. Central to the curricula of virtually all academic programs that prepare public managers, policy analysis provides a methodology to define policy problems, generate options, and evaluate them systematically on a set of policy relevant criteria. In so doing, analysts are expected to predict and measure all the likely impacts of a given policy choice.

However, comprehensive policy analysis models have generally failed to appreciate the cognitive limits that beset analysts and managers. Because so many obstacles and environmental constraints are hidden at the design stage, the trial-and-error process of actual implementation is often required to reveal what can work. Careful policy planning is costly and time-consuming and seldom provides the kind of learning that comes through actual implementation, which facilitates and telescopes the learning and feedback process. In short, John Wheeler's view of science—"our whole problem is to make errors fast enough"—also applies to policy making.[5]

Researchers are providing strong evidence that more often policy is made at the implementation stage and at every step along the way. Following Michael Lipsky's pioneering analysis, more recent analysts are demonstrating that prior planning and analysis may not be as useful as is often supposed, nor may they predict what actually happens when a policy is implemented.[6] A myriad of obstacles reveal themselves during the implementation stage that could never have been anticipated by program planning.

Robert Behn has suggested, "Public managers do and should grope along. They need to have a clear sense of mission for their agency. But they will never know precisely how to realize these purposes. The public manager cannot develop the perfect plan from the beginning. Rather, he or she must experiment with various initiatives, trying to determine what works and what does not."[7]

There is a dialogue in the field of public policy about the relative roles of formal analysis—as opposed to experiential, adaptive, field-based program development—in creating successful public enterprises.[8] This dialogue is at the heart of the field: analysis has always been advocated as the preeminent way to improve performance. The role of management was, to some extent, subordinate to analysis in the policy planning model, and its status and intellectual claims were seen as secondary.

A contending view—one that we put forth in this chapter both descriptively and prescriptively—is that successful program development is rarely based on formal analysis of alternative choices. Instead, policy innovation develops through learning from the field, especially through informal means and what we call evolutionary tinkering.

Policy scholars have just as much to contribute by studying the management of innovation as it occurs, with an eye toward improving it, as by studying how to analyze the prospects for innovative policies in advance. We found that innovation derives from experiential lessons. Managers alter their general course in the field on the basis of operational results. Evolutionary tinkering, however, suggests more directly the way the process of innovation proceeds: through the novel combination of old and familiar things in new ways. Innovative managers rely on the assemblage of bits and pieces of old stuff to create the new.

Innovation in the Natural Sciences: More Evolutionary than Revolutionary

Innovations in the natural sciences are very often more evolutionary than revolutionary—despite Thomas Kuhn's apparently misleading emphasis on scientific development occurring as the breakdown of one scientific paradigm by another through a "great set-piece battle."[9] The history of the development of molecular biology illustrates this.[10] Central to the world-changing development that resulted in the discovery of the structure of DNA was the use of old stuff (physics concepts) in a new setting (biology): "The move from physics [by] . . . Szilard, Crick, Maurice Wilkins and from physical chemistry by Pauling has been the intellectual migration that has mattered most to biology."[11]

Molecular biology's iterative and evolutionary development also proceeded through a process of error correction and a willingness to throw out incorrect hypotheses.

> The insight, however exalting, is not the discovery; it is a moment at the end of a process and the beginning of another. What the insight touches off, even before anything gets published, is the familiar and most characteristic work of the scientific community: criticism, modification, and the development of consequences. . . . DNA is an outstanding example of how a discovery twists and grows. What is still called the Watson-Crick structure of DNA is dif-

ferent today in factual detail from their first short paper in *Nature*.[12]

Analysis—careful analysis—is important in science. But Crick tells us that boldness, overly simple hypotheses, and a willingness to throw out the errors were just as essential in the development of molecular biology.[13]

The character of innovation in the public sector is similar: old stuff used in new ways. So too is the process. In the course of tinkering, wandering, and listening, the innovative manager often picks up old stuff and uses it in a new context. This applies to both innovative policy approaches and innovative management of routine policies.

Our Data

As described in Chapter One, the data for our model of innovative managers come from a diverse group of more than thirty successful public programs and agencies over the past two decades.[14] A brief description of each program can be found in Table 3.1.

Let us focus on a few.

Massachusetts Department of Revenue and Ira Jackson

Ira Jackson, appointed commissioner of the Massachusetts Department of Revenue (DOR) in 1983, developed and implemented several innovative programs through creative development of existing tools to improve tax enforcement. In 1982, the DOR had been seriously marred by a major scandal leading to a suicide, investigations, indictments,

Table 3.1. Programmatic Descriptions of Innovations in State and Local Government Award Winners.

Program	Jurisdiction or agency	Type	Function	Programmatic description
CARE (Computer Assisted Report Entry)	Saint Louis County Police Department	Application of new technology	Public safety	Enables police officers to phone in reports to a computer in a fraction of the normal time; shift from written to verbal reports frees police from clerical tasks so as to have more time for police work.
DAIP (Domestic Abuse Intervention Program)	City of Duluth, Minnesota, Police and Attorney departments	Administrative and management	Social services	Seeks to reduce incidence of domestic violence with aggressive use of enforcement tools.
Family Learning Center	State of Michigan	Direct client service	Social services	Brought counseling and support services into schools where it was needed for pregnant teens in an effort to promote educational attainment of this group with a typically high dropout rate.
Foodnet	Los Angeles County Department of Community and Senior Citizen's Services (DCSCS)	Direct client service	Social service and food delivery	Started as means to distribute extra cheese in 1982; now distributes broad range of food to low-income persons.
Fort Worth Storm Drain	City of Fort Worth, Texas	Administrative	Public works	Used old-fashioned technology to test water in storm drains widely and inexpensively.
HSN (Homeless Services Network)	Saint Louis Department of Human Services	Direct client services	Housing	Provides two phases: (1) intake and referral for employment and case management, (2) efforts to stabilize for permanent placement.
Integrated Wetland Enhancement	City of Arcata, California, Department of Public Works	Capital improvement	Public works	Produces from lagoon and wetland sewage high-quality effluent for use in marshes, recreation area, salmon fishery.

Program	Organization	Category 1	Category 2	Description
K-SIX Early Intervention Partnership	Fresno County, California	Direct client service	Social services	Seeks to integrate case-managed comprehensive services to at-risk elementary school kids and their families.
Medical Care for Children Project	Fairfax County, Virginia	Direct client service	Health services	Insures health care coverage for the children of uninsured working poor families through a cooperative arrangement between the county welfare department, health care providers, local businesses and other local actors.
New York City Department of Juvenile Justice	City of New York Department of Family Services	Direct client service	Rehabilitation service	Developed social and support services for youths in detention to change what was dead time into a productive experience.
New York Department of State	New York Department of State	Administrative	Management development	Changed from investigatory, adversarial function to a consultative, cooperative function by offering support to its client agencies, such as environmental policy advice for small towns.
Nova Ancora Projectc	City of New York Department of Probation	Direct client service	Job training and placement	Places probationers into small businesses and light industry.
One Church, One Child (Minority Adoption Campaign)	Illinois Department of Children and Family Services	Direct client service	Social services	By using the black clergy in an outreach effort, increased the number of adopted black children dramatically, with the goal of every black church congregation adopting at least one black child.
Open Net (Open Public Events Network)	North Carolina Agency for Public Telecommunications	Information	Science and technology, public information	Produces weekly two-hour TV show. First hour: taped hearing on a social issue. Second hour: viewers can call in and talk with participating state officials.
PACE (Parent and Child Education Program)	Kentucky General Assembly	Direct client service	Social services	Attempts to break Kentucky's cycle of undereducation by educating parents in order to educate their children.

Table 3.1. Progammatic Descriptions of Innovations in State and Local Government Award Winners, Cont'd.

Program	Jurisdiction or agency	Type	Function	Programmatic description
Parents Too Soon	Illinois Office of the Governor	Direct client service	Social services	Designed to help potential and actual teenage mothers through "comprehensive adolescent services."
Philadelphia Anti-Graffiti Network	City of Philadelphia	Direct client service	Criminal justice, rehabilitation, and neighborhood beautification	Through community cleanup and beautification projects, provides alternatives to prosecution for graffitists who sign a legal pledge to desist and agree to make restitution.
PPPE (Public/Private Partnerships in Education)	Tupelo, Mississippi, Municipal School District	Direct client service	Education	Designed to improve the quality of education in a weak school system.
Project Deliver: Assuring Quality Obstetrical Care	Montgomery County, Maryland	Direct client service	Health care services	A collaborative strategy between the medical society, local hospitals, and the Department of Health to provide low-cost obstetrical services to indigent patients.
Project Match	Illinois Department of Public Aid	Direct client service	Job training and placement	Moves welfare recipients toward stable employment through realistic, short-term goals in job training and job retention, which are used to achieve long-term goals of stable, long-term employment.
QUIP (Quality Incentive Program)	Illinois Department of Public Aid	Direct client service	Health	Provides financial rewards to high-quality long-term care facilities and seeks to provide incentives and education for further improvement.
REP (Rehabilitation Engineering Program)	State of New York Division of Rehabilitation Services	Direct client service	Rehabilitation (physical)	Arranges for REP engineers to visit handicapped at their homes and to recommend and design assistance tools for them.
School-Based Youth Services Program	State of New Jersey	Direct client service (health and social services)	Health, recreation, job training, and social services	Seeks to integrate health, social services, recreation, and job training services for at-risk teens in school to prevent dropping out and school and job failure.

Program	Location	Type	Area	Description
SRO (Single Room Occupancy Hotel Program)	City of San Diego, California, Planning Department	Legislative	Housing	Seeks to support SRO hotels, which are the last form of housing before homelessness.
Statewide Library Automation Project	Vermont Department of Libraries	Application of new technology	Science and technology	Designed to provide rural access to library systems and materials through use of microcomputers.
STEP (Strive Toward Excellence in Performance)	State of Minnesota	Productivity improvement	Management development	Operates as business-state labor partnership to improve state delivery of services through support for midlevel managers and employees at selected projects. Goal is to get agencies closer to clients who are supposed to receive the services.
Timber Bridge Program	Milford Township, Pennsylvania, Township Secretary	Capital improvement	Transportation	Uses new timber bridge technologies to build bridges of high stress capability at low cost for building and maintenance.
Trauma Intervention Programs	San Diego County, California	Direct client service	Social and support services	Seeks to provide support and services to victims of traumatic events at the site (for example, fire, crime, and so forth).
Work Force Unemployment Prevention Program	City of Cambridge, Massachusetts, Housing Authority	Direct client service	Job training and youth development	Builds self-esteem and school performance through job training, work skills, and exposure to adult role models and interventions.
XPORT, The Port Authority Trading Company	Port Authority of New York and New Jersey	Direct client service	Business services, economic development	Seeks to increase business activity in region by providing a diverse set of business services to small companies engaged in international trade that otherwise would be unable to increase business or launch new trading ventures.

Sources: Program applications and site visit reports from the files of the John F. Kennedy School of Government on the 1986–1991 award-winning programs for Innovations in State and Local Government—based on programs for which site visit reports were available and for which there was interview access to program executives.

and low employee morale. Incompetence and neglect were costing millions in lost revenue. Jackson's ambitious efforts significantly increased revenue collection without increasing taxes. Through aggressive enforcement, including commercial property seizures, the DOR recouped more than $200 million in unpaid taxes. Jackson then successfully proposed the Revenue Enforcement Protection Act (REAP), giving the DOR additional enforcement powers and creating a tax amnesty program yielding over $60 million in back taxes. REAP became a model for other states.[15]

New York City Health Services Administration and Gordon Chase

Gordon Chase, head of New York City's Health Services Administration (HSA) under Mayor John Lindsay from 1969 to 1973, developed and implemented a wide range of innovative programs during an era when it seemed that nothing could get done. He took on, and triumphed over, many seemingly intractable problems that had stymied politicians and administrators for years. His remarkable successes became national models, including lead paint poisoning screening, treatment, and repairs; dramatic improvement of the wretched health programs in the city's jails; establishing a massive methadone maintenance program for heroin addicts; supplementing city garbage collection to reduce rat bites among poor children; setting up hypertension testing outside medical institutions; and opening the first public abortion clinics (between New York State's legalizing of abortion in 1971 and the U.S. Supreme Court's

1973 decision legalizing it nationally). He successfully insisted on delivering services not just at a few pilot or demonstration sites but to very large numbers of clients.[16]

Environmental Protection Agency and William Ruckelshaus

The Environmental Protection Agency (EPA), created during the Nixon administration to consolidate environmental protection efforts, brought together fifteen separate agencies and almost six thousand personnel. William Ruckelshaus, appointed as the EPA's first administrator in 1970, took a fuzzy mandate and created a functioning and sometimes even powerful agency to protect the environment. He stressed the EPA's enforcement duties and built a powerful advocate for environmental concerns.

The challenge was to coordinate the preexisting agencies and to establish goals for the new agency. Ruckelshaus molded a strong agency, though coordination problems remained. Earlier pollution control authorities had a reputation for studying a problem to death. But Ruckelshaus selected pollution abatement as the EPA's initial goal. He used a vigorous legalistic enforcement policy involving litigation against major industries and cities. (In the agency's first two months, it brought five times as many enforcement actions as all its predecessors had in any two-month period.) That policy was very effective in attracting publicity and constituent support, distancing the EPA from the White House, and ultimately making the EPA a powerful advocate for the nation's environmental concerns.[17]

ET Choices in Massachusetts, Charles Atkins, and Thomas Glynn

Under Commissioner Charles Atkins and Deputy Commissioner Thomas P. Glynn, the Massachusetts Department of Public Welfare (DPW) seized the opportunity given them by the 1981 Omnibus Budget Reconciliation Act's authorization for states to launch demonstration programs. With federal authorization of Massachusetts as a demonstration site already in place under the previous governor and Atkins's experience as undersecretary of Human Services in 1978, they introduced Employment and Training Choices—an innovative employment and training program for welfare recipients—in 1983. The principal innovation was the creation of a new mission for the DPW that transformed its limited function of providing eligible clients with correct and timely payments into one that developed a route out of poverty through a broad range of employment and training options bolstered by coordinated support services such as child care, transportation, and job placement.

ET Choices was highly successful. It attracted large numbers of participants and alternative job placements (in the first eighteen months, fifteen thousand clients found jobs). Wage rates were twice as high as the welfare grant for full-time workers, and recidivism was low.[18] ET Choices introduced not only innovative policy but also innovative management. Line workers were treated as partners, and responsibilities for developing implementation approaches were pushed down into the organization. Success was strongly rewarded and publicized. Managers were held accountable for defined targets and rewarded in both concrete and symbolic ways. The DPW's changing mission was communicated constantly to all levels of the organization as well as to its clients and the larger community.

Innovations in State and Local Government Award Winners

The 1985 to 1991 winners in the Ford Foundation—Kennedy School Innovations in State and Local Government awards program developed innovative programs of enormous range. Half provided direct client services. But even here the range is great; innovative service strategies included, for example, job training and placement, food distribution, and education. Other types of innovative initiatives involved building physical infrastructures and applying new technologies to improve public safety or provide rural communities access to statewide library resources. In some cases, the innovation was the policy idea; in others, it was the management application of a rather prosaic idea. In many cases, the innovations involved both elements. Table 3.1 briefly summarizes their program details; we highlight a few of them here. The Saint Louis CARE program used computer technology (substituting a voice-activated computer for written police reports) to free police time for more patrol work. Pennsylvania's Timber Bridge Program used a new technology to build badly needed bridges out of wood and resulted in both many bridges and considerable savings. Simple technologies were key elsewhere: for example, California's wetland program in Arcata modestly treated wastewater to convert it to a natural resource for wetlands, and Fort Worth's Storm Drain program used old-fashioned technology to inexpensively test water in storm drains.

Other programs were innovative by changing bureaucratic relationships. Changing from an adversarial to a cooperative relationship, for example, was key to success for the New York Department of State. That unit's function had been investigatory—telling localities what they had not done. It was shifted to providing consulting services to small towns to help them develop local sewer and other similar programs. New York City's Department of Juvenile Justice innovated by adding social and support services to its detention function, thus moving beyond criminal justice into the realm of social service.

Private sector tools and public-private partnerships were essential for many of the Ford winners. For example, New York's Nova Ancora program was a rehabilitation effort that brought together small businesses and the Probation Department. One was interested in profits, the other in rehabilitation, but each helped the other. By hiring probationers, the businesses helped rehabilitate them; by connecting the probationers with the businesses, Nova Ancora helped solve some of their labor shortages. Similarly, Illinois's QUIP program brought together the interests of nursing homes and the Department of Public Aid (DPA). The latter's inspection program saved the state $15 million (largely by avoiding unnecessary expenditures), and the nursing homes received $18 million in free and friendly consultation and inspection from the DPA. The result was improved nursing home conditions.

Simple provision of support services in an area previously bereft of them was the key to Michigan's Family Learning Center's success. The program began with an exclusive focus on educating teenage girls who dropped out when they became pregnant. But the director found that the pregnant teens' needs negatively affected their capacity for schooling. Expansion into counseling and support services improved the teens' school performance and family functioning as well.[19]

In the next section, we summarize a general model that emerged from this case material. The accompanying tables summarize how well the model fits our sample. Table 3.2 indicates how each case fared with respect to the specific characteristics of the innovation, Table 3.3 indicates the process by which they were generated, and Table 3.4 indicates the management style of the primary manager or management team. The remainder of the chapter provides the specific case evidence that supports and elaborates the first part of our model.

The Character of Innovation

Successful public sector innovation rests on evolutionary ideas and on novel and creative combinations of familiar things, especially their adaptation in new contexts. Our data indicate that the character of innovation is not dominated by revolutionary ideas, by new approaches or techniques, or by new programs or institutions. Rather, the character of innovation is found in the evolution of ideas and in the use of old stuff in new ways, in new combinations, and in new contexts. For example, some of the most

Table 3.2. Character of Innovation in the Model Programs.

Program	Evolutionary tinkering	Using old stuff in new ways	Using novel combinations	Changing relationships between existing institutions
Massachusetts Department of Revenue (Massachusetts)	x	x	x	o
Monroe County Maternity Center (Tennessee)	x	x	x	x
New York City Health Services Administration (New York)	x	x	x	x
Environmental Protection Agency (Washington, D.C.)	x	x	x	x
Education and Training Choices (Massachusetts)	x	x	x	x
CARE (Computer Assisted Report Entry) (Saint Louis)	x	x	x	o
DAIP (Domestic Abuse Intervention Program) (Duluth, Minnesota)	x	o	x	
Fairfax County Medical Care for Children Project (Virginia)	x	x	x	x
Family Learning Center (Michigan)	x	x	x	x
Foodnet (Los Angeles)	o	x	x	o
Fort Worth Storm Drain (Fort Worth)	x	x	x	x
HSN (Homeless Services Network) (Saint Louis)	x	x	x	o
Integrated Wetland Enhancement (Arcata, California)	x	x	x	x
K-SIX Early Intervention Partnership (Fresno, California)	x	x	x	x
New York City Department of Juvenile Justice (New York)	x	x	x	x
New York Department of State (New York)	x	x	x	x

Program			
Nova Ancora (New York City)	x	x	o
One Church, One Child (Illinois)	x	o	o
Open Net (Open Public Events Network) (North Carolina)	x	x	o
PACE (Parent and Child Education Program) (Kentucky)	x	o	o
Parents Too Soon (Illinois)	x	x	x
Philadelphia Anti-Graffiti Network	x	x	x
PPPE (Public/Private Partnerships in Education) (Tupelo, Mississippi)	x	x	o
Project Deliver: Assuring Quality Obstetrical Care (Maryland)	x	x	x
Project Match (Illinois)	x	x	o
QUIP (Quality Incentive Program) (Illinois)	x	x	x
REP (Rehabilitation Engineering Program) (New York)	x	x	x
School-Based Youth Services Program (New Jersey)	x	x	x
SRO (Single Room Occupancy Hotel Program) (San Diego)	x	x	x
Statewide Library Automation Project (Vermont)	o	x	o
STEP (Strive Toward Excellence in Performance) (New York)	x	x	o
Timber Bridge Program (Milford, Pennsylvania)	x	x	x
Trauma Intervention Programs (San Diego)	x	x	x
Work Force Unemployment Prevention Program (Cambridge, Massachusetts)	x	x	
XPORT, The Port Authority Trading Company (New York and New Jersey)	x	x	x

Note: x = yes
o = no

Table 3.3. Nature of the Innovative Process in the Model Programs.

PROGRAM	MANAGEMENT APPROACHES UTILIZED				
	Iterative	Aim-Fire-Ready	Management by wandering around	Interest convergence	Error correction
Massachusetts Department of Revenue (Massachusetts)	x	x	x	x	x
Monroe County Maternity Center (Tennessee)	x	x	x	x	x
New York City Health Services Administration (New York)	o	x	o	x	x
Environmental Protection Agency (Washington, D.C.)	x	x	x	x	x
Education and Training Choices (Massachusetts)	x	x	x	x	x
CARE (Computer Assisted Report Entry) (Saint Louis)	o	o	o	x	o
DAIP (Domestic Abuse Intervention Program) (Duluth, Minnesota)	o	o	x	x	x
Fairfax County Medical Care for Children Project (Virginia)	x	x	x	x	x
Family Learning Center (Michigan)	x	x		o	o
Foodnet (Los Angeles)	o	o	o	o	o
Fort Worth Storm Drain (Fort Worth)	o	o	o	x	o
HSN (Homeless Services Network) (Saint Louis)	o	o	o	x	x
Integrated Wetland Enhancement (Arcata, California)	x	o		o	x
K-SIX Early Intervention Partnership (Fresno, California)	x	x	x	x	x
New York City Department of Juvenile Justice (New York)		x		x	o
New York Department of State (New York)	x	o	o	x	o
Nova Ancora (New York City)	NA	NA	NA	x	NA

Program				
One Church, One Child (Illinois)	o			o
Open Net (Open Public Events Network) (North Carolina)	o			o
PACE (Parent and Child Education Program) (Kentucky)	o	o	o	x
Parents Too Soon (Illinois)	x	x	o	x
Philadelphia Anti-Graffiti Network	x	x	x	x
PPPE (Public/Private Partnerships in Education) (Tupelo, Mississippi)	x	x	o	x
Project Deliver: Assuring Quality Obstetrical Care (Maryland)	x	x	o	x
Project Match (Illinois)	x	o	o	x
QUIP (Quality Incentive Program) (Illinois)	o	x		x
REP (Rehabilitation Engineering Program) (New York)	x	x	o	o
School-Based Youth Services Program (New Jersey)	x	x	o	x
SRO (Single Room Occupancy Hotel Program) (San Diego)	x	x	x	o
Statewide Library Automation Project (Vermont)	o	o	o	x
STEP (Strive Toward Excellence in Performance) (New York)	x	o	o	x
Timber Bridge Program (Milford, Pennsylvania)	o	x	o	o
Trauma Intervention Programs (San Diego)	x	x	o	x
Work Force Unemployment Prevention Program (Cambridge, Massachusetts)	x	x		x
XPORT, The Port Authority Trading Company (New York and New Jersey)	x	x	o	x

Note: x = yes
o = no
NA = not available

Table 3.4. Feature of Management Style in the Model Programs.

Program	Tinkerer	Mission Developer	Mission Outsider	Action-Oriented Manager	Opportunistic Manager	User of Hiding-Hand Strategy
Massachusetts Department of Revenue (Massachusetts)	x	x	x	x	x	x
Monroe County Maternity Center (Tennessee)	x	x	x	x	x	x
New York City Health Services Administration (New York)	x	x	x	x	x	x
Environmental Protection Agency (Washington, D.C.)	x	x	x	x	x	x
Education and Training Choices (Massachusetts)	x	x	x	x	x	x
CARE (Computer Assisted Report Entry) (Saint Louis)	o	x	NA	NA	NA	NA
DAIP (Domestic Abuse Intervention Program) (Duluth, Minnesota)	x	x	x	NA	NA	NA
Family Learning Center (Michigan)	x	x	x	x	x	x
Fairfax County Medical Care for Children Project (Virginia)	x	x	NA	x	x	x
Foodnet (Los Angeles)	NA	NA	NA	NA	NA	NA
Fort Worth Storm Drain (Fort Worth)	NA	NA	NA	NA	NA	NA
HSN (Homeless Services Network) (Saint Louis)	NA	NA	NA	NA	NA	NA
Integrated Wetland Enhancement (Arcata, California)	NA	NA	NA	NA	NA	NA
K-SIX Early Intervention Partnership (Fresno, California)	x	x	x	x	x	x
New York City Department of Juvenile Justice (New York)	x	x	x	x	x	x
New York Department of State (New York)	x	x	x	o	x	o
Nova Ancora (New York City)	NA	NA	NA	NA	NA	NA

Program	C1	C2	C3	C4	C5	C6
One Church, One Child (Illinois)	x	x	x	NA	x	o
Open Net (Open Public Events Network) (North Carolina)	NA	NA	NA	NA	NA	NA
PACE (Parent and Child Education Program) (Kentucky)	NA	NA	NA	NA	NA	NA
Parents Too Soon (Illinois)	NA	NA	NA	NA	NA	NA
Philadelphia Anti-Graffiti Network	x	x	x	x	x	x
PPPE (Public/Private Partnerships in Education) (Tupelo, Mississippi)	NA	NA	NA	NA	NA	NA
Project Deliver: Assuring Quality Obstetrical Care (Maryland)	x	x	NA	x	x	x
Project Match (Illinois)	x	x	x	NA	NA	NA
QUIP (Quality Incentive Program) (Illinois)	x	x	x	NA	NA	NA
REP (Rehabilitation Engineering Program) (New York)	NA	NA	NA	NA	NA	NA
School-Based Youth Services Program (New Jersey)	x	x	x	x	x	x
SRO (Single Room Occupancy Hotel Program) (San Diego)	NA	NA	NA	NA	NA	NA
Statewide Library Automation Project (Vermont)	NA	NA	NA	NA	NA	NA
STEP (Strive Toward Excellence in Performance) (New York)	NA	NA	NA	NA	NA	NA
Timber Bridge Program (Milford, Pennsylvania)	NA	NA	NA	x	x	o
Trauma Intervention Programs (San Diego)	x	x	NA	x	x	x
Work Force Unemployment Prevention Program (Cambridge, Massachusetts)	x	x	NA	x	x	x
XPORT, The Port Authority Trading Company (New York and New Jersey)	x	x	NA	x	x	x

Note: x=yes
o=no
NA=not available

novel and innovative initiatives we studied derived from common practices applied in a new setting, a new sector of the economy, or a new population. The use of old stuff in a different context often generates novel approaches and yields what we call "prosaic profundities."

Evolutionary Innovation

Innovation in the public sector is typically evolutionary; it is not produced from scratch. One state will borrow a program idea from another. Innovation at the EPA, for example, occurred through evolutionary tinkering and evolved from existing programs. William Ruckelshaus used old ideas in new contexts and combined bits and pieces of existing programs and old laws with new approaches to forge a successful agency with innovative policies. Legalistic enforcement—an old thing—was used in a new context, pollution abatement. (The EPA's predecessor had used a consensual, negotiating approach to pollution abatement.)

Ruckelshaus considered alternatives. Many were proposed by the carryover staff he inherited, including seeking new, broader legislative authority. Eschewing the political uncertainty of a legislative effort, however, he turned to an old law to provide the EPA's authority: the 1899 Refuse Act, originally passed to keep navigable waters free of shipping obstructions!

Similarly, the innovations characteristic of most of the Ford Foundation winners were evolutionary. For example, the Integrated Wetland Enhancement program improved wetlands through an evolutionary shift. Instead of viewing wastewater as a by-product to be discarded, it was approached innovatively as a natural resource that could be used, after treatment, for irrigation.

With the help of some new processes, the Timber Bridge Program used wood for bridges—hardly a revolutionary idea—to build, at low cost, many bridges with high-stress capability to ease a bridge shortage in the area. CARE, a program of the Saint Louis police department, made a small evolutionary shift in the method beat officers used to report incidents. Replacing written reports with verbal reports via radio to clerical staff yielded large increases in the officers' active time in the field, producing increased productivity and cost savings. The Nova Ancora program was able to accomplish the difficult task of placing probationers in jobs by shifting its program focus from large to small businesses, which were much more open to providing training. In all these cases, small shifts evolved in the use of existing program elements. This evolution produced innovation.

Innovation at the Massachusetts Department of Revenue was also evolutionary. Several old things were used in new ways, new contexts, and toward new ends. Ira Jackson's first innovation was aggressively implementing enforcement and collection procedures. He turned existing but seldom used tax enforcement laws into innovative vehicles for tax compliance and collection by wrapping these procedures in a lot of publicity. Because general tax compliance relies largely on the taxpayers' perception of the likelihood that evaders will be caught and punished, public pillorying of offenders often has a significant impact. Commercial properties were seized for delinquent business and sales taxes, and highly visible retail businesses like restaurants were closed down. Boats and airplanes were impounded for delinquent personal property taxes.

These cases reveal that successful innovation evolves from preexisting ideas and resources. Ruckelshaus used existing ideas and laws in the new context of an environmental bureaucracy. The Ford winners adapted existing programs and concepts to new purposes. Jackson used existing DOR procedure in a high-profile manner.

Old Stuff in a New Context

As we have emphasized, public sector innovation, be it innovative policy approaches or innovative management of routine approaches, is often simply the use of old stuff in new ways. The new ways may be the use of a routine approach in a new context, such as the efforts to deliver social services to youths in a detention center by the New York City Department of Juvenile Justice.

New ways can also be the use of techniques in the public sector that are typically associated with the private sector. Old stuff serving in a new and different context often yields prosaic profundities. ET Choices used marketing—unheard of for a welfare department—to attract welfare clients to a work-welfare program. Another new way is the use of a routine treatment mode but with a new delivery system or to a new population at a new location. Gordon Chase's blood pressure testing of low-income populations by paraprofessionals at mobile neighborhood sites

USING OLD STUFF

is a good example of this kind of innovation. Though commonplace today, hypertension testing outside a medical facility by nonphysicians was a radical idea at the time. A small change in the mode and context had a dramatic impact, increasing access and thus preventive therapy.

In the 1960s, the synthetic chemical methadone was developed in the Netherlands to block heroin craving and was used there and in Hong Kong to treat heroin addicts. Then it was used in a small-scale methadone maintenance program at a New York hospital. The development of a methadone maintenance program by Chase was therefore tinkering with both an established idea and an existing program. The innovation was in placing it in two new contexts: first, having the city sponsor a chemical treatment program (previous programs had been limited to "talking therapies") and, second, defining a new target population—all addicts—and using an aggressive outreach program to reach it. Previously, successful drug treatment programs had focused on a small group of stable, highly motivated addicts.

The Innovations awards often hailed initiatives based entirely on using old stuff in a new context. For example, an old thing, consulting, being used in a new context, the public sector, led to innovation in the New York Department of State program. Historically, the department pursued an investigatory compliance role: it told localities what they had not done. The innovation was a shift in how they viewed their role, moving from a negative to a positive relationship with localities by offering them consulting services. This helped local governments develop sewer systems and other similar programs that their limited planning expertise would not otherwise have permitted. Such a consulting role was old stuff commonly provided by the Agriculture Department's County Agent program, which offered technical advice to municipalities too small to be able to obtain it themselves. But the Department of State used it in a new context—environmental policy advice for small towns.

Other Ford award winners that used old stuff in a new context included QUIP, which came up with significant innovations for nursing homes (including large cost reductions and free consulting services) by using old stuff (economic incentives) in a new context (a public sector program). Similarly, the Vermont library program was innovative simply by using the existing technologies of microcomputer networks in a new setting, rural libraries. This produced important changes by providing rural users access to statewide library resources. Fort Worth's Storm Drain program had similar success using an old-fashioned, simple technology in a new context—testing water in storm drains, thereby reducing pollution.

Probably no method is as old as midwifery. But nowhere was it used as the principal birthing approach outside a hospital setting. Tennessee's Monroe County Maternity Center (MCMC) used a nurse-midwife-staffed birthing center to meet the prenatal and obstetrical needs of poor rural women. Far from the urban hospital center in Knoxville, MCMC provided a freestanding facility for normal deliveries and thus used existing practice in a new setting.

At the Massachusetts Department of Revenue under Jackson, old stuff became innovative by applying to a public agency approaches that were fairly standard practice in the private sector—another example of prosaic profundities. Jackson converted a classic bureaucratic, catch-22 agency into, of all things, a responsive, service-oriented organization that treated its captive clients as good customers rather than victims. By providing services like rapid refund checks and a problem resolution office to respond to customer complaints, he redefined his organization's function as customer service.

Several of the Ford winners also successfully used private sector approaches in the new context of the public sector. New Jersey's School-Based Youth Services program, like Jackson at the DOR, took a customer-centered approach. Organized to meet the needs of kids rather than the needs of participating agencies, the New Jersey program made kids the center of the service delivery system. As such, it confronted the institutional logic of the service providers that had resulted in fragmentation of services and in the orientation of the delivery systems, which were more likely to respond to kids' needs following their failures rather than preventing them.

The New York–New Jersey Port Authority's XPORT program was developed basically to perform a common private sector function: to act as a broker for small companies seeking access to capital, an unusual role for the public sector. Both the function and the clients were novel for a public activity. Indeed, even in the private sector, banks seldom bothered with small loans like these.

At the DOR, Jackson seized another old thing, tax evasion, and placed in a new, more powerful, and visible context, criminal prosecution. He redefined tax evasion. Eschewing the conventional view of tax evasion as a "victimless crime," he argued persuasively for emphasizing its criminal aspect: "Honest taxpayers, God willing that's the majority, end up subsidizing those who evade, cheat, and don't file."[20] This redefinition, and follow-up enforcement as criminal cases, increased the deterrent value of enforcement and yielded additional revenue.

Under Chase, innovation at the HSA evolved from known procedures used in new, often controversial contexts. Hypertension testing was a familiar procedure in 1970 but available only in medical facilities. Chase tinkered with it. He had the temerity to propose that this routine procedure could be provided outside medical facilities to reach the much broader low-income population that did not regularly visit them. Today this prosaic profundity is widely practiced outside medical facilities. Similarly, his rat bite control program used a most prosaic procedure, garbage collection, but Chase tinkered with the delivery agent. The HSA took on part of the collection procedure in the context that the Sanitation Department would not touch—inside buildings. It was a new conceptualization of garbage as a source of rat bites of children.

The lesson of these cases is that old stuff often becomes innovative when a routine approach is used in a new context or when private sector techniques are adapted for the public sector.

Novel Combinations of Familiar Things

Innovation is often a novel assemblage of familiar elements. Altering relationships between existing institutions is one such example. For ET Choices, success depended in part on the Department of Public Welfare's changed relationship with the Employment Security Department, a collaboration to achieve joint goals. In general, ET Choices was an innovation that evolved almost entirely from existing programmatic and management ideas that were creatively recombined. (Welfare Commissioner Atkins had been exposed to these ideas in previous positions in the employment field.)

The innovations of several of the Ford award winners sprang from novel combinations of services and approaches that are quite familiar but generally found independently. At New York City's Department of Juvenile Justice, Ellen Schall turned the dead time of detention into a more productive period for kids by providing social support services to meet more fundamental needs. By combining her agency's custodial function with more proactive social and support services, she redefined the role of her agency.

At Cambridge's Work Force unemployment prevention program, Steven Swanger developed a highly effective youth development and employment program through a novel combination of multiple services and interventions. Identifying the optimal place to reach at-risk youths as their place of residence, Swanger combined a housing and a social service function. Further, understanding the importance of self-esteem as motivating success and contributing to continued effort, Swanger shaped a unique program that combined work skills, exposure to role models on the job, and training to improve school performance and employment prospects. Work Force achieved its success by linking education and employment and providing the necessary programmatic supports to assist youths to achieve success in both. The innovation was in the assemblage of these familiar elements.

Similarly, Ed Tetelman of New Jersey's School-Based Youth Services program created an innovative social service program in the schools designed to help teenagers in trouble and prevent more serious problems through dropout prevention and work training. The objective was to make available an array of services not typically combined in the same setting—health, mental health, employment, and family counseling—and to encourage their use by making it voluntary and linked to recreational activities. The program gave adolescents the opportunity to complete their education, to obtain skills that lead to employment or additional education, and to lead physically and mentally healthy lives. Tetelman arranged this by bringing together historical adversaries—schools and social service agencies—in a unique collaboration.

Philadelphia's Anti-Graffiti Network was a novel combination of law enforcement and community beautification. A collaborative effort, it combined multiple objectives to control and clean graffiti while providing youthful offenders with alternative outlets for their energies. It is a classic example of innovation derived from combinations of unexpected elements. Police, volunteers, professional artists, and community organizations work together in unexpected ways. The result has been enforcement, cleanup, neighborhood beautification, and youth development.

The DOR's amnesty program evolved from novel combinations of familiar things. Amnesty is not a new concept in the public sector or even in the annals of tax collection; the DOR picked it up from other states. But using it as the carrot combined with the big stick of enforcement efforts was novel and produced a greater success than in other states where it had been tried. Similarly, the Philadelphia Anti-Graffiti Network used an amnesty program (persons guilty of applying graffiti could sign a pledge not to do so again and be exempt from prosecution for prior offenses). It was also used in combination with a strong law enforcement crackdown, which helped convince local courts to treat graffiti writing as serious vandalism. Combined with a strong commitment to prosecute and the designation of a special unit of the police department's Juvenile Division to target major graffiti vandals and repeat offenders, the program became a creative combination of incentives and sanctions, of carrots and sticks.

At the EPA, innovation was also characterized by novel combinations of familiar things. Often one of the most effective ways of implementing a new program is to create a brand-new agency for it. But this was not how the EPA developed. Instead, it was created by amalgamating existing federal agencies and programs.

In one of his innovations at the HSA, Chase delivered a familiar product (health care) in a new and controversial context (the city's prisons) by changing the character of relationships between existing institutions. The HSA contracted with Montefiore Hospital to provide health care to the city's prisons. Until then, the HSA had ignored the city's prison population, whose health was poor and for whom inadequate health care had become an increasingly volatile issue. (Before this innovative intervention, responsibility for health care services to prisons resided with another cabinet agency, the Human Resources Administration.)

These cases show that innovation grows from novel combinations of familiar things more than from the birth of a wholly new concept.

Conclusion

The central lesson of these cases is that successful innovation springs from evolutionary ideas, the use and adaptation of routine approaches in new contexts, and novel and creative combinations of familiar things. Jackson at the DOR, for example, successfully redefined the context in which tax evasion was understood. He adapted private sector customer-centered techniques in the context of a public sector bureaucracy while using familiar amnesty and enforcement ideas in a novel and effective combination. Jackson did not need brilliant new ideas or intricately devised new initiatives to turn the DOR into an innovative agency.

The implications are clear. Innovation is not the sole domain of genius, nor does it spring from a thunderbolt of inspiration. Innovative concepts generally derive from evolutionary tinkering with established practices. Using old stuff in new ways can create novel and highly effective new initiatives. Novel combinations of familiar elements can produce altogether different outcomes.

Managers at all levels of public organizations can improve their activities by understanding these sources of inspiration. All managers can be innovative. They simply need be aware of a broader inventory of existing practice than what they are likely to observe in their narrow domain. Further, our findings suggest that scanning the environment, being open to existing resources, and incremental tinkering are most often the ways in which novel and effective interventions develop. These are lessons for aspiring managers.

Notes

1. David Osborne and Ted Gaebler, *Reinventing Government* (Reading, Mass.: Addison-Wesley, 1992); Robert D. Behn, *Leadership Counts: Lessons for Public Managers from the Massachusetts Welfare, Training and Employment Program* (Cambridge, Mass.: Harvard University Press, 1991); Richard J. Merritt and Anya J. Merritt (eds.), *Innovation in the Public Sector* (Newbury Park, Calif.: Sage, 1985); Alan Altshuler and Marc Zegans, "Innovation and Creativity: Comparisons Between Public Management and Private Enterprise," *Cities,* February 1990, pp. 16–24; Olivia Golden, "Innovation in Public Sector Human Services Programs," *Journal of Policy Analysis and Management* 9 (1990): 219–248.
2. François Jacob, *The Possible and the Actual* (Seattle: University of Washington Press, 1982). We wish to thank Eugene Bardach for first suggesting the relevance of Jacob's work on evolutionary biology to man-

agement. The concept applied to public policy was first introduced by Gerald Garvey in *Constitutional Bricolage* (Princeton, N.J.: Princeton University Press, 1971).
3. Thomas Peters and Robert Waterman, *In Search of Excellence* (New York: HarperCollins, 1982), pp. 119–123, 155. Robert D. Behn, in "Management by Groping Along," *Journal of Policy Analysis and Management* 7 (1988): 648, has modified this to "aim, fire, ready" because he suggests that executives often know what they are aiming at but need to know how to fire a gun, which guns to fire, or whether they need to design new guns.
4. On bounded rationality and cognitive limits, see Charles Lindbloom, "The Science of Muddling Through," *Public Administration Review*, September 1959, pp. 79–88, and, more generally, the works of Herbert Simon.
5. John Wheeler, quoted in Aaron Wildavsky, *Speaking Truth to Power* (Boston: Little, Brown, 1979), p. 6.
6. Michael Lipsky, *Street Level Bureaucracy* (New York: Russell Sage Foundation, 1980). In particular, Lipsky demonstrates the singular and independent role that public service personnel—police officers, social workers—play in determining how a policy is actually implemented in the field and thus what the actual impact is.
7. Behn, "Management by Groping Along." See also Alan Altshuler, "A Comment on 'Groping Along,'" *Journal of Policy Analysis and Management* 7 (1988): 664–667; and Golden, "Innovation."

8. Another contribution to the reexamination of the field was Olivia Golden's 1990 article "Innovation in Public Sector Human Services Programs." She used data from the innovative programs identified by the Ford Foundation–Kennedy School Innovations in State and Local Government awards program to test Behn's argument that managers "grope along" by testing and adapting policy to the realities they find in the field. Though she limited her analysis to human services programs, her critical contribution was to confirm, for the most part, the role of managerial experimentation and learning in the field in the development of innovative programs.
9. Thomas Kuhn, *The Structure of Scientific Revolutions* (University of Chicago Press, 1970).
10. Horace F. Judson, *The Eighth Day of Creation: Makers of the Revolution in Biology* (New York: Touchstone, 1980).
11. Ibid., p. 612. Judson suggests that the pattern of innovation in biology is more common in the sciences than suggested by Thomas Kuhn and others who rely almost exclusively on examples from physics:
   > Historians of science, in trying to account for revolutionary change, have relied upon the history of physics almost exclusively, and in physics have appealed to certain great set-piece battles. . . . The rise of molecular biology asks for a different model. Copernican astronomy, Newtonian physics, relativity, quantum mechanics—but biology has

> no such towering, overarching theory save the theory of evolution by mutation and natural selection. . . . Biology has proceeded not by great set-piece battles but by multiple small-scale encounters—guerrilla actions—across the landscape. In biology, no large-scale, closely interlocking, fully worked out, ruling set of ideals has ever been overthrown. In the normal way of growth of the science, variant local states of knowledge and understanding may persist for considerable periods. Revolution in biology, from the beginnings of biochemistry and the study of cells, and surely in the rise of molecular biology and on to the present day, has taken place not by overturnings but by openings-up (p. 612).

12. Ibid.
13. Ibid., pp. 612–613:

    > Just as important as having ideas is getting rid of them. . . . From Bragg and Pauling I learned how to see problems, how not to be confused by the details, and that is a sort of boldness; and how to make oversimple hypotheses—you have to, you see, it's the only way you can proceed—and how to test them, and how to discard them without getting too enamored of them. All that is a sort of boldness.

14. Several of these cases are well known. However, our analyses differ from the conventional view of them.

For example, in some instances we offer critical insights even of these successful executives.
15. Robert D. Behn, *The Massachusetts Department of Revenue: Sequel* (Durham, N.C.: Duke University, Institute of Policy Sciences and Public Affairs, 1986).
16. Martin A. Levin, Bonnie Hausman, and Sylvia B. Perlman, "Gordon Chase: The Best and the Brightest Doing Good Deeds in New York City," paper presented at the Association for Public Policy Analysis and Management Research Conference, 1986; Diana Gordon, *City Limits* (New York: Charterhouse, 1973), pp. 17–106; Charles Morris, *The Cost of Good Intentions: New York City and the Liberal Experiment, 1960—1975* (New York: Norton, 1980); Mark Moore and M. Ziering, *Methadone Maintenance in New York City* (Cambridge, Mass.: Harvard University, John F. Kennedy School of Government, 1976).
17. Joseph Bower and Gregory B. Mills, *William D. Ruckelshaus and the Environmental Protection Agency* (Cambridge, Mass.: Harvard University, John F. Kennedy School of Government, 1974); Alfred A. Marcus, *Promise and Performance: Choosing and Implementing an Environmental Policy* (Westport, Conn.: Greenwood Press, 1980).
18. See Robert D. Behn, *The Management of ET Choices in Massachusetts* (Durham, N.C.: Duke University, Institute of Policy Sciences and Public Affairs, 1989); Office of Research Planning Evaluation of Public Welfare, *An Evaluation of the Massachusetts Employment and Training Choices Program: Interim Findings on Participation and Outcomes* (Boston: Commonwealth

of Massachusetts, 1986), pp. 484–485; and Massachusetts Taxpayers Foundation, "Training People to Live Without Welfare" (Boston: Massachusetts Taxpayers Foundation, 1987). More recent evaluations reported by the Urban Institute generally support the view that ET Choices is a highly successful program; see, for example, Demetra Nightingale, "Use of Transitional Child Care and Health Assistance in Massachusetts's ET Choices Program," paper presented at the Association for Public Policy Analysis and Management Research Conference, Arlington, Virginia, November 1989.

19. Pamela Varley, *Ellen Schall and the Department of Juvenile Justice* (Cambridge, Mass.: Harvard University, John F. Kennedy School of Government, 1987); Anna M. Warrock, *Finding Black Parents: One Church, One Child* (Cambridge, Mass.: Harvard University, John F. Kennedy School of Government, 1988); Leslie Brunetta, *Jean Ekins and the Family Learning Center* (Cambridge, Mass.: Harvard University, John F. Kennedy School of Government, 1988); Kristen Lundberg, *XPORT: A Public Sector Trading Company* (Cambridge, Mass.: Harvard University, John F. Kennedy School of Government, 1990); David M. Kennedy, *Spreading the Gospel: The Origin and Growth of the DARE Program* (Cambridge, Mass.: Harvard University, John F. Kennedy School of Government, 1991).

20. Behn, *The Massachusetts Department of Revenue,* 1986.

4

Not from Blueprints
The Process of Innovation

Innovative interventions evolve. Managers who want to invigorate government organizations need not generate an entirely new or original concept. Indeed, we discovered a remarkable process of adaptation of familiar elements among the most effective and novel programs. Evolution is incremental and follows a carefully managed process whereby program elements are adapted in response to actual field conditions. Successful innovation depends primarily on a flexible manager who engages in learning in the field.

How a manager who seeks new and effective initiatives goes about the process is the central question of this chapter. If effective managers share a set of skills that can be learned, the prospects for improved performance are infinitely better. Our review of the many cases of successful innovation reveals useful and replicable practices that most managers pursue. This is the process of innovation, of exploration, filled with trial and error, adaptation, iteration, and error correction.

Innovation Through Evolutionary Tinkering

We found that public sector innovations did not spring forth spanking new, as if from blueprints. Their novelty was more often in their assemblage, often of familiar parts. Like natural selection, the evolutionary tinkering that ultimately produces innovation is messy. Organisms change and adapt; their fate is tested in the field. Evolutionary tinkering—using bits and pieces of what's around in new ways to meet changing circumstances—is iterative, incremental, and disorderly. Failure—error—becomes the basis for evolutionary learning. Analysis occurs at the implementation stage after a process that is begun to "do the doable." Implementation helps practitioners detect errors in ideas and designs and then correct them. It gives them the opportunity to make errors, which is the most realistic way to detect weaknesses in policy ideas.

Iteration and Adaptation

Innovation at the Environmental Protection Agency was iterative, experimental, adaptive, and full of efforts at error correction. William Ruckelshaus was a tinkerer. He faced an ill-defined mix of existing agencies and programs and a vague legislative mandate. He decided to start small—to take a narrow focus and move incrementally. He also wanted to avoid the dangers of defining his mandate too broadly or too narrowly, which he had seen limit the effectiveness of other new agencies. The National Aeronautic and Space Administration's mission was too narrow ("a man on the moon in ten years") and as a result almost put itself out of business; the Office of Economic Opportunity's was too amorphous ("let's do something about poverty"), and hence its success was too difficult to measure.

Managing by groping along is a process whereby managers move incrementally but without a detailed road map because they are unlikely to know precisely how to realize this objective.[1] This was Ruckelshaus's approach. He did not follow the policy analysis model—undertaking a systematic examination of all of his policy alternatives. Instead, he defined a rather discrete mission for his enterprise—pollution abatement—and pursued an aggressive program of legalistic enforcement. He undertook a series of highly visible lawsuits in his first two weeks in office. Later the agency might have to backfill. It was management by groping along, but it was action. It was dramatic. It provided a jump start for his enterprise, creating what he felt he needed: immediate credibility for both him and the EPA.

Ruckelshaus's decision to begin with lawsuits had an additional benefit. Because the technical experts at the EPA were mostly transferees from old-line agencies (such as the Department of Agriculture) and were sympathetic to the industries they regulated, using a litigation approach was also designed to loosen their dominance. Instead of regulation writing, which would depend greatly on these "quasi-captured technocrats," litigation allowed Ruckelshaus to transfer power and hence direction to his new cadre of highly committed environmental lawyers.[2]

Innovation for many of the Ford Foundation's award winners also was iterative, incremental, and adaptive. Take, for example, the Family Learning Center's unplanned expansion into counseling and support services. The program began as an alternative school to allow teens who dropped out when they became pregnant to complete their education. But the director found that the pregnant teens' personal needs were a much greater determinant of their educational outcomes than she anticipated. The teens' presence in an alternative school environment became an opportunity to address these other critical and even more fundamental needs. These insights, however, were learned along the way, and the program was continually adapted to meet the teens' psychological and personal needs. To the classroom activities contemplated at the outset were added additional counseling and support services that turned out to be essential in improving school performance.

The Fort Worth Storm Drain program developed through evolutionary tinkering—broad and inexpensive water testing was achieved by small changes in an old-fashioned technology. Tennessee's Monroe County Maternity Center began simply as a rural facility designed to give low-income women access to prenatal care and a midwife-staffed birthing center. But along the way it evolved into a women's community resource that provided an increasing number of services to meet needs not originally anticipated: well-women care, sex education, and general health care were all services that evolved incrementally in response to newly identified needs. Indeed, though initially planned for the indigent, the center grew to attract 40 percent of its clients from people with third-party coverage.

New York–New Jersey Port Authority's XPORT program exhibited classic adaptive abilities. It initially sought to become the agency's subsidiary export trading company. That, however, required legislation to allow the new company to assume a variety of functions, including taking title to goods, operating warehouses, issuing insurance, offering legal assistance, and providing trade documentation. These roles, in addition to freight forwarding, foreign exchange, and financial services, were not performed by the Port Authority. But the legislation failed to pass because of opposition from both the private sector (which did not want the competition) and the legislature (which worried about its susceptibility to corruption).

The basic concept of XPORT did not die, however. Instead, its director, Herb Ouida, in an evolutionary and iterative manner, designed what he called a public-private partnership: XPORT would provide logistical support, financial brokering service, and consulting guidance to small companies. For example, by handling dozens of export transactions, XPORT could obtain favorable terms for small clients who could not have afforded to get into the export business on their own. Similarly, most banks were not interested in the small loans that XPORT's small clients needed. So XPORT played the role of a broker to help these small companies get access to capital.

All of these cases suggest that successful innovation does not require the intricacy of carefully drawn road maps. Rather it is a function of action and adaptation, often achieved by groping along. Innovation was a response to a change in the landscape, and it was carried out in an iterative and adaptive manner. Vigilant managers constantly assessed changing circumstances and program performance during the implementation process.

The Ready, Fire, Aim Process

The iterative and incremental process of innovation is often characterized by the "ready, fire, aim" approach. Action is rarely based on thorough prior policy analysis. After defining a fairly specific mission, managers take actions they believe necessary to further their missions—they fire. Then they assess the effects of their actions. This allows them to improve their aim in subsequent iterations.

Agencies likely to innovate often begin in crisis. Opportunity is a great engine of innovation here, as it is in science. Constraints loosen in a crisis because there tends to be more acceptance of the need for radical change, and this provides considerable freedom to innovate. Rather like the impetus provided by natural selection when old biological solutions and structures cease to meet the needs of a changing environment, crises in public organizations provide the fuel for change. Crisis often quiets natural opposition and provides the political and organizational support for innovation.

None of the innovators in our study relied much on thorough prior analysis of options or systematic program planning. Instead, they more often relied on operational data during the implementation process to assess performance as they went along. They started out with only the approximate aim provided by their new missions and began operations before they did much formal analysis (for example, seizing property and closing stores or opening methadone clinics before budgetary authorizations cleared). Reevaluating after an analysis of program performance, they could readjust their aim if necessary.

Los Angeles's Drug Abuse Resistance Education (DARE) program, now a national program model, was successful in its hometown in the early 1980s and expanded to other California cities. In 1986, as part of the Reagan administration's war on drugs, the National Institute of Justices's Bureau of Justice Assistance (BJA) was searching for a program to get behind that focused on reducing the demand for drugs rather than the supply. The BJA offered to fund a major DARE training effort. DARE proposed creating regional training in Illinois, North Carolina, Virginia, and Arizona, and the BJA accepted. By 1989, DARE was training three thousand officers annually. Soon the program spread to four thousand police departments in all fifty states and covered 150,000 classrooms and five million students.

All this began without any formal judgment on the program's actual effectiveness in preventing drug abuse. DARE had signed an evaluation contract with the Evaluation and Training Institute (ETI) at the start of the program, but by 1986, when the Reagan administration suggested DARE's expansion, ETI had made only preliminary reports. Not until 1988 did ETI release its first formal analysis of DARE's effectiveness in preventing drug abuse.

Massachusetts's ET Choices was born not in a crisis but rather in an opportunistic response to a federal option for states to develop new welfare demonstration programs. The Reagan administration, in its efforts to reduce federal involvement and budget commitments, allowed state discretion under the Omnibus Budget Reconciliation Act of 1981 to experiment with welfare reforms. Motivated by a desire to cut the rolls and reduce spending, the new federal waivers, which had been authorized under the previous governor, were seized by Department of Public Welfare Commissioner Charles Atkins and Deputy Commissioner Thomas P. Glynn as an opportunity to reform welfare according to their own values. With the general goals of providing high levels of service to clients and voluntary opportunities for education, employment training, and job placement, they undertook an action-oriented plan following a classic ready, fire, aim approach. They did not ask *whether* their program would work but rather *how* to make it work. Atkins's experience as undersecretary of human services in 1978 provided the experience; the federal waiver provided the opportunity. (Atkins's experiences in this field from 1978 to 1982 meant that when he became welfare commissioner in 1983 he brought to the job a good deal of knowledge of the research and programmatic models of how to assist the dependent poor. Thus, though ET Choices did not perform formal policy analysis in developing its policy approach, Atkins did engage in planning ahead of time based on these models.)

Similarly, One Church, One Child—a Ford winner—evolved from a pragmatically improvised effort: Illinois Children and Family Services faced continued failure in improving the adoption rates for minority children. After failing in their attempts to increase adoptions through expanded publicity, they tried something else: linking up with black ministers.

A ready, fire, aim approach often characterizes successful innovation because it induces an incremental and adaptive process by producing a real field test. Ira Jackson, William Ruckelshaus, and Gordon Chase all launched activities without firmly defined programs and with only an approximate idea of their new missions. Systematic analysis came after action. Los Angeles's DARE program began, expanded, and grew again without any formal judgment on its effectiveness in curbing drug abuse. ET Choices asked not whether its programs would work but rather how to make them work. One Church, One Child did not adopt its linkage with black ministers out of a thoroughly designed program but out of desperation because their original goal had failed. Bureaucratic innovation demands action. This pattern of action first and analysis later is not surprising. It results from a realistic assessment of what analysis can deliver. As James Q. Wilson has persuasively argued, social science has much more to contribute by evaluating what has happened than by trying to predict what will happen.[3]

Error Correction

Error correction was essential to this evolutionary, iterative process. Management by wandering around facilitates this process because it helps the practitioner learn about errors and about what resources are available.[4] Indeed, failures, and a continual process of error correction, become the basis of learning. Implementation helps practitioners detect errors in ideas and designs and then correct them. It gives them the opportunity to make errors, which is the most realistic way to detect weaknesses in policy ideas. Ira Jackson relied heavily on error correction at the Massachusetts Department of Revenue. By just wandering around and asking questions, Jackson literally stumbled onto one of his most important first steps on a routine field visit—determining how many of the DOR's own employees had not filed tax returns. This, rather than thorough policy analysis of the systems and options before him, led him to his first narrow definition of his task: integrity. Learning much from his first few weeks of wandering, he moved to management by groping along. While still at the most elemental level, he moved to rid the department of corruption and to create administrative systems.

Then without much pause or analysis, Jackson tried to correct the previous error of too little tax enforcement. As he wandered, he picked up one of the most obvious and most familiar revenue department tactics—enforcement of the tax collection—and began a pattern of continual action. Closings and seizures were pursued iteratively, with a lot of learning by doing. There was more firing than aiming. At the outset, as he increased enforcement, little time was taken for formal policy analysis. As he continued to act, however, Jackson began to take better aim and learned about his targets and their surroundings. Then he moved forward and sometimes sideways to develop new policies, such as aggressive enforcement and criminal prosecution.[5]

Pretty soon he had developed bigger targets and an even bigger vehicle to reach them—a tax amnesty plan. But even this plan developed in an iterative, adaptive, and even sideways manner. First, the DOR borrowed the idea from other states. Second, when a tax amnesty plan was first proposed, the governor's office turned it down. It was later suggested by a legislator, not as a clever policy or as a good way of producing additional revenue (as it was later to be viewed), but as a moderating element: the legislator advised the governor's staff, "Give people a chance before you come down on them with the heavy hand of the law." Jackson, ever tinkering, opportunistically grabbed at the sideways suggestion because he could use it as a forward step. (Though formal policy analysis was not used, a good deal of thought went into the choice of policies: Jackson and his staff thought much about what innovations other states were carrying out and informally considered the costs and benefits of borrowing from them for Massachusetts.)

There was a similar pattern of ready, fire, aim and error correction at ET Choices. The executives at the Massachusetts Department of Public Welfare knew what their objective was: to move welfare recipients from dependency to self-sufficiency. They knew exactly what they were aiming at. (In developing their policy, they did not perform formal policy analysis. However, they did do prior planning based on their experiences in the field.) But they did not know entirely how to use their resources—or even which program elements to use, or whether they needed to design some completely new ones—to achieve their goal. But rather than get completely ready before beginning, they launched year one's program. When they saw where that first shot went, they got a little more ready and launched another program for year two. This continued in an interactive process. Their aim was a process of continual improvement. For example, in the second year of ET Choices they improved the wage level that they had found to be insufficient in the first year.[6]

The ready, fire, aim approach teaches us the benefits of accepting the presence and correctability of error. It helps integrate error correction into the evolutionary process. And error correction is essential to innovation. Learning by doing, aiming more precisely later, and correcting errors along the way allowed these programs to develop iteratively and adapt by evolution.

Speed and Action, Not Careful Analysis

Gordon Chase's process of innovation at New York's Health Services Administration was iterative and adaptive but not slow or incremental. It was a ready, fire, aim process rather than deliberate, thorough analysis of options. Chase emphasized speed—not just in program results but also in choosing programs. More than the other managers in our study, he emphasized firing immediately and quickly. He sought results, but even they were secondary to his perception of the need to act. At the end of Mayor Lindsay's first term in 1970, in a city where "nothing seemed to work" and in an era when "nothing could get done," no symbolism seemed as positive as action.

Chase quickly understood that he must rapidly set up

focused programs to establish his own credibility and that of the often criticized HSA. He had come into office under fire because he was a manager with no health policy background and, unlike previous commissioners, was not even a physician. He started managing by wandering around and asking a lot of questions. But he did not ask or listen as much as, say, Ira Jackson did in Massachusetts because the New York media focused enormous attention on the city's health and bureaucracy problems.

Chase quickly shifted to a ready, fire, aim process. The city faced a heroin epidemic, and its programs (mainly drug-free residential treatment centers) were a failure. Chase quickly chose a large methadone maintenance program as the city's primary policy. A young doctor, Robert Newman, and others pressed the idea on him. Following Dr. Newman's brief and not entirely systematic presentation (which did not discuss the range of alternative options for heroin treatment), Chase read a three hundred–page analysis of methadone maintenance over a weekend. He came back on Monday with his decision to pursue the methadone route as the HSA's primary drug program. Neither then nor later did he pay much attention to more complicated analysis or to various alternatives and their direct costs and opportunity costs.

Having chosen methadone maintenance, he acted immediately. He got the program off the ground even before it received official budgetary authorization. And he kept acting. First, there was a need to locate sites for clinics and open them. Then there was the need for outreach: recruiting large numbers of addicts into the program. His aim was very broad: attempt to treat all heroin addicts in the city. The HSA started small but focused on the two immediate targets of clinics and clients. Throughout the early implementation stage, the administrators were learning about these targets, increasing the number of targets, and adapting to problems in the field. They were redesigning where the clinics should be located and learning how to cope with and overcome opposition to the location of clinics.

Interest Convergence

Patterns of interest convergence, especially between public and private institutions, are often important for leveraging the process of innovation. The development of patterns in which private (or individual) and public interests coincide is often politically and institutionally important in building support for innovative approaches.

Interest convergence resembles the ideal outcome of individuals operating in a private market. But in public sector activities like the implementation of a complex public program, there is no "invisible hand" to lead interests to coincide. Indeed, the inherent tension between private and public interests is a constant obstacle to socially desirable actions in the public sector. In effect, a manager's actions in creating interest convergence provides the public sector's missing "political hand" and creates a public use of private interest.

Innovations award winners illustrate the importance for successful implementation of developing patterns of interest convergence. The talent to do this was different from coalition building in several ways. First, these executives found instances of converging interests among actors and organizations who usually did not work together, such as public and private sector organizations and businesses or competing and jealous public agencies. Second, developing patterns of interest convergence is more of an active and complex process than mere coalition building because it requires creating ways in which apparently diverse objectives can be achieved through common intervention. It means more than standing together. It involves an exchange relationship: one actor or organization makes a contribution to the process that the other cannot, and the other usually reciprocates the exchange with a contribution that has been absent before.

The Nova Ancora program was a rehabilitation program that brought together small businesses (whose main interest was profit) and the Probation Department (whose main interest was rehabilitation). Each helped the other. By hiring probationers, businesses helped rehabilitate them. By connecting the probationers with these businesses, the department helped solve their labor shortages. Similar patterns developed in the programs of QUIP; One Church, One Child; and the New York Department of State. In these programs, managers made it clear to nursing homes, black churches, and small towns, respectively, that their interests overlapped with public programs. Thus the two cooperated to produce innovation. Indeed, creating and exploiting patterns of interest convergence was one of the Ford Foundation's programs' dominant innovative themes: it was part of their widespread "connecting" with the private sector. For example, QUIP brought together the coinciding interests of private nursing homes and the Illinois Department of Public Aid (DPA). Through the latter's inspection program, the state of Illinois saved $15 million and the nursing homes received $18 million in incentives tied to the inspections, as well as free and friendly consultation and inspection from the DPA.

Many of the executives among the Ford award winners moved their programs toward success by bringing out latent patterns of interest convergence among actors and organizations who seldom worked together (schools and social service agencies, county health departments and private hospitals). Indeed, a key to success in a large number of these programs was creating incentives for historical adversaries to cooperate.

Cambridge, Massachusetts's Work Force unemployment prevention program's success was to a great extent a product of the development of patterns of interest convergence between the program and the city schools. School systems rarely work closely with outside agencies, but Work Force's Steven Swanger got them to do just that. Protective of their turf and threatened by ever-increasing criticism of their performance, school systems are notoriously insular. However, to succeed, Work Force required cooperation from the schools and access to student records. Grades, attendance, and behavior were important ways to monitor youth performance and success. Similarly, the mutual interests of private employers to provide training and employment opportunities to youths and of Work Force to provide businesses with better-trained employees and good community public relations benefited both parties.

New Jersey's School-Based Youth Services (SBYS) program faced similar obstacles of competitive agencies. But the schools and human service providers, well known for their past independence, were induced to put aside many differences to cooperate in SBYS. Corporate participation, especially by AT&T, which assisted in job training and devoted one full-time staffer to SBYS, was also key to its success.

In Philadelphia's Anti-Graffiti Network, success came from developing a convergence of interests among an even more diverse group of actors: law enforcement agencies cracking down on graffitists, art museums and local artists collaborating on public arts projects such as wall murals, and community action agencies providing services to rehabilitate former graffitists.

Connecting with the private sector was the essential motor driving the success of Virginia's Fairfax County Medical Care for Children Project (MCCP) and Maryland's Montgomery County Meeting Obstetrical Needs of Indigent Women Program. In Fairfax County, the notion of private doctors providing low-cost medical care to the indigent was the conceptual power behind the program's success. But it required a partnership of many cooperating institutions and actors to make this concept a reality: the HMOs, the Fairfax County Department of Community Action, and doctors in both private and group practices. A unique public-private partnership was formed in the county. The business community has undertaken the responsibility of raising operating funds for the MCCP, and HMOs and private physicians provide preventive services. The county continues to pay salaries and other administrative expenses. Similarly, Montgomery County's success in providing low-cost obstetrical services to the indigent was derived from the development of a cooperative relationship between the county Health Department, the medical society, and private hospitals. Through the efforts of the county health director and the medical society's president at developing interest convergence, the initial reluctance and resistance of the hospitals to participate yielded, and a sense of ownership of the program emerged.

These executives brought out latent patterns of interest convergence among organizations that rarely worked together. Indeed, in Los Angeles's DARE program, two unlikely institutions found a convergence of their interests. The cooperation between the schools and the police, often suspicious of each other, was key to DARE's success. By ensuring a role for teachers and full participation of educators, the police were able to enlist the schools' support in the mutually attractive objective of communicating an antidrug message in the schools.

Gordon Chase also relied on developing many patterns of interest convergence to achieve his program goals. For example, HSA helped Montefiore Hospital develop its ambitious community programs by putting the large and expensive prison health programs under Montefiore through a contracting procedure. In turn, Montefiore operated an excellent program for the HSA that neither the agency nor the Corrections Department had been able to do. Similarly, the HSA contracted with private hospitals and clinics to run its methadone maintenance program. Not only were the private hospitals eager for the financial benefits of their contracts, but they also viewed these devices as a way to get into the growing substance abuse area without making their own investment. This arrangement enabled them to avoid assuming any overhead and to benefit from the city's assumption of the marketing and outreach costs. The city got its methadone program faster than it would have if it had depended on city hospitals or new city clinics. Understanding these diverse needs of independent institutions was crucial in both the selection and the development of innovative mechanisms to achieve these public health objectives.

These cases indicate the critical importance that developing patterns of interest convergence plays in producing innovative solutions. Much innovation, we have argued, results from new combinations of familiar elements. In many cases, we see that increasingly that means crossing sectors and institutional barriers. Establishing relationships among diverse institutions and between sectors derives from an active process of developing and promoting common interests. More active and complex than coalition building, interest convergence depends on connection and exchange.

Conclusion

This chapter demonstrates that innovation generally derives not from new ideas and approaches but from novel or untried ways of combining often familiar things. The novelty is often the assemblage. New plans change and adapt. Most innovative initiatives are developed as a result of experiential learning derived from experimentation at the implementation stage. Good ideas were tested quickly in the field and subjected to evaluation and feedback from informal operational experience. Formal analysis, contrary to the reigning paradigm of public policy schools, was more helpful after implementation. It served as an evaluative function by exposing the deficiencies of poor options.

We found that the process that generated innovation was iterative, incremental, and sometimes even disorderly: it used bits and pieces of what was around in new ways to meet changing circumstances.

The Ford winners frequently adapted their programs because of either difficulties with their original objectives or recognition of greater potential. Neither of these came from the drawing board; they came from experience in action and implementation. A ready, fire, aim approach was used frequently to initiate action first, and program experience served to refine original ideas and program elements later. Interest convergence, especially among public and private sector institutions, was a frequent and important technique used to generate support.

Ira Jackson asked questions at the DOR, then acted quickly within a narrow scope. He gradually expanded, learning to aim better as he went along. Gordon Chase began implementing programs right away. He, too, learned as he went, incrementally expanding his target group and his scope. DARE expanded without formal assessment of its effectiveness.

Each of these innovating organizations chose to act without detailed, carefully designed plans of action. Action generated the data needed to assess success by allowing for a process of incremental and iterative adaptation. Action without a plan presumed the need for error correction and for learning with experience. Through a trial-and-error process, the implementation of initial goals is altered accordingly as new information is received and as early shots hit or miss. These findings differ significantly from those suggested by formal models of program development and policy analysis. Further, they point to qualities of management that emphasize risk taking, flexibility, and opportunism. Successful innovation is marked by a willingness to act without a complete plan and to make mistakes. Not only is a tolerance for mistakes and misfires necessary, but it is also desirable because the lessons it teaches allows for a process of continual error correction. Managerial innovation is an iterative and adaptive process, a process of action and involvement by a vigilant and highly responsive manager.

Notes

1. Robert D. Behn, "Management by Groping Along," *Journal of Policy Analysis and Management* 7 (1988): 648.
2. In regulation writing, lawyers tend to be the subordinates of technicians. In litigation, technicians are the subordinates of lawyers. Thus by choosing litigation first and backfilling with regulation later, Ruckelshaus shifted power within his agency from old, slow hands to quick, younger new recruits who had chosen the EPA because they wanted to regulate. We are indebted

to Martin Shapiro for suggesting this point. See also Marc Landy, Marc Roberts, and Stephen Thomas, *EPA: Asking the Wrong Questions* (New York: Oxford University Press, 1991).
3. James Q. Wilson, "Social Science and Public Policy," *Public Interest,* Spring 1983.
4. Thomas Peters and Robert Waterman, in *In Search of Excellence* (New York: HarperCollins, 1982), pp. 119–124, suggest that successful managers get information personally and directly from their employees, suppliers, and customers. Such managers get out from behind the desk, out of the office, out of meetings. They wander around, talk to people, and observe. Their approach, according to Henry Mintzberg, in *The Nature of Managerial Work* (New York: HarperCollins, 1973), pp. 31–39, is characterized by "brevity, variety, and fragmentation." Peters and Waterman conclude that "the name of the successful game is rich, informal communication." Mintzberg's conclusion is that the job of managing "does not develop reflective planners; rather it breeds adoptive information manipulators who prefer a stimulus-response milieu."
5. Robert D. Behn, "Ira Jackson and the Massachusetts Department of Revenue," Case Study Prepared for the Duke University Policy Studies Institute, 1986.
6. Robert D. Behn, *Leadership Counts* (Cambridge, Mass.: Harvard University Press, 1991).

5

Bureaucratic Entrepreneurs
A Bias Toward Action

In Chapters Three and Four, we considered the character of innovative solutions to public problems and the process by which each was brought about. Here we examine the style of the manager of innovation.

Natural selection is a random process of trial and error, of natural adaptations tested in changing environments. And in the private sector there can be coordination and innovation without a coordinator.[1] Public sector innovations, however, proceed only with executive direction. The manager defines the agency's mission, develops an organizational culture that can generate change, and rewards behavior that supports the process.

Making government work does not require genius. It does, however, require an executive—an active, highly focused, flexible, adaptive performer. It also requires particular strategies and approaches. Five strategies characterize successful executives: they are driven by a mission, they behave opportunistically in the face of rapidly changing environmental circumstances, they have a bias toward action, they are willing to take risks, and they employ a strategy of intentionally underestimating the difficulty of achieving their objectives.

Managers of innovation may grope along testing, evaluating, and redesigning their approach. But they do not wait for random accidents to determine the fate of their enterprise. Rather, they behave opportunistically, picking up resources lying around, seizing advantages (even in crisis), and taking risks.

We examined a variety of cases in Chapters Three and Four. They differed in the sources for the innovative idea, in the course that it took from conception to implementation, and in the process of learning and refinement. Nevertheless, one profound element characterized them all: the firm stewardship of an entrepreneurial manager was central to the success of innovative programs. The process proved fluid and uneven. Fraught with false starts, revisions, and continual refinement, innovative initiatives evolve. They do not spring full-grown from the mind of the manager. But through all this, the direction of these executives was clear. Further, the executive strategies and approaches that mattered most were very similar among diverse cases. We spell them out here.

The Innovative Manager as Entrepreneur

Innovative managers are both tinkerers and bureaucratic entrepreneurs. Thus their managerial style is not comprehensive or synoptic; they do not start from scratch. For them, it is an evolutionary process, consisting, in part, of using old approaches in areas where they have not generally been used before. Entrepreneurship in public sector organizations is one of them. As tinkerers, they use what already exists. But they also assume the managerial style of an entrepreneur. So they move these old approaches one level beyond where they were: they take risks with them, with an opportunistic bias toward action.

For them, being entrepreneurial did not necessarily mean that they assumed the style of managers in the private sector. They clearly did not exclude private sector techniques like marketing. But what distinguished them most was their willingness to scan the broader environment for approaches that suited their objectives: they were not captives of sectoral conventions or institutional traditions. They were entrepreneurial in specific ways.

Creating New Missions

Public executives often face diffuse or vague mandates. In our heterogeneous society, consensus is often lacking on many basic values. Conflicting and contradictory objectives often result in legislative compromises that purposely obscure an agency's mission to win legislative consensus. The EPA was created in just such a context, and its vague legislative mandate reflected that.

In the face of such vagueness, successful managers were greatly aided by their creation of new missions for their agencies. Under Ira Jackson, the Massachusetts Department of Revenue's narrow and conventional mission was transformed into a new, broader one as he operated as an evolutionary tinkerer, using what was at hand and repairing the broken bits and pieces of the DOR's power and image. First the mission was "honest, firm, and fair tax administration." Then it moved to the even more ambitious goal of increasing revenue without new taxes through a combination of aggressive enforcement and tax amnesty. Finally, Jackson redefined the role of the taxpayer as a good customer rather than a victim. This approach was so new and broad that it attracted national media attention for both him and his boss, the governor.

Gordon Chase, too, faced an ill-defined mandate to improve the health of New Yorkers, but he developed many personal missions for the HSA. Through his project management approach, he created specific programmatic, concrete, and visible responses to this vague mandate. His contribution was in redefining a specific programmatic role for the HSA in responding to the health problems he selected to tackle. Those problems, and the programs he developed, defined his mission. For example, testing and treatment for lead paint poisoning, rat bite control, and hypertension testing among the underserved became just some of the targets for the agency. In seeking to improve health care in the city's prisons, he took on a mission beyond his agency's traditional jurisdiction.

Even in specific problem areas, Chase faced a diffuse mandate. For example, heroin was an obvious problem, but who should deal with it and how were not at all clear. The HSA had never done much about drug addiction. In fact, the Human Resources Administration (HRA), not the

HSA, was the city agency with primary responsibility in this area. Further, there were many possible approaches to the heroin problem, such as prosecution and incarceration, and many treatments, ranging from talking therapies to behavior modification. Thus what to do and how became issues of his personal vision. The final element of Chase's vision for the HSA's mission was a commitment to the principle that programs should aim to treat the entire relevant universe (all heroin addicts) rather than participants in a pilot or demonstration program.

Few of the managers of the award-winning Ford programs came to their positions with a discrete public mandate or even much guidance. Some worked in existing agencies with ongoing activities; others developed new institutions to respond to a perceived need. But in both cases, many of them forged a clear and compelling personal vision. For instance, when Ellen Schall took over the troubled New York City Department of Juvenile Justice (DJJ), the mayor gave her only two orders: "Don't let any of them get out" and "Do as much as you can for them." But Schall created a new mission for the DJJ by turning the dead time of juvenile detention into a productive period when social and support services were delivered to troubled kids. She moved the DJJ beyond its traditional mission of custodial warehousing by adding a social service function. By simply changing the bureaucratic schedule, which involved waiting weeks or months for the recommendations of the juvenile judge, she started educational and rehabilitative services immediately after the kids were arrested.

Similarly, Jean Eakins had no broad mandate at the Family Learning Center. She had only opposition. Nevertheless, she created an increasingly broader mission for the center that transformed its role beyond classroom education for pregnant teens to one that embraced their social and psychological development. At One Church, One Child, the Catholic priest who inspired the program and worked closely with its managers made the program's mission quite personal when he adopted a child himself.

Just as Schall in New York created a productive social service program by moving the DJJ beyond custodial warehousing, Cambridge's Steven Swanger created a new youth employment and training mission for the Work Force unemployment prevention program by expanding the concept of public housing services beyond mere shelter. When he arrived at the Cambridge Public Housing Authority as the director of tenant services, he had only a fuzzy notion of what the unit was supposed to do. It had had seven directors in four years and was in disarray. It had no clear goals, no accountability, and no professionalism. Moreover, the agency had a real institutional reluctance to embrace a social service role in public housing. Swanger nevertheless developed a new mission for the unit by molding housing and social services functions to create a youth employment and training program with the ultimate goal of improving self-esteem among-at-risk kids.

The director of New York–New Jersey Port Authority's XPORT created a new mission for his enterprise under quite adverse circumstances. When legislation necessary to authorize its mission as an export trading company for the Port Authority failed, it appeared that its reason for being no longer existed. But Herb Ouida created the new, albeit less ambitious mission. XPORT became a public-private partnership with small companies by providing them with financial brokering services, logistical support, and consulting guidance. XPORT flourished in its new mission because it filled a vacuum for these small companies. Most banks were not interested in providing the small loans that XPORT's clients needed, and thus the program's mission as broker was crucial in helping small companies get access to capital. This in turn supported the Port Authority's larger mission to improve and increase commerce in the region.

Dr. Martin Wasserman developed a new vision for the Montgomery County Health Department by assuming the responsibility for providing low-cost obstetrical services for indigent women. He operationalized his mission through an innovative partnership between his own agency and private obstetricians, private hospitals, and the local medical society.

The direction given an agency by its executive is crucial for successful innovation, especially when operating under a vague mandate. Jackson transformed the DOR's narrow and conventional mission into a new, broader one that was a first step toward many innovations there. Chase and Schall—like many of the Ford winners—also reinvigorated their agencies at the outset by setting out a new concrete purpose and vision for them.

The Entrepreneur as Opportunist

Opportunism was the second element of innovative managers' entrepreneurial style. They took advantage of by-products and excesses and made virtues of them. These findings support the conclusion that success depends on selecting the appropriate objectives and resources to support them given the environment in which one must operate.

Ira Jackson opportunistically turned the crisis of institutional corruption to his advantage. It provided him with an initial advantage to marshal new public support and to seize new tools and powers. DOR employees' morale and public image were so low ("they were ashamed to talk about work in the supermarket") that Jackson had freedom and support to innovate. The employees were in a weak position to offer resistance. Many even welcomed change as a way of improving their own morale and image. Jackson used this freedom from internal resistance to seize the existing tools at the DOR and to reorient them for new, unusual means.

Gordon Chase opportunistically used crises besetting the city and the HSA to his advantage. He used media and public outcry to allow the agency to take bold approaches. Public outcry over the heroin epidemic softened the natural resistance to radical solutions and created a willingness to consider methadone maintenance.

William Ruckelshaus's Environmental Protection Agency did not face a crisis. Nonetheless, he innovated by using increased public concern over the environment in the early 1970s to give him license to act more boldly than earlier environmental officials. A few years later, he seized on weakness in the Nixon White House to distance the EPA from it and thus create a certain advantageous independence. Yet he never allowed the EPA to move far enough away to become pitted against it. Ruckelshaus also opportunistically used the media, which gave the EPA a great deal of attention—most of it rather adversarial. He turned their rough questioning to his benefit by using the media as "the equivalent of an internal audit . . . . I learned a lot from the media's wandering around the agency."[2]

As we noted in Chapter Four, crisis presents problems but also great opportunities for the freedom to innovate. Loosening ties to failed policies and programs, crisis often subdues natural opposition and mobilizes political and organizational support for innovation. Among the Ford award winners, One Church, One Child increased adoptions by focusing on the growing number of children languishing in foster care.

In Montgomery County, Maryland, Dr. Wasserman found an innovative opportunity in the crisis created by the increasing unwillingness of private hospitals to deliver the babies of indigent women. Because they viewed delivering babies of indigent women as posing significant medical risks (due to mothers' poor prenatal care, malnourishment, and drug abuse), local doctors feared for their reputations and for the adequacy of their malpractice insurance.

The crisis that induced cooperation on an innovative solution was the eventual refusal of one of the two remaining hospitals still providing care to continue to do so. Responding systematically to the concerns of both doctors and hospitals, the health care emergency thus created a climate that enabled Wasserman to get the president of the county medical society to commit to joint action with the county health department—an unprecedented outcome. In this atmosphere, they jointly developed the award-winning Meeting Obstetrical Needs of Indigent Women program, in which private physicians became part-time employees of the health department.

The lesson for managers is that crisis is not always negative. Executives seldom seek crises as a means to further their goals; indeed, what manager wouldn't be better off with a budget surplus than with a cut? Crises, however, can be manipulated to create opportunities for action and innovation. Crises feed the demand for change, and innovation is about change. Successful innovators are opportunistic. That includes turning the disadvantage of a crisis situation to the benefit of their agency.

Risk Taking

Most of the successes we observe would not have been possible were it not for the entrepreneurship of managers. A willingness to assume risk (and a tolerance for some mistakes) is central to launching something new. Having a personal vision that manifests itself in staking out a new organizational mission involves considerable risk. Though crises may foster change, redefining an organizational role involves a real danger of failing.

New missions are fraught with the risk of taking on too much.[3] Ira Jackson's first substantive policy—vigorous tax enforcement—was a risk. It is seldom popular with the public, nor does it have political benefits for a tax collector's elected boss. Tax amnesty was just as risky. Similarly, ET Choices' risky opportunism used the conservative

Reagan administration's welfare reform option to develop its generally liberal welfare reform program.

Gordon Chase's appetite for risk led him to focus on the city's most intractable problems—heroin addiction and reforms in large, recalcitrant institutions like prisons. Moreover, he sought to deal with the whole problem all at once, without the benefit of learning through pilot projects.

Dr. Wasserman's transformation of the Montgomery County Health Department involved considerable risk taking. Assuming the helm of an agency facing a critical public health crisis whose historical role was reactive and responsive, Wasserman chose a new vision for his organization and selected an innovative means to meet his objectives. Open to risk taking and oriented toward action, he mobilized his department to become proactive and to engage a host of community actors historically unengaged in meeting public health objectives.

Committed to developing a collective community solution to the serious shortage of obstetrical services for poor women, he built a constituency for a public-private partnership. His strategy involved considerable risk because it depended for its success on the willingness of private physicians, hospitals, and the county medical society to collaborate with the Department of Health. No previous experience had ever suggested that such a relationship could be developed or that the Department of Health could be viewed as a credible representative of the practitioners' interests. His approach was thus highly entrepreneurial and characteristic of an executive with a taste for risk taking.

A Bias Toward Action

A fourth characteristic of these bureaucratic entrepreneurs was a bias toward action. Public sector executives are typically cautious, constrained by political factors, legislatures, and more restrictive budgets than the private sector's. Because they operate under more pervasive oversight and accountability mechanisms than private managers, their tolerance for failure is low, and incentives for boldness are inherently weak. But public sector managers' bias toward action—especially Ruckelshaus, Chase, and Jackson—was often crucial to their success because it helped establish immediate visibility and credibility with the public.

They emphasized rapid and visible indicators of their success by developing concrete and measurable outputs. Lacking the clear bottom lines available to private entrepreneurs, who use them to measure and trumpet their policies, Ruckelshaus, Chase, and Jackson sought public sector proxies.

For instance, from the outset, Jackson used action—even just the image of it—to establish his credibility. He emphasized rapid, visible success: enforcement with quick results instead of drawn-out court cases, which were slow and invisible. He opted for property seizures and closings of familiar retail establishments. Closing well-known restaurants frequented by politicians and seizing the yachts of wealthy persons for tax evasion established initial visible success in enforcement. But the DOR's most concrete and measurable output was the collection of unpaid taxes, which gave the DOR an unusual bottom line for the public sector. Like a private sector manager, Jackson had actually generated new resources.

Chase had a bias toward action from the outset. He too used action to help establish his credibility, which was suspect because he was not a physician. Mimicking the private sector manager in his emphasis on rapid, visible, and concrete outputs, he got methadone maintenance off the ground even before receiving formal budgetary authorization. He picked programs in which success could be easily operationalized and in which outputs were easily measured. Thus his performance could be trumpeted concretely and visibly to the media: the number screened for lead paint poisoning or tested for hypertension, the number of doses dispensed daily at methadone maintenance clinics, the tons of garbage collected per day by his rat control program.

Similarly, Ruckelshaus took immediate action, moved quickly, and emphasized measurable outputs. He selected a legalistic enforcement approach, rejecting the agency's previous consultative one. He decided to bring major suits against large cities and large corporations in his first two weeks. Indeed, the EPA brought five times as many enforcement actions in its first two months under Ruckelshaus than all its predecessors had in any two-month period.

In the face of adversity, Herb Ouida showed a strong bias toward action by defining the XPORT program's new mission of providing small companies with financial brokering services, logistical support, and counseling guidance. The legislature's failure to authorize XPORT's initial mission as an export trading subsidiary for the Port Authority did not stop him from shifting gears and adapting his enterprise to a different role.

The Hiding-Hand Principle

A fifth approach in their management style was their use of a principle dubbed the "hiding hand" by Albert Hirschman.[4] Hirschman argued that a conscious underestimating of bureaucratic and political obstacles would help development projects. Imbalance, ignorance of all the conditions at hand (hence all the limitations), and even a touch of foolhardiness are needed to give initial impetus to development. He urged executives to ignore the overly cautious conclusions that are usually drawn from focusing on the obstacles to implementation and instead to overextend their reach and not to be constrained by knowledge of the implementation difficulties.

Ruckelshaus followed the hiding-hand principle in everything he did, disregarding bureaucratic and political obstacles as he took on the many elements flowing from the broad mandate that he created. He later admitted, "If I had known what I was doing at all times, I might not have done all of it."[5]

Similarly, one of Chase's staff said, "Gordon's vision of achievement was never cluttered by reality."[6] In a similar vein, another aide said:

> He was conscious of the significance of the strategies he pursued—like contracting out [with private vendors]. . . . From the beginning, all his strategies were deliberate. It was all conscious;

you could see the mind behind the mind. . . . He realized that if you accurately estimated the difficulties, you would never get anything done. But deep down he knew . . . how hard it was. He just never talked about it. . . . He had just a few minutes of despair . . . just a few.[7]

Jackson also seemed consciously to underestimate bureaucratic and political obstacles. Vigorous tax enforcement is seldom popular. Institutionalizing and broadening this type of enforcement, as the Revenue Enforcement Protection Act legislative package did, is probably even less so. Because of its breadth, state budget officials said that REAP had "zero probability of passing." Jackson shared some of the pessimism, but added: "They're probably right. . . . But you only go around once. And let's hold it together. The only offense is a totally concerted, straight, nose-guarded, up the middle with this thing. Don't allow anyone to touch it in any of its parts."[8] Jackson's strategy was right on the money—the bill passed in its entirety.

Getting Top Political Executives' Support

Many of our successful entrepreneurs developed their enterprises independently from a strong political base. But support from a top political executive was crucial to the ultimate management success of a number of program executives we studied. After all, chief political executives can kill even a thriving and well-established enterprise. The programs in our sample show that some innovators depended on the support of a political executive to initiate or sustain them. Some, like Philadelphia's Anti-Graffiti Network, developed early mayoral support. Others, like Swanger's Work Force, earned political support and then resources through its success.[9]

The innovative managers' relationships to their top political executives—mayor, governor, cabinet secretary—were significant, but there was a dual pattern. In some instances—in crises or for large programs—the relationship was close and supportive at the outset. In others—indeed, most of them—the relationship with a top political executive proved important only in sustaining an already successful enterprise. These smaller programs, not facing crises, seemed to benefit from the initial freedom to experiment that came from their distance from top political executives.

Meeting the political needs of a political executive significantly helped support the agendas of several of our bureaucratic entrepreneurs. Innovative managers often developed their programs with an eye on winning the support of their top political executives. When trying to launch large programs or when confronting city or state crises, as in the cases of Ira Jackson and Gordon Chase, they often relied on the intervention and active support of their top political executives. The resources, support, and protection that the political executives brought to these programs contributed significantly to their success.

To interest a political executive in a program, these managers selected policy areas high on the executive's agenda. Chase, for example, chose to develop a program that would deal with the heroin epidemic, despite its seeming intractability and controversy. This program met the political needs of his top executive, Mayor John Lindsay, who faced strong criticism in this area. The mayor then provided significant budgetary resources and political support for Chase's controversial choice of methadone maintenance to combat heroin. Further, he exerted political pressure to locate the methadone clinics in neighborhoods that opposed them.

Chase similarly undertook reforming the health system in the city's prisons. This was not only a controversial area but one outside his agency's jurisdiction and within that of another cabinet agency, the Human Resources Agency. Again the mayor reciprocated the favor with financial and political support for Chase's controversial moves, such as contracting out with Montefiore Hospital rather than using the New York City Health Department's doctors.

Ira Jackson was sensitive to Governor Michael Dukakis's political needs: his top political executive had competing and seemingly incompatible desires to hold the line on taxes (during Dukakis's first gubernatorial term a tax increase cost him reelection) and to increase revenue generation. In developing the policies of tax amnesty and increased tax enforcement, Jackson served the governor's dual needs. Yet both policies were controversial and potentially unpopular. Thus Jackson needed and received the governor's protection of these innovations from their many potential enemies in the legislature, the media, and even in the DOR itself.

Support from New York's Mayor Edward Koch contributed much to Ellen Schall's success at the Department of Juvenile Justice. Fearful of the impact of continued breaches of security, Koch wanted to avoid the embarrassment of escapes from its detention facilities. By bringing control and order to this previously chaotic agency, Schall was able to gain the mayor's support for her innovation of bringing social services into the agency's detention environment. Again, protection from potential opponents of this innovation was the key aid provided by the political executive.

Philadelphia's Anti-Graffiti Network's initial efforts were controversial and complicated. The program's contribution of tougher enforcement and amnesty had something for everyone to oppose. Its initial survival owed much to a popular mayor's early protection and support.

But there was another, more predominant pattern. Most of these successful programs flourished without any initial relationship with a top political executive. Programs that were not large or did not face crises did not seem to need a large degree of support from top political executives. Indeed, many of these programs seemed to benefit from their relative neglect by political executives. This distance or even marginality and isolation gave their executives the freedom to experiment and take the risks that led to innovation.

This dual pattern in the role of top executives in initiating rather than simply sustaining a successful innovation helps explain our findings from the Xerox and IBM PC cases described in Chapter Two. These cases suggested that bright ideas are not enough without effective top executives. Effective top executives were necessary there because the organizations were very large and faced crisis. But for most of the programs analyzed here that were not large or did not face crises, top executives' lack of attention may have actually encouraged innovation by creating an environment in which program executives felt free to be entrepreneurial.

Conclusion

Most of these bureaucratic entrepreneurs came to agencies that had weak or diffuse mandates. In response, they carved out new and personal missions for their organizations and sustained them by developing supportive organizational cultures. As entrepreneurs, they were opportunistic, taking advantage of both available resources and crises. They capitalized on crisis situations, often turning what seemed to be intractable and pressure-laden situations into attractive opportunities. Crisis creates opportunity, removes much opposition to change, and provides the freedom to experiment. All this was achieved not through the use of comprehensive or synoptic analyses but through a process of continual tinkering with known or existing practices.

Finally, all these executives were willing to take risks, often ignoring and consciously underestimating the bureaucratic and political obstacles and preferring a bias toward action. Taking action quickly, often without considered aim, their goal was to create visible and marked achievement early. This enhanced the public image of their enterprises, and the picture of action made future initiatives easier.

What, then, are the lessons for a beleaguered public manager? Developing innovations and furthering an ambitious public agenda do not depend on exceptional brilliance or rare managerial talent; they depend on learning from success. The lessons are clear. Innovative solutions require openness to good ideas from broad environments and a willingness to test them in the field. Success is evolutionary. It derives from systematic assessments of what works and continual adjustment and refinement through field-based learning. Analysis is required during the implementation process so that original ideas can be shaped by realistic constraints and opportunities.

Managers who develop public initiatives in this way share common approaches. They are flexible, adaptive, and opportunistic. Whereas formal advance analysis of options assumes that all obstacles and impacts can be anticipated, successful implementers try to take advantage of opportunities that develop. Opportunism is not a negative characteristic in this fluid environment but rather a significant asset.

Willingness to take risks is a basic entrepreneurial characteristic. Some individuals may be born with that orientation, but others can be trained to become less risk-averse (we discuss ways of doing this in Chapter Nine). Though the public sector provides few inherent incentives to do so, moving quickly to achieve a clear articulated mission offers considerable rewards. If goals are operationalized and ongoing implementation systematically evaluates how well they are being achieved, action-oriented program development can benefit profoundly from visible and rapid demonstrations of success.

Many of these approaches require changing the basic decision rules for moving forward. Although executives can benefit significantly from analysis ahead of time, there is more to fear from the paralysis of analysis than from developing a clear vision of objectives and moving forward rapidly with continual scrutiny and vigilance. This represents a significant difference in orientation and training for a new generation of public managers. We develop this in Chapter Nine in our proposals for the training of future public managers.

Managers can use these lessons to improve the success of their enterprises. Moreover, success is greatly facilitated by an adaptive environment of managers and workers who embrace the executive's vision and support organizational goals and values. Developing and managing an innovative organizational culture is an additional vehicle for improving agency performance. How this should be done and rewarded is considered in the next chapter.

Notes

1. Economists argue persuasively that in the private market, people can coordinate without a coordinator by means of exchange relationships.
2. William Ruckelshaus, personal interview, October 1989.
3. Obviously, there is also the danger of taking on too little or taking on the wrong thing, either of which can result in failing to accomplish organizational goals. The danger in taking on too much, however, is being unable to assemble the resources (financial, human, or political) to achieve the objectives. Because many of our cases chose large and difficult problems, not his-

torically amenable to simple or available treatments, the dangers of taking on too much were especially great.
4. Albert D. Hirschman, "The Principle of the Hiding Hand," *Public Interest, 6,* Winter 1967, pp. 10–23.
5. William Ruckelshaus, personal interview, October 1989.
6. Martin A. Levin, Bonnie Hausman, and Sylvia B. Perlman, "Gordon Chase: The Best and the Brightest Doing Good Deeds in New York City," paper presented at the Association for Public Policy Analysis and Management Research Conference, Chicago, 1985.
7. Ibid.
8. Ibid.
9. The fate of the Work Force was ultimately threatened by a new governor and a wave of legislative budget cuts. The withdrawal of the support of a political executive threatened the ultimate resource base of the program.

6

The Crucial Role of Organizational Culture

In the preceding chapters, a wide range of highly innovative public initiatives were identified. But even highly innovative ideas often fail to produce effective policy outcomes due to defeat at the implementation and management level. As we have shown, policy is difficult to operationalize because executive autonomy is constrained in public institutions by rules, regulations, and clearance points. Although these impediments result from well-intentioned efforts to advance significant public values, in practice they operate to tie the hands of entrepreneurial executives.

Nevertheless, successful innovators find ways to use or work around the constraints to manage effectively. Some innovators have enjoyed considerable success by changing the rules in some way—altering the incentives, values, and relationships that shape how people inside and outside the organization make decisions and set priorities. Ira

Jackson at the Massachusetts Department of Revenue and Charles Atkins at the Massachusetts Department of Public Welfare are two dramatic examples. However, altering the mission of an organization and as a result changing the rules that members follow in carrying out their roles is not self-effectuating. Indeed, altering the values and behavior of individuals is one of the most challenging activities an executive undertakes. It requires that individuals at all levels of the organization abandon the routine, predictable, and safe and embrace a new vision of their work. It requires that they substitute new values and operating procedures of unknown outcome. As a result, they may perceive of change as involving considerable risk.

Even if there is general agreement that organizational functioning is poor (as after a scandal or consistently poor performance evaluations), demands for fundamental change can be threatening and hence strongly resisted. Further, organized interests often have stakes in the status quo that are not easily abandoned.

Rather than altering existing organizations, many of our innovative entrepreneurs developed new enterprises. Barbara Levin's birthing center in Monroe County, Tennessee, and Wayne Fortin's Trauma Intervention Program in California, for example, required establishing new entities capable of fulfilling a precise mission. In the case of the maternity center, that mission was to build a health care institution oriented toward early prenatal care and routine delivery outside the hospital setting. In California, it involved developing a highly motivated and skilled volunteer corps to intervene with the victims of traumatic events (fire, assault, or accident) with supportive counseling and practical assistance at the scene of the event.

Rather than facing existing constraints and recalcitrant workers, the charge was to develop a lean, focused, and highly motivated staff to carry on nascent operations. This provided a unique opportunity to establish at the outset a shared mission as well as a set of decision rules and organizational values to shape the behavior and motivate the efforts of a new staff.

Whether developing a new enterprise or seeking to change an existing one, managers who understand and use an organizational culture perspective seem to have a considerable advantage over those who do not. Indeed, although we did not observe executives consciously designing and using this approach in most of our cases, many did, in fact, embrace the basic concept. Further, we observed that this approach can make an important contribution to executive success.

As we have argued throughout, management matters even when the "best" policy choice has been selected. Here we will explore the importance of managing the organizational culture in a range of specific cases. In particular, we will analyze the management approach of Thomas Glynn, general manager of the Massachusetts Bay Transit Authority. We will illustrate the significance of organizational culture by comparing the unsuccessful management of Xerox's unprecedented product innovation, Alto, the first personal computer, with IBM's successful introduction of its own PC shortly thereafter.

The lesson appears equally salient for public and private

managers, even if public managers, given their unique constraints, have a greater need for creative tools. Management is especially critical in an organization that by necessity or choice is about to undertake something new. The cases analyzed here all deal with bringing about change. Our analyses of them suggest that an underappreciated instrument in the bureaucratic entrepreneur's tool kit is management of the organizational culture.

When Thomas Glynn arrived at his offices to assume his new job as general manager of the Massachusetts Bay Transit Authority (MBTA), he observed a striking contrast with the commissioner's office at the Department of Public Welfare, where he had recently been the deputy commissioner. Whereas the welfare offices were adorned with photos of clients and workers, children and parents, the general manager's suite displayed photographs of various trains, subway cars, and trolleys standing alone, vacant, on the test tracks. They were not occupied by riders or operated by employees. The contrast was stark, and the message that these organizational artifacts conveyed was not wasted. Indeed, it was the first symbolic manifestation of what would turn out to be strong organizational values.[1]

The cues from the photos led him to understand that the strongest cultural value of the organization was equipment, not people. Dominated by the old transit engineering perspective, the organization focused on managing and maintaining equipment. Glynn's challenge was to move the organization to a newer transportation perspective, one that emphasized serving its customers and valuing its employees.

The cars in the photographs were antiseptic—without users or operators, they memorialized technology and hardware. The organization defined itself by the physical aspects of the business. Glynn was sensitive to these cues in part because the message stood in such stark contrast to those communicated by his previous organizational setting. But he was also actively looking for such cues. Successful executives understand the importance of organizational culture as a tool or a constraint in realizing their mission and accomplishing their goals. They understand that the successful use and management of an organization's culture is a very powerful determinant of organizational effectiveness.

The use and management of the organizational culture remains, however, an underappreciated tool in the public manager's bag of tricks. It is given little attention in the public management literature even as the lessons of its importance seem so clear in some of the most popular and widely used public management cases. This chapter is an effort to identify the value of an organizational culture perspective for public managers. Using cases of some extraordinary corporate and public successes and failures, we will lay out what a cultural perspective is, why it is important, and how failure to understand and manage the culture produces needless impediments to organizational effectiveness and change. Further, we will outline the ways in which public managers can take culture into account in shaping their goals and implementing their initiatives.

The lesson is that creating and maintaining a supportive organizational culture is difficult and time-consuming.

It requires a longer time horizon and more interpersonal involvement at all levels, inside and outside the organization, than most public executives are comfortable with.[2] It is nevertheless possible to move organizations slowly to internalize positive and functional assumptions, values, and behavioral norms through constant attention to communication and participation. Not attending to these dimensions can have serious consequences for an executive with a new agenda: at best, failure; at worst, active resistance and sabotage from both internal and external constituents.

What Is an Organizational Culture?

An organization's culture has been compared to a person's character or personality—it is not easily changed by a pronouncement, a command, an emotion-laden description of a new vision, or a careful calculation of a rational plan. It is changed through a process of growth rather than engineering.[3] But culture is very difficult to change when it is deeply held. It is often the product of a long history in which people develop personal stakes in the current way of doing business.

Because it is very hard to alter in a short time a world view that is based on history and shared experience, a successful executive must see management of the culture as a critical imperative. Though change is most often necessary to realize a new vision, successful entrepreneurs must approach the existing culture in the short run as something to be shaped and redirected toward uses more compatible with their objectives. This will not happen in the absence of a plan that recognizes the singular importance of an organizational culture perspective.

An organization's culture provides consistency and predictability for its members. It manifests what is important, valued, and accepted. It derives from a shared set of values and assumptions about a wide range of solutions to broad human issues. As such, cultures are infinitely variable from setting to setting. Distinct and different cultures may be found in military organizations, social service bureaucracies, and schools. And although history, necessity, professional norms, and idiosyncratic characteristics of individual leaders can shape a particular institution, even institutions in the same line of work can vary enormously in culture.

The usefulness and appropriateness of any given culture is likely to vary according to its mission and the environment in which it operates. Hierarchy, obedience, and service are necessary in a military organization. But the unique history of any organization (often a function of the professional norms that have shaped it) and the particular values of its most influential leaders are important in shaping its cultural identity. "Housers" differ from social service workers in their values and assumptions about how to improve the lives of tenants in public housing projects or homeless families. These dominant values, which motivate policy and programmatic responses to social problems, are often in conflict. Thus, when Steven Swanger assumed a social service function within the Cambridge Public Housing Authority, he met with initial resistance from the dominant housing culture.

Many theories of human motivation support the notion that an appeal to compelling values that provide meaning and dignity to the people who embrace them is a very powerful way to induce initiative and commitment. Because public sector employees generally seek public service rather than private employment in order to contribute to society in a concrete way, managing the organizational culture provides a very potent way to harness the organization's resources and improve and change performance. We do not attempt here to elaborate the infinite kinds of cultures that could be developed, but those that create meaning and value for managers and workers by articulating clear and consistent messages about the fundamental purposes of the organization and the kind of behavior that is admired and rewarded can be very effective in directing initiative. The values, beliefs, and justifications that belong in an organizational culture are matters of normative judgment. We will not attempt to develop a prescriptive model here, but there is clearly no more important role for a public executive than to address and enunciate these critical choices.

The remainder of the chapter is organized to explore the organizational culture perspective for the bureaucratic entrepreneur. It will identify the relevance of the perspective to all of the management decisions that need to be made in staking out a new direction for an enterprise. We will examine how a cultural perspective influences decisions about organizational structure, personnel, incentives, and rewards. Further, we will outline the opportunities and constraints of changing an organizational culture and the particular challenges of managing organizations with multiple cultures.

Constituencies

"I'm not sure what it is, but I know it when I see it." The message that Glynn inferred from the photos of trains in the manager's office was a manifestation of the culture of the MBTA—the shared philosophies, ideologies, assumptions, beliefs, and behavioral norms that permeate the community.[4] New employees often do not understand or appreciate an organization's culture when they arrive, but they learn quickly.

New police recruits in New York City generally join the force to fight and deter crime. Crime, however, is epidemic on the New York streets, and former Police Commissioner Lee Brown's mission was to change the basic philosophy of policing in New York. Current police methods keep most officers patrolling in cars and responding through 911 dispatchers to calls for help. The system has kept officers off the streets, isolated from the community and reacting to crime rather than deterring it.

Community policing is an effort to change the way police understand their role and do their jobs. Philosophically different from prevailing methods, community policing is designed to put officers back on the street in neighborhoods where they come to know and understand community problems. Working cooperatively with community residents and with considerable discretion in methods and approach, officers are expected to be involved in preventing rather than simply responding to crime.

The commissioner understood, however, that reconceptualizing the police function and reorganizing where, when, and how police work takes place are not merely matters of assertion. Brown was quoted as having said, "I have a role to determine the culture of this organization. That's the role of a leader in any organization. . . . I happen to believe that values are a key element in terms of helping to mold that culture. If you don't know what you stand for, then you can't provide the guidance to the organization to go in the direction that you want to go."[5]

Structural and cultural impediments to change abound. Regulations intended to prevent corruption and respond to citizens' concerns about overzealous for overly aggressive policing have reinforced officers' reluctance to develop friends on the beat or to seek arrests aggressively. Excessive fraternization can be grounds for punishment, officers claim, and high numbers of arrests often meet with charges from superiors of overtime padding or of citizen complaints about excessive force or harassment.

> "The less you do, the less trouble you get," Officer Comisky said. "You get the idea they don't want you to make collars. They just want you to drive around and stroke people." . . . Another veteran police officer in Bushwick who asked not to be identified said: "We virtually can't do anything because every time you do something, there are repercussions inside the station house. You keep making arrests day after

day, and you see what's happening. Right away perpetrators start making allegations and they transfer you to another area. After a while you learn. You stay in a neutral corner. You collect your paycheck. You get your pension. It stinks."[6]

New recruits may not know what the culture is at the outset, but all the implicit messages of superiors and the behavioral norms evidenced by their fellow officers define the organizational culture quite distinctly. Very clear messages are conveyed through organizational handling. And patrol cops are unusual in the level of discretion they can theoretically exercise.[7]

If community policing is to have any real opportunity as an effective strategy to deter crime and increase citizens' actual and perceived safety, the values, assumptions, and behavioral norms of the department are going to have to change dramatically. A culture will be necessary that supports, reinforces, rewards, and values very different philosophies and behaviors. To realize Brown's vision, the new police commissioner, Raymond Kelly, is going to have to give very serious attention to changing the message of what business the police are in and what is valued by the organization. He'll have to do that at every point—in the way reporting relationships are organized, symbols are created, and officers are trained, rewarded, promoted, and recognized. And it will not be enough to assert these values. Cultures are very pervasive. They become internalized at all levels. New cultures must be marketed internally and externally. They require the support and participation of employees and constituents at all levels. Citizens will have to think about police in a new way and understand their new role. The commissioner will have to attend to these things through direct and indirect communications at every level. Observers have likened his role to that of a preacher, seeing his mission as the "gospel" and trying to sell it wherever and whenever he can. It must be a critical concern if he is to exercise leadership as he sets his goals and develops an implementation plan.[8]

New Executive Task: The Management of Organizational Culture

In Chapter Five, we identified the unique qualities of highly successful executives who generated innovations in their organizations. They were often highly committed actors who had a personal vision or defined a mission for their organizations. Success was often characterized by the development of discrete and measurable goals by which success could be monitored and judged over both the short and the long term. Then they developed an implementation plan that included organizational structures that would be compatible with the new mission and developing rewards and incentives capable of enlisting the commitment and cooperation of employees at all levels of the organization.

Many of these activities depended on the involvement of people throughout the organization. Though the vision itself might depend more on the personal commitments of the executive, implementation and means more often relied on expertise farther down in the hierarchy. This was a critical recognition by Atkins and Glynn at the Massachusetts Department of Public Welfare and a strong finding in the recent literature on corporate innovation.[9]

The most successful executives relied less on getting people to do as the executives wanted and more on getting people to *want* to do as the executives wanted.[10] Highly successful executives were most often entrepreneurial—opportunistic and risk-taking. But those able to change the direction, focus, or business of their organizations were very sensitive to building and maintaining a compatible culture around which to generate organizational allegiance and commitment to the mission.

When Charles Atkins was commissioner of public welfare in Massachusetts, his mission was to change the role of the agency from providing income and support for eligible recipients to one providing employment and training to assist in achieving independence. However, income maintenance specialists and social service workers would be critical to reorienting the agency's activities because their contact with clients was direct and frequent. The success of the program depended on investing clients with a desire to enter employment and training, and that depended on how well the personnel with whom they interacted sold the program.

The success of the program is often attributed, in part, to the phenomenal success of Charles Atkins and Thomas Glynn, his deputy commissioner, in marketing their mission to their employees and various critical external constituencies—the governor, the legislature, the business community, and the voters.[11] Their marketing was clearly top-notch. However, their strategy (and the one developed at the MBTA) used marketing as a vehicle to change the *culture* of the welfare department.

The strategy of successful bureaucratic entrepreneurs, inside and outside the government, is to change the message of what is important and what is valued in the organization, explicitly and implicitly.[12] It is an effort dependent on the development of a shared set of assumptions, values, and practices. This is done through a variety of means and vehicles—marketing is clearly one. But it is more than being sophisticated about press and media relations or skillful at written and verbal communication. It is an organizational culture perspective that affects executive decisions at every level.

The Massachusetts Bay Transportation Authority: Successful Managing of Organizational Culture

Communicating the Mission

The most important initial activity of an executive is clearly to identify the mission of the organization. But existing cultures often run deep, and asserting a new mission or a new way of doing things is seldom in itself effective. It requires considerable attention to the various means that an executive has to communicate and the frequency and visibility with which the communication is undertaken. It further depends on a clear strategy to reach a range of constituencies and a sensitivity to the wide range of implicit and symbolic messages that can be communicated throughout the life of an organization.

When Thomas Glynn arrived at the MBTA, he met with

120 of his top managers, introduced himself, and told them he preferred to be called by his first name. A young woman raised her hand and asked, "Do you prefer Tom or Thomas?" Within two years, considerable change had been made in the organization. Customer service and employee morale replaced equipment performance as the main goals, and performance indicators were developed to evaluate how successful improvements in these two areas have been. Managers became accountable for meeting targets, and in the first year most were met. But the old-time MBTA managers continued to call their boss "Mr. Glynn."[13]

The MBTA has been described as very hierarchical, even paramilitary. Customer service and employee morale did not initially appear compatible with such formalized culture. Further, for an organization that lionized equipment, reorienting around people was going to involve a dramatic shift in the basic assumptions of the organization and the behavioral norms that reflect them. It was going to require a culture more compatible with the mission and goals of the new executive. However, Glynn saw that a hierarchical organization would have certain strengths in the short run because it consisted of levels comfortable with receiving direction from above.

Communication and leadership are key to altering an organization's mission and shaping a culture capable of supporting it. Management strategies that take organizational culture into account provide a systematic opportunity to communicate the message of what is valued and to reinforce and reward conforming behavior.

One particularly effective vehicle that combined an

educational function—teaching managers about the mission—and a morale or reward function—recognizing individuals' importance to the organization—was a program that Glynn designed with Professor Leonard Schlesinger at Harvard Business School, where Schlesinger is a leader of the customer service approach to management. Within three months of assuming the directorship, Glynn took his top ninety managers to a two-day training session at Harvard Business School. This gave his customer service agenda external validation. Indeed, it provided a way for Glynn to shift the focus from the capital and equipment goals of the previous regime to a new and growing need for rider services. While never minimizing or denigrating the earlier organizational goals, the Schlesinger program was used to teach senior managers throughout the organization by having a credible actor lay out a new vision for the organization.

At the sessions, videos of focus groups with public transit customers were shown to help all managers learn about the service program at the same time. Even the heads of bus garages were in attendance. This inclusiveness was an important element in shifting the attention away from the engineering values of the past without ever criticizing or undermining their importance. In this way, the shift in cultural values was articulated clearly without threatening existing interests. Indeed, by embracing them at the outset, Glynn sent the message that they were important to organizational success. After the battlefield mentality of his predecessors, it was a vehicle to reinforce the positive and put the issue of change on the table.

Both the dean of the business school and the governor addressed the attendees. This had tremendous symbolic and substantive significance in building self-confidence and self-esteem. The prestige of Harvard Business School greatly impressed the managers, and they felt valued by attending. At the same time, this "reward" afforded an occasion to engage them in learning about customer service. During the second day, the session ended with an unexpected downpour. Schlesinger presented each manager with a Harvard Business School umbrella. These remain important symbolic rewards and are cherished.

The second year, the second-level managers—one hundred of them—were sent to a two-day, Schlesinger-led session titled "More, Better, Faster, with Less." This constituted an effort to move down in the organization and establish a commitment to the new program. By this time, positive press response to changing organizational performance provided continual reinforcement for the new agenda. Employees at all levels of the organization could take pride from the tangible payoffs of the new organizational success.

On the day of his swearing in, Glynn identified his mission: providing high-quality service to customers and improving employee morale. But the symbolism and action of the day were probably more effective in communicating those goals than the speech itself. Glynn chose the swearing-in ceremony, with the governor and five hundred employees in attendance, as his first opportunity to recognize particularly outstanding employees. To those who manifested in their performance the most highly valued goals of the new organizational mission, he awarded his first customer service awards. By handing out a simple certificate at his own swearing in, he was able to make a statement about two critical priorities of his mission: customer service and employee morale.

Numerous occasions provided opportunities for rewarding many other employees. For both internal and external communication of the organization's mission, these award winners were recognized on large advertisements in all the subway cars and in Glynn's executive suite. Once adorned by sterile subway cars on test tracks, his suite became filled with the "car cards" displaying pictures of customer service award winners. They were also displayed in what he called the Customer Service Hall of Fame.

Reinforcing the Message: Seeing Every Executive Decision as an Opportunity

Communication, reinforcement, and recognition are all critical strategies for changing the culture of an organization. Organizational change is a long-term objective, and every organizational decision should be seen as an opportunity to reinforce the most fundamental values. Early in his tenure at the MBTA, Glynn faced the need to implement a fare hike—a highly unfortunate reality, given his desire to become a sensitive and "user-friendly" service provider. The fare increase did not engender vocal opposition in part because no increase had been implemented in eight years despite considerable visible investment in the system over the period. However, like other successful bureaucratic entrepreneurs, he saw this obstacle as an opportunity.

He ran a media campaign of fresh and clever posters with a headline reading "Boston Still in Last Place," cleverly reminding riders that of all major American cities, Boston's fare still remained the lowest. On the buses, where the fares remained the same as before, he had posters stating "Fare Hike Misses the Bus." Externally, therefore, he told customers, "We're on your side." He also provided the transit system, known as the "T," with a voice to speak the new message of customer service—a voice with personality and humor.

Internally, Glynn used the implementation of the fare increase as an opportunity to teach his managers how he was going to do things. He organized a task force on the fare increase to develop response plans. Rather than meeting exclusively with his top level managers—typical of the hierarchical MBTA—his task force consisted also of third- and fourth-level managers from many departments. He realized that the task force provided an opportunity for meetings, and he understood the value of meetings as a fundamental cultural experience where values can be enunciated and reinforced, behavioral norms can be established, and culturally desirable behaviors can be rewarded.

The task force on the fare increase served as a vehicle to teach several important lessons about how problem solving would be approached—cooperatively and with consultation—and what values would prevail—customers and employees. Further, instead of depending on communications trickling down to lower levels of the organization, opportunities like the task force were used to make communication direct and experiential for managers and, as a result, affecting employees far lower in the organization.

Establishing Credibility Through Concrete Results

Finally, the fare increase provided an opportunity to demonstrate the credibility of management to carry out its goal and to teach internal and external constituencies that the mission could be operationalized. Posters were used well in advance of the fare increase to prepare riders for the change so that there would be no surprise on the day of implementation. Hoarding of tokens typically prohibited by other transit systems when fares are raised, was not discouraged or punished. (It was another way to say, "We are on your side.") And the needs of customers for information and assistance at stations on the day of the fare change were anticipated. Managers were placed in all critical stations to assist riders with the transition. Press and career employees described it as the smoothest fare increase in memory.

Organizational Decisions: Opportunities to Enunciate Key Values

Using the fare increase as a tool to elucidate a new set of values was a calculated and deliberate strategy central to the organizational culture perspective. Yet it was but one example of how sensitivity to culture and the need to send continual messages about critical values shape every element of an implementation strategy. Even decisions about organizational structure are potentially shaped by the need to reinforce critical cultural values. When Glynn arrived, all sixteen coequal department heads reported directly to the general manager.

His first personnel decisions involved bringing in four new managers who had come from other state agencies—the Department of Revenue and the Department of Public Welfare—where they had implemented a similar strategy. He placed them in key positions (budget, marketing, chief of staff). He elevated the operations director to the status of a deputy. This put him at the same level as the deputy for administration, a more traditional deputy's role. Though somewhat unconventional, doing this strongly reinforced the message that "operations is the business we are in."

Penetrating the Organization:
Building Organizational Allegiance
and Individual Commitment

Successful management of the organizational culture requires having a message and communicating it often, to everyone, in every management decision or action. All activities of routine decision making and management ought to be seen as vehicles to underscore important organizational values.

Communicating with employees, explaining what the objective is and why it is important, is critical. But communication, even if flawlessly accomplished, is rarely sufficient. Existing cultures are hard to change. In the absence of crises or a generally perceived need to change—such as falling market share in the private sector or a new political mandate in the public sector—change requires the cooperation of the new managers and employees at levels in the organization that chief executives seldom see. Nevertheless, it is often at these levels that the business of the organization is actually carried out. A police commissioner without the cooperation and commitment of the officer on the beat is unlikely to be successful at implementing a community-based initiative.

The key to developing organizational allegiance and individual commitment is for an executive to convince employees first of the desirability of the mission and then of their own credibility. Employee commitment is therefore based on shared values of "moral commitment."[14] Employees must also be given opportunities to be successful in accomplishing the missions—they must be given what they need to do their work.[15] That means sharing power, information, and resources. Finally, to reinforce the value of individual contribution and commitment, a strong system of rewards and incentives is critical.[16] But rewards need not be material. Indeed, simply celebrating the accomplishment of employees through a variety of "culture rites" including public recognition and ceremonies is often enough to provide support for continued effort.

Glynn recognized the singular symbolic and material significance of developing a cooperative environment and providing incentives, rewards, and support for behavior that reinforced the mission. In addition to developing an employees' hall of fame and publicly announcing and disseminating the winners of the customer service awards, he resuscitated an employee newsletter and increased its publication to once a month. He developed new ways to use celebrations of employees' tenure to inspire, entertain, and reward. He created videos to commemorate their twenty-five or forty years of service by pulling together cultural images, songs, and memorabilia from the time they began work at the "T."

Similarly, he endorsed and expanded an employee event called the Rodeo at which bus and subway workers would compete at making repairs and driving. He invested in the event and provided it with internal visibility, arranging for winners to meet the governor and having their pictures taken with him. The Bus Rodeo dinner had only 225 in attendance his first year. After Glynn focused on it as a way to recognize and reward employees, it attracted 550 the second year. These small and symbolic rewards have an important cumulative impact on changing the culture deep into the organization. The executive with an organizational culture perspective looks for ways to improve rewards—formal, intrinsic, and symbolic. The message of these rewards is, "You are important, and the 'T' is important." Similar occasions to reward and recognize were used by Atkins and Glynn at the Public Welfare Department.[17]

Finally, giving people the tools they need to do a good job—both resources and authority—is critical to developing credibility among employees. When fare beating became a problem in suburban "T" stations because middle-class passengers couldn't always find correct change (they needed seven quarters per trip), drivers complained. They could not do their job and monitor fare compliance because they couldn't provide change. The response was to install change machines at some suburban stations. This solved the problem, allowed drivers to do their job, and demonstrated responsiveness on the part of management.

Similarly, providing authority but holding managers accountable for achieving specific goals was effectively used throughout the organization to empower managers, giving them broad authority on approaches but holding them to firm accountability on organizational goals. For example, using this strategy resulted in changes in the hiring process that halved the time it took to fill a vacancy while expanding the gains made in achieving affirmative action goals.

Thomas Glynn was not unique in his understanding that an organizational culture strategy can be central to organizational change. Some of these techniques can be found in the management practices of Gordon Chase, Ira Jackson, Charles Atkins, and Ellen Schall. Likewise, Barbara Levin depended strongly on the inculcation of organizational values about women's empowerment and professional relationships in the development of the Monroe County Maternity Center. Sandra Steiner Lowe depended on developing shared community values to generate diverse support for her child health initiative.

A particularly good example of shifting an agency's dominant culture to achieve a new mission is the actions of William Ruckelshaus at the EPA. Having inherited environmental protection efforts scattered among numerous old-line federal agencies, Ruckelshaus first wished to establish a clear, aggressive, and focused initiative. This meant acting quickly and decisively. However, previous federal efforts relied primarily on activities (in the Department of Agriculture and elsewhere) of scientists who had been closely allied with the industries they were responsible for regulating. The dominant culture of science that he faced at the outset was very cautious, more apt to wait for the definitive scientific conclusions before advocating regulatory action.

Poised to move more quickly to establish the new agency's credibility as independent and aggressive, he strategically moved to replace the dominant culture of the scientists with that of litigation and advocacy dominated by idealistic and mission-driven young lawyers. However, instead of abandoning the scientists whose expertise he needed, he shifted their roles, using them more as expert witnesses to provide evidence to support the activities of the litigators. Rather than waiting for the slow and cautious regulatory approach led by the scientists, in his new agency Ruckelshaus adopted an adversarial legalistic approach that brought in a new culture through the dominance of lawyers. He drafted scientists from the existing agencies to support his new aggressive orientation.[18]

Most successful innovators implicitly understand the importance of these practices. Glynn's use of the approach was among the most systematic and most clearly articulated.[19] An examination of two private corporate cases—one of extraordinary success and the other of failure—demonstrates the importance of managing the organization's culture.

New Mission at IBM: Understanding and Managing Organizational Culture

A great deal of IBM's success in creating its innovative and standard-setting PC was the product of its top executives' ability to understand organizational culture and then to manage it well. The IBM executives were particularly effective at managing multiple cultures. Their ability to communicate down through the organization made a special contribution to their innovative success.

Managing Multiple Cultures

A good deal of strength derives from having different cultures and different approaches in a single organization. The successful executive is the one who can manage multiple cultures by maintaining a creative tension among them. The advantages of multiple cultures are so significant that when they do not exist, they are sometimes created to achieve this creative tension. A good example of this is the creation of internal venture groups known as independent business units (IBUs) within IBM and the use of one such unit to develop the IBM PC.

IBM's top executives had set up the Entry Systems Division Unit as an independent unit in Boca Raton, Florida, in 1968 to experiment with small, low-cost computers. In 1980, its director, Bill Lowe, made a presentation on the personal computer business to IBM's corporate management committee (CMC). He argued that the crisis—IBM's zero share of the growing PC market—should be viewed as a major opportunity. The PC industry was now a viable opportunity for IBM, but getting into it would mean going outside IBM's culture: "The only way we can get into the personal computer business is to go out and buy part of a computer company or buy both the CPU [central processing unit] and software from people like Apple or Atari—because we can't do this within the culture of IBM."[20]

He argued that the IBM culture was not hospitable to PC development because it was dominated by its mainframe division and disfavored by the general orientation toward mainframes as IBM's core business. Also, many other IBM divisions, such as sales, were hostile to the PC. Ostensibly this was because it was a "toy" in their view. More likely it was because it would conflict with the way they were accustomed to doing business. The sales division, for example, had exclusive control of the sale of all IBM products, and no outside retailers were selling IBM products.

A Challenge to IBM's Culture

The CMC gave Lowe one month to prepare a plan. He came back with one that departed radically from three of IBM cultural tenets: (1) IBM would use outside vendors for all the computer elements and off-the-shelf components that had already survived in the market. (2) The new machine would have an open architecture. (3) It would be sold through outside retailers rather than exclusively through IBM's own sales force.

The CMC responded by authorizing these approaches with a twelve-month deadline to bring the product to the market to "fill this embarrassing gap at the low end of the product line."[21] The essential breakthrough in developing the IBM PC was Bill Lowe's shrewd understanding of IBM's organizational culture: "We can't [develop a PC] within the culture of IBM."

This realization was the necessary but not sufficient condition for the ultimate success of the IBM PC. The chief executives at the top of IBM understood the need to create an environment that would first encourage and then protect the innovations that would bubble up from below them in the organization. In particular, these chief executives understood the necessity and difficulty of managing multiple cultures in a large organization. Thus they had encouraged independence by setting up the IBU at Boca Raton. Even more important, they then protected it from the mainstream IBM divisions that had potential differences with it on the grounds of both substance and power.

Beyond creating this independent unit and then allowing it to carry out this new mission, the top executives effectively managed these multiple cultures in a variety of ways. They sent the message by both word and deed that they were serious about developing an IBM PC. They did this by their willingness to depart radically from IBM's central cultural tenets and use outside vendors, an open architecture, and outside retailers.

IBM achieved extraordinary success by working around its dominant culture and tolerating and nurturing multiple cultures, but the result did not endure. Recent downturns in IBM's dominance seem to be in large part the result of the abandonment of its successful efforts to encourage independence and innovation by breaking away from this dominant culture and from corporate centralization. Confirmation of the accuracy of our analysis as to these causes of IBM's recent ills is that the new CEO, Lewis Gerstner, has advocated an effort to assert a new culture of decentralization, flexibility, and innovation as precisely the route to reemergence in the mid 1990s.

Words Are Not Enough: Ineffective Managing of Organizational Culture at Xerox

Xerox's president, Peter McCoulough, wisely saw the need to develop controls in the mid 1960s to cope with the corporation's rapid and unwieldy growth. By 1970, McCoulough had perceived the need to develop a new and additional corporate mission because of the future changes in the market for the company's copier and the approaching end of its patent-based monopoly. He thus called for a new mission of creating an "architecture of information." But McCoulough and the other top Xerox executives were ineffective in managing organizational culture, especially multiple cultures. They instituted controls that were inappropriate for Xerox's organizational culture. Xerox's new mission was quite appropriate for the company. But both the old and new organizational cultures around this new mission were managed poorly by the top executives and the managers at the program level.

An Inappropriate Culture of Control

Controls are necessary in a large organization. At Xerox in the mid 1960s, they were especially needed because Xerox's huge growth had seriously overloaded its management capability, leading to "a complete lack of control."[22] However, the culture of control that McCoulough imposed at Xerox was probably inappropriate for both Xerox's culture and its product.[23]

Controls were of course necessary, but the particular controls that McCoulough and his top executives, such as Archie McCardell, who came from the Ford Motor Company, instituted were antithetical to the very culture of innovation and risk that had fueled growth at Xerox. Indeed, they were transplanted from an organization with a very different culture and product. The controls were appropriate for an automaker like Ford, with model years, high fashion consciousness, low technology, and enormous numbers of blue-collar workers. But these controls didn't fit Xerox, a high-technology company where product development was critical and the sales and service organizations dominated.[24]

New Mission, New Organizational Culture

In setting a new mission for Xerox—to create an "architecture of information"—McCoulough was far ahead of his time. The simultaneous creation of a generously funded computer research unit, the Palo Alto Research Center (PARC), was also quite prescient. And PARC's proposal to build a personal computer was absolutely trailblazing.

But McCoulough failed to understand the essential attribute of an effective manager of organizational culture—communication. For this new mission to be effective, it required constant communication downward through the organization and reinforcing symbolic actions. McCoulough's "new mission" speech pointed toward a corporate transformation—a new organizational culture. But it was so new that it "both mystified and threatened his organization. Thousands of Xerox employees—from factory workers to salespeople to executives—had, at most, a vague notion about the need for, or content of, an 'architecture of information.' And at worst, they believed McCoulough's goal unnecessary or irrelevant."[25]

To instill conviction among the doubters and to provide direction to the doers would require constant explanation and hands-on experience—experiential management and communication. But McCoulough did not do this. Instead, he distanced himself from daily operations. Upon ascending as chairman, he turned over the presidency to the number-crunching Archie McCardell from Ford. But McCardell was a poor communicator, especially poor in explaining down the organization the new controls that he instituted. He was described by one Xerox colleague as an "extremely bright individual."

> But he managed by the numbers. He wasn't a very good communicator. There would be meeting after meeting of whomever with him at which decisions would not be made at the meeting. Then shortly thereafter a decision would come out but with no explanation of why that decision was chosen and no communication of its implications to those affected by it. His management style was not one that communicated much to the troops. It was not well understood why the company was doing what it was doing—whether good, bad, or indifferent. And that lack of understanding went to all levels.[26]

In other words, McCardell did not understand that meetings are important cultural experiences. They are important opportunities to repeat messages, reinforce basic values, and teach a way of looking at things. This was precisely the understanding that Tom Glynn developed so well.

PARC's Executives: Poor Managing of the Organizational Culture at the Program Level

The people at PARC were very bright. But they had poor communication skills and little understanding of how to bridge differences in organizational culture.

Bob Taylor was the dynamic and charismatic head of PARC's Computer Science Lab (CSL), to whom his group was very loyal. He was described by a fellow PARC executive as "extremely skilled at building an espirit in his group. However, it was very much a 'we-they' phenomenon. His idea was that his group was better than everyone else. And they were better. But they were not skilled at communicating with the 'theys.'"[27] They did not build bridges with the rest of Xerox. In fact, they went about burning bridges.

PARC's executives had the same poor communication and interaction with SDS, Xerox's computer subsidiary. This contributed to SDS's billion-dollar failure, as well as to the failure of Xerox's PC, the Alto. Perhaps most stunning was PARC's poor communication with Xerox's headquarters. Neither Taylor, the program advocate of both PARC and the Alto, nor Pake, PARC's chief executive, spent much time at the Stamford, Connecticut, headquarters. They mistook isolation for insulation and thus failed to explain their product.

The PARC executives did not seem to understand the message of what one consultant called their "haughty, im-

ORGANIZATIONAL CULTURE

mature disposition."[28] It told people everywhere in Xerox (at headquarters, at SDS, at the Dallas office-products division) that PARC thought it did not need any of them and could go it alone. They were highly critical of the computer scientists at SDS and of Bob Potter, the head of the Dallas unit, who would have been the natural outlet to implement PARC's research. (Eventually in 1980 the Dallas unit did develop a personal computer for Xerox, but in reciprocal hostility to PARC, it was not based on the Alto, and it quickly failed.) PARC complained that Potter made a one-hour presentation without ever mentioning the word *software* once! But instead of patiently proselytizing Potter, Dallas, or SDS, the young PARC scientists rudely snickered.

We should also note that whereas IBM was successful in managing multiple cultures, Xerox's difficulties were probably more typical. For example, Kodak and Apple also saw the need to bring differing cultures into their organization. Kodak, like IBM, went the formal route of creating IBUs within the company. They were much praised by Rosabeth Kanter and others for being a "giant learning to dance."[29] But a more recent evaluation showed that the outcomes of these IBUs have been quite modest.[30]

Conclusion: The Manager's Imperative

The broad lesson of all these cases is obvious: management matters. Management turns out to be especially critical in an organization that by necessity or choice is about to undertake something new. In the public sector, where politics can change leadership and create new mandates regularly, organizational change is constant. Why, then, when change in leadership is so inevitable and frequent, is the mark of an executive's mission so rarely observed?

Part of the failure of public executives to realize their visions is the result of inadequate attention to the management of organizational culture. Culture is stubborn and often pervasive and has unanticipated power to undermine even brilliant and bold policy initiatives. Cultures develop over a long period of time and can provide employees of an organization with a set of assumptions and values that provide a sense of control over how they do their jobs. They internalize a set of behavioral norms and decision rules that help create predictability. Over time, new recruits become initiates, and many develop strong stakes in the status quo.

Public managers bringing new values and assumptions to their organizations can therefore face formidable resistance. Success depends largely on making subordinates want to do what you want them to do. Our research suggests that in both the public and private sectors, management of organizational culture is a key variable in successful organizational change. We propose six management imperatives.

1. Diagnose the culture before you develop a strategy for implementation.

Executives who fail to understand the assumptions, values, and behavioral norms that are strongly held will not be able to anticipate where resistance will be encountered. Further, understanding and using the culture as it exists is much easier than trying to change it, particularly in the short run. Strategies that take the existing culture into account have a greater chance of success.

2. Communicate your mission with an eye toward shaping a culture capable of supporting it.

Communication is a major vehicle for exercising leadership. Communication must be seen as more than asserting a position or a plan. Executives who have an organizational culture perspective identify all the explicit and implicit ways in which the message of a new mission can be communicated. All written and verbal communications can support the mission. But virtually all organizational activities provide opportunities to communicate and to teach key values; meetings, celebrations, reward systems, organization charts—all can be seen as vehicles to communicate what is valued. The strategy to shape the culture requires attention to the potential of all these cultural "artifacts" to reflect a new emerging set of values and norms.

3. Reinforce the message.

You can never emphasize your primary values and objectives too much or too often or to too many different people. Cultures take a long time to develop. They take almost as long to change. Executives with an eye toward fundamentally altering an organization must be there for the long term and see in their role an opportunity for virtually every executive decision to communicate a set of principles about what is important in the organization.

4. Establish credibility through concrete results.

No matter how convincing the communication or what the rewards for supporting an executive's new mission, there is no better method for demonstrating the credibility of your position than producing the desired result. Celebrating the success further reinforces the value of what you have accomplished.

5. Reach down into the organization to build allegiance and commitment.

Executives must look for ways to reach employees at successively lower levels in the organization. Communicating to lower levels exclusively through upper- and mid-level managers dilutes the messages and makes remote the values that need to be internalized often at "street level." This can be achieved in part through formal and symbolic efforts to reward and recognize performance and behavior that reinforce organizational goals. But it is also strongly achieved by building cooperative and nonhierarchical structures that bring various levels together to develop collective solutions and to demonstrate that senior management is willing to give workers the tools they need to achieve the new mission.

6. Use and manage multiple cultures.

A full understanding of the organization's culture or cultures is the first imperative. Among other things, this means getting executives who are appropriate for the particular cultures, especially those with communication and interaction skills.

Executives also need to understand what a culture is. Executives at the top must be sensitive to the fact that almost every one of their statements and acts sends a cultural message. They must be sensitive to the role of all the organization's cultural artifacts. Most of all, they must recognize that management matters: orchestration and coordination will not occur automatically.

Another aspect of this understanding is the extent to which one or more cultures are appropriate for the organization today. Failing to understand this through organizational egocentricity can be a serious blow to the organization, be it a large and apparently secure private organization or a public one. For both types of organizations, competition may be just around the corner. The organization may be vulnerable if it is operating with an inappropriate culture.

Even if cultural change is necessary, it may not be feasible. It may be wiser to add another culture or subculture to the organization. This is most likely to be initiated or at least implemented from the top. Executives then must be sensitive to tensions between the organization's multiple cultures. Tensions are not likely to be eradicated, nor should they be. Such tensions, especially in the form of competition, are likely to be healthy for the organization.

Once this awareness has been established, executives need the management skills of orchestration and coordination—communication, interaction, protection, and nurturing—in order for multiple cultures to coexist and be jointly productive for the organization as a whole. In short, management matters.

Though the role of the top executives is most important in managing the potential tensions between cultures, the effectiveness of executives below that level is also essential: middle managers and project managers must master the skills of communication and interaction so as to explain, exhibit, and protect the new culture or subculture in which they work. Their efforts at coordination and orchestration with other cultures in the organization will have positive effects that are both manifest and latent.

Notes

1. Descriptions of the management of the Massachusetts Bay Transit Authority come from our research. Though not a candidate for the Ford Foundation Innovations award, Thomas Glynn had previously been a finalist for the award while serving as deputy commissioner for the Massachusetts Department of Public Welfare. Though at the MBTA for less than three years, he is generally credited with having made dramatic and positive changes in the organization. One leadership challenge is documented in Ellen Herman, "Massachusetts Bay Transit Authority," Harvard Business School case no. 9-391-202, June 1992, pp. 1–12.
2. Short time frames are most often imposed by the short cycles of elective and appointed office. Thus there is a constant tension between moving quickly to get things done and investing in the organizational infrastructure—here, the organizational culture—which will then allow mobilization of organizational resources and support for change.
3. Alan Wilkins and Kerry J. Patterson, "You Can't Get There from Here: What Will Make Culture Change Projects Fail," in *Gaining Control of the Corporate Culture*, ed. Ralph H. Kilmann, Mary J. Saxton, Roy Serpa, and associates (San Francisco: Jossey-Bass, 1985), pp. 262–291.
4. Kilmann et al., *Gaining Control*, p. 5.
5. George James, "Brown's Gospel: Community Policing," *New York Times*, August 14, 1991, p. B1.
6. James C. McKinley, Jr., "Policy Plan Facing Hurdle in

Precincts: Cynicism," *New York Times,* October 4, 1990, pp. A1, B3.
7. Michael Lipsky, *Street Level Bureaucracy* (New York: Russell Sage Foundation, 1980).
8. Commissioner Brown has resigned, but community policing has been cited to explain New York City's improved police performance as measured by crime data. Most observers believe that this strategy has great promise.
9. Robert D. Behn, *Leadership Counts: Lessons for Public Managers from the Massachusetts Welfare, Training and Employment Program* (Cambridge, Mass.: Harvard University Press, 1991); Thomas Peters and Robert Waterman, *In Search of Excellence* (New York: HarperCollins, 1982); Rosabeth Moss Kanter, *The Change Masters* (New York: Simon & Schuster, 1983).
10. James M. Kouzes and Barry Z. Posner, *The Leadership Challenge: How to Get Extraordinary Things Done in Organizations* (San Francisco: Jossey-Bass, 1987), p. 27.
11. Behn, *Leadership Counts.*
12. Many of the cases we analyzed paid implicit attention to culture; far fewer had a systematic strategy. The cases we highlight here are ones in which the executives had a clear and systematic approach to changing the organizational culture.
13. Thomas P. Glynn, "Workshop on Public and Private Entrepreneurs," presentation at the Gordon Public Policy Center, Brandeis University, Waltham, Massachusetts, 1990.
14. Barry Z. Posner, James M. Kouzes, and Warren H.

Schmidt, "Shared Values Make a Difference: An Empirical Test of Corporate Culture," *Human Resource Management* 24 (1985): 293–310.
15. Kanter, *Change Masters;* Kouzes and Posner, *Leadership Challenge.*
16. Nirmal K. Sethia and Mary Ann Von Glinow, "Arriving at Four Cultures by Managing the Reward System," in *Gaining Control,* ed. Kilmann et al., pp. 400–420.
17. Behn, *Leadership Counts.*
18. We are indebted to Martin Shapiro for his suggestions on this point.
19. In addition to the documentary evidence we cite to support this conclusion, many hours of interviews with Thomas Glynn revealed a highly conscious and systematic program to change the organizational culture. As the new United States deputy labor secretary, he now seeks to extend these approaches to the Labor Department.
20. James Chposky and Ted Leonis, *Blue Magic: The People, Power, and Politics Behind the IBM Personal Computer* (New York: Facts on File, 1988).
21. Ibid., p. 9.
22. Douglas K. Smith and Robert C. Alexander, *Fumbling the Future: How Xerox Invented, Then Ignored the First Personal Computer* (New York: Morrow, 1988).
23. Because these control systems did not work well, there was still a great deal of inefficiency. Not only was the cure as bad as the disease—it stifled innovation—but it was also an ineffective cure.
24. The zeal to drive down manufacturing costs caused Ford to make products that broke down too often. The

same self-defeating spiral began to bedevil Xerox in the late 1960s. Hughes, chair of the strategy review committee, criticized the Ford financial people who came to Xerox for their inappropriate approach: "They would be very concerned about getting modest amounts of savings because in automobiles, modest savings added up to big dollars. If you saved a penny, you were a hero. However, if the result of saving a penny is that every time you do a repair job on the copier, you spend a penny, it's dumb economics" (Smith and Alexander, *Fumbling the Future,* p. 221). (Those of us who during the period got to know the Xerox repairman almost as well as our spouse would be inclined to agree.) Executives like Hughes argued that Xerox should reduce overall "life cost" by spending more to build a better copier that would need less service later.
25. Smith and Alexander, *Fumbling the Future.*
26. Ibid., p. 134.
27. Ibid., p. 144.
28. Ibid., p. 140.
29. Rosabeth Moss Kanter, *When Giants Learn to Dance* (New York: Simon and Schuster, 1990).
30. *Wall Street Journal,* August 17, 1990.

7

Balancing Innovation and Accountability

The preceding chapters show that skillful executives can make government work. They achieve innovation often through a willingness to confront (and sometimes circumvent) intransigent institutions and inhospitable political and bureaucratic environments to realize their missions. Executive talent is scarce in government, yet our research reveals that there is considerably more available than many people have supposed.

Executive Talent: Scarce or Just Hamstrung?

In explaining frequent policy failures and government ineffectiveness, many observers have pointed to the scarcity of executive talent in government.[1] We agree that executive talent is scarce, but, as Chapters Three through Six showed, there are nevertheless more talented executives than many people have supposed. Rather, certain institutional constraints often overwhelm. Efforts to ensure accountability and respond to the multiple and often conflicting demands in large, complex bureaucracies result in an abundance of routines, procedures, and decision points. These are designed to provide oversight and compliance with various goals, but they also suppress and discourage executive talent. Indeed, oversight overload can create a drag on the energetic and innovative manager.

Analysts have pointed to the critical role that external context plays in constraining the opportunities for policy and program innovations in government. Conflicting political mandates, short time horizons, and a distrustful political culture provide limited support for initiative. Further, structural and systems characteristics of public organizations can suppress the exercise of creative initiative and discourage otherwise talented executives. The scale and complexity of public organizations, coupled with often rigid personnel, budget, and accountability systems, serve to reduce the opportunities for the exercise of creative managerial discretion.[2]

But discretion to act is a fundamental precondition to exercising managerial initiative. And the demands for accountability in the public sector, along with other values such as equity and access, ultimately produce organization constraints that affect even minute practices of management on a daily basis. For example, hierarchical organizational structures may impede efforts that rely on cooperation or collaboration. Similarly, rigid personnel systems may prohibit efforts to reward success. These and dozens of other characteristics of public organizations and their political contexts affect managers' options at virtually every level. Their impact is pervasive, and they limit the depth and breadth of entrepreneurial activity of even the most energetic and creative manager.

Innovation and managerial initiative are encouraged by environments that stress autonomy and risk taking and eschew hierarchy, centralization, and routines. Accountability, by contrast, is ensured by very different organizational structures and rules. Accountability requires an environment that allows for continual sources of information about who is responsible for doing what and for significant certainty about what will happen when. The need in a democratic society to ensure that government is accountable to citizens and that it responds to their demands results in efforts to standardize procedures and decision points and establishes rules and regulations that make behavior predictable. These characteristics of public organizations produce dramatic tensions when they are confronted by the equally compelling values of improving public performance through innovation and initiative.

Other organizational requirements also suppress and discourage executive talent. For example, analytical requirements for evaluating trade-offs among alternative policy or program investments provide important insights for improving the payoffs from any given intervention. Analysis, however, can be time-consuming and controversial as different organizational actors support alternative goals and decision rules. In practice, these requirements can easily lead to the paralysis of analysis.

Similarly, other organizational characteristics develop in response to political requirements: oversight, access, and equity goals impose the demands of bureaucratic routines with their formal rules and procedures, which also suppress the legitimate exercise of executive initiative. These procedures, in combination with ongoing legislative and budgetary oversight, spring from the appropriate desire to maintain accountability over executives. If they are lacking, public enterprises risk fraud, waste, and the compromise of democratic principles. But these safeguards often have perverse effects.

Cumulatively, these elements often act as a brake on talented executives. They reduce the executives' ability to improve the effectiveness and performance of public enterprises. Inadequate accountability and participation can compromise democratic values and can easily result in waste and fraud. Indeed, these are all the flip side of insufficient oversight. Throughout this chapter, we explore these tensions. These are the dilemmas of overregulation and underregulation. In the next chapter, we describe the ways that effective managers can act to produce a more acceptable balance between the need for freedom to act and citizens' rights to hold accountable the people responsible for conducting the public's business.

Bureaucratic Entrepreneurs: Succeeding Through Creative Subversion

Successful public executives are so frustrated by the difficulty of getting things done that they proceed with a compensatory bias toward action and a risk-taking emphasis on quick results. Moreover, there has been a backlash against the rules and procedures that limit their authority and impede their efforts to act. Success in this context often depends on creative subversion. An increasingly common response to management's frustration with excessive oversight and regulatory requirements is for executives to seek innovative ways to circumvent the formal rules—to short-circuit organizational clearance points and to gather enough informal power to surmount implementation obstacles. The successful executives we analyzed often operated outside the normal bureaucratic chain of command.

Gordon Chase: Creative Circumvention

Gordon Chase's response to New York City's heroin epidemic, described in Chapter Four, illustrates this pattern. The city's initial response—primarily drug-free residential treatment centers—had been slow to develop and, once started, proved ineffective. When Chase took over the city's Health Services Administration (HSA), he chose a large methadone maintenance program as the city's new policy. A young doctor, Robert Newman, and others pressed the idea on him. Following Dr. Newman's brief and not entirely systematic presentation (which did not discuss the range of alternative options for heroin treatment), Chase read a three hundred–page analysis of methadone maintenance over a weekend. He came back on Monday with his decision to pursue the methadone route as the HSA's primary drug program. Neither then nor later did he take the time to pay much attention to more complicated analysis or to consider a full range of alternatives.

Having chosen methadone maintenance, he pushed ahead immediately. His first creative circumvention was to get the program off the ground even before it received official budgetary authorization. He located sites, rented them, and opened clinics immediately. He kept acting. Outreach was needed to recruit large numbers of addicts into the program. He ignored a more cautious approach, such as a pilot program. This was despite the fact that methadone maintenance was very new and had never before been launched on a large scale in any city. Instead, his aim was very broad: attempt to treat all heroin addicts in the city.

Moreover, to circumvent creatively the normal bureaucratic channels that could impede progress in dealing with this crisis, Chase contracted with private hospitals to provide on-site clinics. A very bold and innovative step at the time, it got quick results and avoided the impediments to implementation normally experienced from depending on existing public agencies for service delivery. Later Chase wrote that when you have problems coping with overhead problems, "if you can't reason and you can't bypass: escape."[3] This was clearly the route that he himself had taken at the HSA.

Navy Secretary John Lehman:
Working Around Formal Constraints

In the 1980s, Secretary of the Navy John Lehman faced a major obstacle to developing innovative policies: the Pentagon's slow, inefficient procurement process. It didn't work functionally or efficiently because, he said, the bureaucracy was "bloated." Lehman responded with aggressive, informal methods of working around formal constraints to improve the efficiency of the procurement process and obtain better outcomes—cheaper, more rapidly developed weapons. Lehman viewed the procurement process as excessively slow and bureaucratic. It resulted in weapons that were imperfect and expensive. The problem at the Pentagon was not the absence of laws and regulations. Rather, it was an excess of them that made the process slow and prompted Lehman to move around them in pursuit of innovation and improved efficiency. To deal with these inadequacies, Lehman engaged in corner-cutting and short-circuiting formal constraints. Private consultants were the instruments he used to achieve greater efficiency.[4]

Lehman felt that insufficient competition among contractors was a key problem. One reason for this was insufficient interaction and information exchange between the military and the contractors about the weapon specifications desired and the excessive formality of the process itself. The procurement process was a classic example of oversight overload.[5]

Lehman sought more competition among weapon contractors, both as a good itself and as an improvement in the efficiency of weapon production. Impatient and convinced that competition needed some stimulation, he turned to informal means. Contractors often did not know enough about Pentagon specifications for a weapon to build it or even to bid on it. Thus Pentagon officials wanted them to know more and as a result create more competition and better weapon systems by stimulating more and better bids. With private consultants, Pentagon officials worked around formal requirements and leaked enough information to contractors to improve the quality of their bids. To stimulate increased competition, consultants were encouraged to leak the weapon plans of company A to company B. Company B could develop plans for that weapon and bid on it competitively. Whereas previously contractors had difficulty responding by the forty-five-day deadline, the number and timeliness of responses improved. All of this led to what most objective observers considered innovative outcomes: a procurement process that was more competitive and that produced weapons more rapidly and more cheaply.

Similar Constraints and Frustrations in the Private Sector

Excessive oversight and bureaucratic routines have similarly frustrated private sector executives. Indeed, the paralysis of analysis was first noted in connection with private sector organizations. The difficulty of getting things done in these organizations has generated a similar backlash of admiration for action-oriented executives.

A leading study of how to improve innovation in the private sector, Gifford Pinchot's *Intrapreneuring*, suggests that there are plenty of good ideas around. But the implementation stage is the most important hurdle. And the requirements of analysis and control are the chief villains. Pinchot tells the typical CEO:

INNOVATION AND ACCOUNTABILITY

Generally, when you or any CEO calls for innovation, very little happens. This is not because of a lack of good ideas but because of the difficulties your people have in implementing them. If you are not hearing good ideas, it is because they are blocked or sanitized before they reach you.... The stagnation of innovation in large organizations is the almost inevitable result of the currently fashionable systems of analysis and control.[6]

Peters and Waterman found that although innovation is often the launching pad for a successful corporation, subsequent organizational development tends to stifle the potential for future innovations. The free flow of ideas that characterizes smaller, looser organizations is replaced by hierarchical structures that do not permit the autonomy at lower levels that is essential for innovative development.[7] The Xerox Corporation's failure to market the first PC is a striking illustration of excessive, poorly managed control that doomed their brilliant idea.

Succeeding Through Creative Subversion in the Private Sector

The difficulty of getting things done in the private sector has resulted in a similar pattern of executives pursuing innovation by subverting these impediments. For example, Pinchot's book on highly effective "intrapreneurs"—entrepreneurs working within large private organizations—identifies the following lessons from the strategies that they pursue in working around bureaucratic constraints.[8]

First, circumvent and work around the formal rules, requirements, and channels: just do it, and don't bother to ask for permission. It takes too long to get an answer, and the answer will usually be cautious or negative.

Second, to sustain yourself until the positive results come in—inevitably, they will take a long time—hide! Stay underground. Third, disguise the real costs and the real time frame, and don't tell anyone you've started the project because people will get impatient during the long wait for results.

*Circumvent Formal Rules
and Regulations: Just Do It!*

This is the first of Pinchot's findings. Innovative entrepreneurs, he found, do not "ask for permission . . . because it is easier to ask forgiveness than permission."[9] For instance, Art Fry, the innovator who developed Post-It Notes for the 3M Company, claimed that "it can't be done through formal channels," even though he worked for a very loose organization.[10] Moreover, Pinchot found not only that formal channels are slow but also that they are often guarded by envious and even vindictive people who are especially jealous of innovators.

> When one group is singled out to innovate, everyone else feels slighted and cheated. "Why do they get relief from bureaucratic restraints when I don't?" people ask. The jealousy can be substantially worsened by a CEO who says: These

brilliant people are creating the future of our company. [This] insures that everyone else will hate them, and that the hated "hot shots" fail. . . . [There is a] danger of success: Venture groups that begin to succeed are particularly vulnerable to attack. . . . Success also threatens to put [them] ahead of their former peers. One highly successful group found themselves so isolated that for months they could not even get routine supplies from other divisions, which company customers could get delivered on twenty-four hours' notice.[11]

Peters and Waterman's findings on innovation parallel Pinchot's on the necessity of working around formal rules and channels. The innovations they observed were often accompanied by "bootlegging"—an explicit strategy of moving beyond the rules to obtain additional resources. Bootlegging activity is especially important during the research stages. Successful innovators garner disproportionate amounts of research and development time as well as funds from other projects: they move money and bootleg time. This extra time and money then permits ambitious researchers to engage in the experimentation required for innovative product development.

Peters and Waterman found bootlegging fairly common at General Electric and IBM. An IBM manager told them: "In every successful big development project there were two or three (about five once) other small projects, you know, four- to six-person groups, two people in one instance, who had been working on parallel technology or parallel development efforts. It had been with scrounged time and bodies. But that's a time-honored thing. *We wink at it.* It pays off."[12]

Bootlegging is necessary because the "creative fanatic"—the mover behind the innovation—is usually outside the mainstream of the corporate culture and therefore not very likely to get needed support. Thus the innovator often needs a sponsor to help move beyond the rules. For instance, the jealousy surrounding formal channels tends to create "antisponsors." Pinchot emphasizes this point well in the story of the product champion at Owens-Corning who developed and tested his brilliant fiberglass idea outside the company with a local patching contractor.[13] "Avoid having to check ideas with all the operating divisions before proceeding. If every division must reject the idea first, . . . the ventures get 'antisponsors'; the division managers who rejected the idea can't wait to see it fail and prove they were right in the first place."[14] Pinchot concludes his findings on circumventing formal rules with this dictum for innovators: "Honor your sponsors."

Work Underground: Publicity Triggers the Organization's Immune Mechanism

Pinchot illustrates this circumventing strategy with the case of Lee Iacocca setting out to create a totally new car for Ford in the 1960s. Iacocca gathered resource people from outside of formal channels and literally hid from top management as they worked underground.

> Iacocca did not sit patiently at his desk. . . . He put together a group that included people from Design (even though as head of the Ford Division he had no authority to draft people from elsewhere in the company) along with people from the advertising agency (who traditionally were not called in until a project was ready to roll). They met at the Fairlane Motel so they could work without any company interference. Working on the fringes of the system meant that the group could present management with a fait accompli. Had the initial work occurred inside Ford's walls, compromise and delay could have ruined it. By stretching the boundaries of acceptable corporate behavior, Iacocca brought his idea to life.[15]

The ultimate product of that group—the legendary Mustang—had great success, which was central in developing Ford's new strength in the 1960s.

Another part of the working underground strategy is disguising how long the innovation process is taking in order to "stop the impatience clock." Bob Adams of 3M explains: "When people hear about a new idea, a clock begins running in their minds—after a certain length of time they run out of patience if they don't see results. . . . Keep your ideas quiet. The clock doesn't start until people hear about it. Also, the more they hear about it, the faster the clock runs."[16]

Skunkworks: Recapturing the Benefits of Smallness

One of the formidable elements to work around in public sector organizations is the organizational structure and hierarchy. Large private organizations face similar obstacles. As organizations grow, the free flow of ideas that characterizes smaller, looser organizations is replaced by hierarchical structures that constrain the autonomy at lower levels that is so important for innovation. Preserving an environment conducive to innovation is difficult in these large corporations.

Peters and Waterman found that a less clandestine way of recapturing the benefits of smallness is through the institutionalization of "skunkworks": groups of eight or ten zealots who are given the autonomy necessary for innovative product development.[17] This decentralization within a centralized structure leads to duplication and overlap, but it re-creates an environment in which the entrepreneurial spirit can flourish. "Performance shootouts" at IBM, the development of Fellows and Individual Contributors programs at Texas Instruments, GE's practice of "hiving off" new divisions, and IBM's encouragement of "mavericks and gadflies" represent successful attempts to reintroduce these small types into big corporations.

In particular, IBM program managers were able to rebound in the PC market, which they had allowed Apple to dominate, by creative end runs around IBM's accountability process. As we mentioned earlier, they short-circuited IBM's thorough but slow testing process by using off-the-shelf components from outside vendors. By contrast, five years earlier, Xerox's executives could not bring their brilliant creation of a PC to market in large part because they were unable to work around the corporation's excessive oversight mechanisms and culture.

The Dilemmas of Innovation and Accountability in the Public Sector

Innovation is often the product of creative subversion of bureaucratic constraints. But in some instances, such action can go too far, and inadequate oversight poses risks for abuse. In others, these bureaucratic entrepreneurs' bias toward action causes them to operate as if theirs were a world without opportunity costs.

The approaches of these bureaucratic entrepreneurs are characterized by tension between management and vision, between effective implementation and considered policy analysis, between getting things done and choosing the right things to do. These are the dilemmas posed by over- and underregulation: overregulation creates a drag on action and the free exercise of executive talent; underregulation leads to waste, fraud, or the subversion of legitimate organizational goals. Before we show how these dilemmas are manifested in the cases analyzed in Chapters Three through Six, we illustrate them in the broader context of the savings and loan debacle. Then we analyze them in the innovative actions of Gordon Chase in New York, John Lehman at the Pentagon, and Herb Onida at the New York–New Jersey Port Authority.

The Dilemmas of Over- and Underregulation: The Savings and Loan Debacle

American savings and loan associations (also known as *thrifts*) were authorized by Depression-era legislation in response to widespread bank failures. They were set up to encourage home ownership. The industry was always tightly structured and highly regulated, restricted to making fixed-rate home loans and limited in the interest they could pay on savings deposits. Stable economic conditions until the 1970s fostered a conservative but solid industry. However, in the 1970s, inflation quickly eroded the value of their portfolios and of long-term fixed-rate loans. At the same time, customers took advantage of higher rates of return by moving their deposits to money market funds, treasury bills, and other unregulated commercial accounts. The convergence of the two events created an industry-wide crisis.

In response, federal regulations over thrifts were relaxed to improve their competitive positions vis-à-vis commercial banks. First the deposit side of their structure was deregulated, and several years later the asset side.

As interest ceilings were eliminated and restrictions on allowable loans loosened, a more market-oriented climate was encouraged. But federal deposit insurance provided to S&Ls insulated most from prudent assessment of risk. Most significantly, just when increased regulatory oversight was needed more than ever, oversight staffs were cut.

Some of the justifications for these cuts were budgetary. The Reagan administration was seeking reductions in all domestic areas. But the dominant motivation was its deregulatory thrust: to the Reagan administration, deregulation meant moving the government away from meddling in the private market, and this included, in their view, less oversight. They did not distinguish between less intervention in setting interest rates or dictating allowable loan categories and general oversight of fraud and accounting practices. The first could be justified as legitimate deregulatory targets; the second could not because they were necessary to ensure system integrity. Without oversight to prevent fraud, deregulation would be discredited and regulation would be brought back. Indeed, both ultimately occurred because of the lack of oversight. (This is analogous to airline deregulation: the fare structure and the granting of new routes were proper deregulatory targets. But regulation and oversight of airplane safety had to be maintained because the markets could not be relied on to provide sufficient safety on their own.)

The deregulation of savings and loans resulted in new institutions being chartered at soaring rates and entering a newly invigorated market. But as they experimented with new financial instruments and amassed riskier loan portfolios, regulatory oversight diminished, leaving the industry vulnerable to fraud and mismanagement, which, in fact, began to occur.

The dilemmas between allowing creative executive initiative to encourage innovation and ensuring accountability and adherence to a number of sacred democratic values are not easily resolved. Balancing these objectives is the challenge of public management.

Gordon Chase Ignores the Obstacles:
A World Without Opportunity Costs

Some of our bureaucratic entrepreneurs, as part of their hiding-hand strategy, often operate as if theirs were a world without opportunity costs. When Gordon Chase became health services commissioner of New York City under Mayor John Lindsay, he developed a policy agenda that was diverse, ambitious, and innovative. But he did not develop a comprehensive plan. Instead, he opportunistically selected critical public health problems to tackle. And his approach was programmatic. The opportunity cost of the programs that he pursued so vigorously and with such ample funds was the forgoing of alternative approaches and programs. Yet whenever his staff sought to raise questions about the large expenditures for new programs or about the competitive merits of alternative programs, Chase would disarm them by responding, "It's only money. And if you want money for some other projects, don't worry: I'll go to the mayor and get it. You know my record of getting money is damn good."[18]

In the face of institutional constraints, Chase had a compensating bias toward action, an emphasis on quick results, and a tendency to work around formal rules and channels. This produced innovative results—programs that dealt with many serious public health problems. But this bias toward action also generated tension between getting things done and choosing the right things to do, between effective implementation and considered policy analysis.

Chase's development of the prison mental health program vividly illustrates this tension. Most of his staff felt that the effort to establish an expensive therapy-oriented mental health program in the city's prisons was ill-advised because it couldn't survive the prison environment. The general feeling was that at worst the funds were being wasted and at best the program had only a marginal chance of success. The comments of one staff person are typical:

> I had a different view than Gordon on spending money. For example, on the prison mental health effort, I felt, first, that it was a large amount of money and, second, that this money could be used better elsewhere. But his style was to focus a lot on the program that he was creating and that he was interested in and to tend to ignore the others. So these others tended to be starved for money.[19]

Another stop staff person expressed similar views on prison mental health: "It was not always great that Gordon didn't see the other side—the other ways of doing what he wanted to get done. . . . He just didn't analyze the prison mental health situation carefully."[20]

In the Health Services Administration under Chase, these tensions were always resolved in the direction of efforts at implementation. Alternatives often were not fully considered. There was little effort to aggregate the direct costs of programs or the total thrust of the agency's policies.

Innovation Can Be Dangerous Without Oversight: Abuse and Scandal at the Pentagon
The history of Pentagon procurement similarly demonstrates the dilemmas of over- and underregulation and the

need to balance innovation with accountability. Underregulation in the 1940s and 1950s had led to abuses at the Pentagon that had in turn led to overregulation. The result was a slow, inefficient procurement process in the 1960s and 1970s. As noted earlier, in the 1980s, Secretary of the Navy John Lehman faced obstacles to developing innovative policies. He responded with aggressive, informal methods of working around formal constraints.

This led to more competitive and cheaper procurement. To achieve these innovations, as described earlier, aggressive Pentagon executives and consultants gathered enough power to surmount implementation obstacles. But this was also enough power to lead to abuses. Their goal was to avoid formal constraints. But then another result was that they were relatively free to abuse their power. The very factors that contributed to the innovative outcomes were also those most susceptible to abuses: working around clearance points and formal rules. Also, the steps that Lehman took may have raised the stakes to the point that contractors felt pressed to take all possible measures, including potentially fraudulent ones, to win work. A scandal involving corruption among these consultants resulted, and it was a significant political wound to Lehman, Defense Secretary Caspar Weinberger, and the Reagan administration. Several years later, Secretary Lehman testified before Representative Les Aspin, who jokingly welcomed him by saying, "We are ready to take your confession." But in his testimony, Lehman scoffed at this dilemma: "I don't see any possibility of any correlation between good, strong management and wrongdoing."[21]

As we spell out in the next chapter, the solution does not lie in the development of additional procedural requirements and regulations. Instead, too many laws and regulations were a large part of the problem. The solution lies in striking a balance between innovation and accountability.

Innovation at the Port Authority:
Dangerous Without a "Reverse Gear"

In starting the XPORT agency at the New York–New Jersey Port Authority, Herb Ouida had a strong bias toward action that risked being out of control. In fact, his boss, the executive director, worried whether, once Ouida's agency got going, he could stop it to evaluate if it was going in the right direction. In Chapters Four and Five, we described how the legislature's failure to authorize XPORT's initial mission did not stop Director Ouida from shifting gears and adapting his enterprise to a different role. This was not quite creative subversion, but it was clearly an end run around the legislature's explicit intention not to allow XPORT to develop.

Indeed, Ouida's bias toward action was so strong that before XPORT's ultimate success became apparent, Port Authority Executive Director Peter Goldmark used it as an example of the Port Authority's lack of a "reverse gear":

> One of the potential problems at the Port Authority is that it doesn't have a very good reverse gear. So the person at the top has to make clear he or she is willing to say, this isn't working,

close it down. Because it's a large institution and once you get chugging around the bases, it's likely to continue right out into center field and into the bleachers if you don't stop it.[22]

Goldmark's concern is not an indictment of working around the rules. Rather, it is a caution that there is risk involved in this bias toward action: even the chief executives of these entrepreneurs may not be able to control them. Thus this bias carries risks.

The Dilemmas of Innovation and Accountability in the Private Sector

These same dilemmas faced the executives in the private sector cases that we have analyzed. Chase, Lehman, and Ouida risked being out of control as they aggressively circumvented institutional constraints. By contrast, the other side of the dilemma dominated at Xerox. There, innovation was smothered in the name of oversight, and Xerox's PC never made it to market. The necessary control mechanisms that McCoulough introduced at Xerox unfortunately developed into a culture of control. And that culture became so predominant at Xerox that executives were not supportive of risk or even innovation.

In contrast to Xerox's innovation-discouraging culture of control, in developing its PC, IBM had a culture of action constrained by oversight that allowed it to balance innovation and accountability. IBM brought its PC to market within its self-imposed twelve-month deadline.

Creative subversion and bias toward action carry risks. The dilemma is that we need the innovation that they produce. But the other side of the dilemma is that too much oversight smothers innovation. In the next chapter, we present ways of balancing these tensions and dilemmas by suggesting the necessity of two management roles.

Notes

1. For example, in explaining the policy failures of President Lyndon Johnson's Great Society, James Q. Wilson made the following influential argument:

> "Talent Is Scarcer than Money" should be the motto of the Budget Bureau. . . . The supply of able, experienced executives is not increasing nearly as fast as the number of problems being addressed by public policy. . . . This constraint deserves emphasis, for it is rarely recognized as a constraint at all. Anyone who opposed a bold new program on the grounds that there was nobody around able to run it would be accused of being a pettifogger at best and a reactionary do-nothing at worst. . . . Everywhere except in government, it seems, the scarcity of talent is accepted as a fact of life. The government—at least publicly—seems to act as if the supply of able political executives were infinitely elastic, though people setting up new agencies will often admit privately that they are so frustrated and ap-

palled by the shortage of talent that the only wonder is why disaster is so long coming.

(James Q. Wilson, "The Bureaucracy Problem," *Public Interest,* 6, Winter 1967, pp. 3–9).
2. Paul Light, "Surviving Innovation: Thoughts on the Organizational Roots of Innovation and Change," paper presented at the Innovations and Organization Conference, University of Minnesota, Minneapolis, September 18–21, 1992. See also Lawrence E. Lynn, Jr., "Innovation and the Public Interest: Insights from the Private Sector," paper presented at the Innovations and Organization Conference, University of Minnesota, Minneapolis, September 18–21, 1992; and Steven Kelman, *Procurement and Public Management: The Fear of Discretion and the Quality of Government Performance* (Lanham, Md.: AEI Press, 1990).
3. Gordon Chase and Elizabeth Reveal, *How to Manage in the Public Sector* (Reading, Mass.: Addison-Wesley, 1983), p. 85.
4. "Former Navy Chief Defends Policies," *New York Times,* September 17, 1992, p. 16.
5. Though not focusing on Lehman, Steven Kelman's book on the process, *Procurement and Public Management,* is an excellent analysis of the limits of regulation and oversight on executive initiative and performance and includes helpful prescriptions for reform.
6. Gifford Pinchot, *Intrapreneuring* (New York: HarperCollins, 1985), p. xi.

7. Thomas Peters and Robert Waterman, *In Search of Excellence* (New York: HarperCollins, 1982).
8. Pinchot, *Intrapreneuring*.
9. Peters and Waterman, *In Search of Excellence*, p. 139.
10. Pinchot, *Intrapreneuring*, p. 154.
11. Ibid.
12. Peters and Waterman, *In Search of Excellence*, p. 205.
13. Pinchot, *Intrapreneuring*, p. 151.
14. Ibid., p. 155.
15. Ibid., p. 123.
16. Ibid., p. 190.
17. Peters and Waterman, *In Search of Excellence*.
18. Interview, with staff person in the New York City Bureau of the Budget, 1985.
19. Martin A. Levin, Bonnie Hausman, and Sylvia B. Perlman, "Gordon Chase: The Best and the Brightest Doing Good Deeds in New York City," paper presented at the Association for Public Policy Analysis and Management Research Conference, Chicago, 1985.
20. Ibid.
21. "Former Navy Chief Defends Policies," p. 16.
22. Peter Goldmark, quoted in Kristen Lundberg, *XPORT: A Public Sector Trading Company* (Cambridge, Mass.: Harvard University, John F. Kennedy School of Government, 1990).

8

The Chief Executive Role

The pervasive dilemmas of innovation and accountability suggest that an anatomy of management requires two different roles. Both a chief executive and a program executive are needed to provide balance and resolution. Because we seek both innovation and accountability, two different roles are needed. When only one is present, significant performance problems emerge.

An Anatomy of Management: Chief Executives and Program Executives

The role of program executive is appropriate at the program level; that of chief executive, at the level of administration policy making. Both are "ideal types."[1] Program executives or advocates tend to have certain common characteristics: their official position is often bureau chief or the equivalent, analogous to that of field commander, rather than commander in chief, in the military. They advocate and run programs; they charge ahead. They generally do not try to consider a full range of alternative approaches for achieving a policy goal. But contemplation of all the options by such managers probably would not result in better decisions. Indeed, they are not well positioned to evaluate the relative contribution of their program to a broader, more strategic set of policy goals. If they tried to consider all the alternatives, breakdowns and inaction at the program level would probably result.

Instead, the choice of the program that they pursue is dictated by incrementalism, expediency, a superior's urging, or some combination of the three. Their major criteria in making a choice include what is good for their program or operating unit or for their own immediate future. They give less consideration to what is good for the administration or city as a whole or for citizens more broadly.

Program executives are enthusiastic not only about the program that they advocate but also about the possibilities of successful implementation. In contrast to chief executives, who tend to evaluate new steps in cold and questioning terms, program executives approach them in warm and accepting terms. They are aware of other programs in the larger administration and in their own department, but they have little concern for this larger program hierarchy.

Chief executives, by contrast, take a very different management approach. Their official position is usually at the top of a large cabinet-level department (secretary), the entire administration (mayor, governor, president), or an oversight or analytical unit (budget chief). Their position is analogous to commander in chief in the military. They do not run or even advocate single programs. They have ultimate responsibility for a large number of programs or for an entire administration. Their responsibilities encompass broad areas, be they functional (such as transportation) or substantive (health). Rather than moving straight ahead on one program, they look at ongoing programs in comparison to others. They tend to make decisions in terms of alternatives and opportunity costs. They ask which of the existing programs in the department or the administration should receive a budget increase? Which should be first in line for new talent? They cannot afford to advocate one program.

Chief executives must view each existing program and each new step in cold and calculating terms. They first ask whether the program will work at all: What are the downside risks involved for the administration? Only secondarily are they interested in how a particular program can be made to work better. This is because chief executives always consider a program as embedded in a larger bureaucratic context—the department or the administration as a whole. Every decision related to a program has to be considered in terms of its relationship to other programs, their budgets, and their needs. Were program executives to have this focus, they would be distracted from developing their own programs.

Again in military terms, chief executives do not ask whether the battle can be won but what it will cost in lives and matériel because there are other battles to fight. Other campaigns must also succeed if the overall fight is to be successful. Because chief executives are responsible for setting broad policy goals for the organization as a whole, they are more likely to consider a full range of alternative approaches and programs. Rather than simply make an incremental change from what was done in the past, they tend to search for other alternatives. In that context, a single program or its advocate may suffer or even be sacrificed for the department's or administration's overall success. The costs of a single program are considered in the context of their impact on the department or administration budget. It is budget making from the top down rather than the bottom up.

Both Roles Are Necessary in a Balanced System

Both of these management roles are necessary; they must be present in the same system. Innovation will proceed blindly without the guidance of oversight and analysis. Oversight and analysis without action will not produce innovation and will usually lead to paralysis. Indeed, in almost all of our cases, program executives provided the initiative, the fuel for generating innovation. Though chief executives were necessary to provide oversight, control, and accountability, they seldom initiated innovation. All the program executives developed their innovations with little guidance from their chief executives. Many had to develop new missions for their agencies wholly on their own. Few of these chief executives even provided much early support for these program executives.

Achieving the Balance

Here we will go beyond analysis of the tensions and dilemmas posed by the two competing management roles of chief executive and program executive to suggest approaches for developing a balanced system to cope with them. Program executives are vital to create a program and get it implemented. But they cannot be too self-questioning about their program, lest that lead to inaction.

For example, as we noted earlier, in New York's Health Services Administration under Gordon Chase, the tensions were always resolved in the direction of efforts at implementation rather than policy analysis: alternatives were not fully or exhaustively considered. There was little effort to aggregate the direct costs of programs or even the total thrust of the agency's policies. However, it would have been neither necessary nor wise for a program advocate like Chase to perform considered policy analysis. That was not his role. If he had, he probably would have been much less successful at implementing his many innovative programs. No individual can be effective at both management roles of innovation and analysis.

Hence chief executives are also necessary. They use analysis and ask whether a given program should be implemented at all. Later, they ask whether it should be renewed or expanded and, if so, what proportion of the administration's scarce total resources should be allocated to it. They must compare each program with the others in terms of the administration's larger goals and its total budgetary capacity.

In most instances, however, chief executives without program executives would be unable to get programs up and running. Analytical considerations often suppress creative program solutions. They would consider so many alternatives, and so many sources of opposition and potential problems, that their ability to get any program started would be limited. Indeed, in virtually all the cases we have analyzed, it was necessary to turn to the program executives to generate innovation. In fact, few even had close relationships with their chief executives.[2] Nevertheless, both management roles must be present in any administration.

Many of the innovators in our sample had unique leadership qualities. These qualities had a significant impact on what they were able to accomplish. But this is more than a book about leadership; the development of an environment that makes innovation possible is even more important than leadership. It is more important because environments supported by positive cultures have the capacity to endure through successive administrations. An organizational environment that encourages innovation can improve public performance by allowing talented executives to exercise their creative abilities. Identifying and attempting to reproduce supportive environments is a more generalizable approach than seeking to develop individual leadership abilities. Thus these insights are more transferable.

More important than leadership, therefore, is changing the current set of incentives in most public sector organizations, which too often discourage executives' innovative behavior in the name of necessary oversight. Most of this oversight is essential to protect important democratic values even though it imposes serious costs. These structures are a product of our political culture, and they ensure oversight, accountability, and predictability.[3] This points to the inherent dilemmas in these two roles: between getting things done and maintaining democratic values. Given these tensions, a balanced *system* is needed, one that nurtures innovation while providing the guidance of oversight and accountability.

But our clear conclusion is that often the balance between accountability and innovation is located at the wrong end of the continuum. Nevertheless, we are also aware of the need for control to meet legitimate public interests. Consequently, managerial imperatives for bureaucratic entrepreneurs to shift the balance within their organizations from control to action are likely to involve working at the margins to change the rules and the culture. The differing development strategies for the personal computer at IBM and Xerox provided some dramatic examples of concrete vehicles for balancing freedom and discretion with oversight and accountability. At the end of this chapter, we will suggest some ways in which successful innovators institutionalize this balance.

Most important at the margin are actions that increase tolerance for error and risk taking, reduce layers and hierarchy to share power and information, increase budgetary flexibility, and reward behavior that supports initiative. These are critical steps in encouraging a culture of action. A balanced system needs both program executives and chief executives. But balancing innovation and accountability depends most on the role exercised by the executive at the top. Our cases indicate that if this chief executive role of balance and restraint is not performed, even otherwise successful executives' administrations end up wounded in both policy and politics. Indeed, this chief executive role is analogous to top-down budgeting or a prospective payment system in health care. For a budget or for an administration's overall policy, guidance and oversight must come from the top. Bottom-up decision making almost always proves inadequate.

Applying an Anatomy of Management

In the cases that follow, we will assess how well the competing roles of program executive and chief executive operate to ensure a satisfactory trade-off between discretion for programmatic innovation and accountability for organizational integrity. In particular, our analysis of these cases will provide some answers to the question that we are often asked: The role of chief executive sounds good in theory, but does anyone actually play that role? These cases will show the critical importance of the dual functions of chief executive and program executive in explaining organizational success. Indeed, in large part, the successes and failures of administrations can be explained by the degree to which they perform both roles and balance the functions of accountability and innovation.

Chief Executive as Guardian
Against the Downside Risk of Innovation

Chief executives consider policy and programming in the larger strategic framework where emphasis is on setting broad policy goals and where success is measured by the performance of the entire administration or organization. They act like the hedgehog in the Greek fable of the hedgehog and the fox: "The fox knows many things; the hedgehog knows one big thing. . . . There exists a great chasm between those, on the one hand, who relate everything to a single central vision, . . . a single universal organizing principle, . . . and, on the other side, those who pursue many ends, often unconnected and even contradictory." We will see that successful chief executives focus on one big thing—the ends of the administration as a whole. By contrast, administrations in which the people at the top do not play this role lose sight of broader policy goals. No one is providing the control, discipline, and analysis that are critical to the success of the administration. Innovation is cultivated primarily at the lower levels of an administration by program executives. Jean Eakins, Barbara Levin, and Steven Swanger, for example, all developed innovative programs outside the executive office. But it was also necessary for their innovation to be moderated by chief executives using different assessment criteria. Barbara Levin's proposal to the state for a community birthing center was a creative means to meet the needs of a particular community. Had it threatened the state's budget constraint or compromised more important policy objectives at the state or county level, the health commissioner, playing a chief executive's role, ought to have intervened further.

This kind of executive scrutiny will improve the innovation's impact on the administration's overall reputation and power. In some instances, it will save an administration from the downside risk of undertaking a predictable failure, no matter how innovative it might appear at the outset: what once seemed to be a clever innovative proposal may come back to haunt the administration in the future because it involves methods that are unethical or cut too many corners. Had Secretary Weinberger exercised a more aggressive oversight and review, perhaps Secretary Lehman's procurement innovations at the Pentagon would not have resulted in public scandal and discredit for the management of military operations more generally.

The bulk of our cases represent acknowledged successes where executive approval, however begrudging, was handsomely rewarded. Nevertheless, the risk of unlimited discretion at the program level is dramatically illustrated by numerous examples. Chief executives and their staffs, who should operate as an extension of those executives, must play three related guardian roles: guarding against predictable failures of innovative action, against the risk to the integrity of the administration generated by cutting corners or using unethical methods, and against the risk of jeopardizing the administration's overall budget limits by failing to control aggressive program executives. Compromising a chief executive's budget limits here refers not only to threatening its size but also to upsetting the balance between competing policy objectives that the budget itself is the formal device for achieving. In short, chief executives must focus on overseeing and not just creating.

A major reason that the chief executive role is insufficiently performed is that there are strong pressures to focus on specific program successes. There is pressure to get things done, to be creative, with little tolerance for failure—whether it is curbing a heroin epidemic or reducing Pentagon procurement costs. These pressures tend to reduce an executive's commitment to the oversight function in favor of these competing objectives. Oversight functions tend to be swept away in favor of emphasizing creative solutions to policy problems.

Reining In Executive Staff

The too frequent tendency of a chief executive's staff to become entangled in operational efforts and program advocacy is another reason that this role is insufficiently performed. Executives who successfully perform the chief executive role seem to do so because they push their staff toward it while resisting the staff's pull toward program advocacy.

Today the staffs of chief executives often tend to be program- and policy-oriented rather than focusing on oversight and control. Thus they often do not assess the broader strategic choices for the administration as a whole. The staff's stature, success, and rewards too often come from attending to particular program goals. The media, for example, put pressure on government to "solve" problems "once and for all." Immediately following his election, the media set a standard for President Clinton to develop solutions to multiple crippling social and economic problems in his first hundred days! And the media focus more on staff because they tend to be more visible than many agency heads. For example, the White House chiefs of staff from 1976 to 1992—Hamilton Jordan, James Baker, Donald Regan, and John Sununu—and the power struggles revolving around them were familiar to every newspaper reader. But during the same period, few cabinet secretaries, beyond the secretaries of State and Defense, had any visibility. This reflects a more fragmentary view of the administration's overall mission.

Because staff people do not have reputations or power bases independent of their staff role, they also have less to lose when initiatives fail. This produces a bias toward risk taking. Thus the staff may be insufficiently interested in ensuring that the administration is seen as upright. The Eisenhower and Ford administrations were not praised much for maintaining this reputation. But when administrations such as Nixon's or Reagan's were greatly weakened by their improprieties, we came to appreciate the political and policy benefits of avoiding these problems.

The chance that unchecked program executives can be imprudent, narrow, or wrong is real. It tends to be inherent in their role. To get things done, be innovative and creative, move quickly, and cut costs, program executives often seek to avoid formal constraints. To achieve these innovations, program executives must gather a great deal of power to surmount implementation obstacles, but often this is enough to lead to abuses. The very factors that contributed to effective implementation are those most susceptible to abuses: short-circuiting the political system's numerous clearance points and formal rules. This was a problem in Lehman's bringing innovation to the Pentagon procurement process.

Further, if program executives have the power to bring together all the necessary elements for implementation, they will probably have the power to get the program extra funds. This, as we will see, was a problem in the Lindsay administration. Many agency heads in his administration were bold and innovative entrepreneurs, but their creative programs were often very expensive. Chief executives must protect their budget, broad policy goals, and the appearance and reality of propriety. This requires control and oversight. But there was little control and oversight of these innovators in the Lindsay administration. That was one of the contributing factors to New York's near bankruptcy, which in turn led to the end of Lindsay's political career.[4]

Staff should help the chief executive play this guardian role, but the incentives run in the wrong direction. Few staff make personal reputations as naysayers who protected their chief executive from undue risk. Few even make reputations for keeping the budget from getting out of control. Frank Keefe, the tightfisted, naysaying budget chief under Governor Michael Dukakis in Massachusetts, for example, did not achieve the public recognition of Dukakis's program executives Ira Jackson, Thomas Glynn, and Charles Atkins. But his actions to balance the budget served the administration well. He helped Dukakis recover from the politically dangerous budget imbalances of his first stint as governor—a mistake that necessitated a large tax increase, which in turn led to his reelection defeat. With Keefe as budget chief in a later second term, no new taxes were required, and Dukakis was voted in for a third term.

The tendency to ignore, avoid, and fail to appreciate naysaying staff and guardian overhead agencies is so great that there is now a compensating pattern: efforts to re-create the guardian and overhead agents and agencies to fill the void left as these older ones are brushed aside. This is manifested in the growing popularity of independent prosecutors and special ethics panels at many levels. The media have also increasingly assumed this evaluative, naysaying role, especially in its scrutiny of political candidates.

Chief executives must guard against the downside risk of the bold and innovative actions of program executives to protect the integrity of the enterprise as a whole. Program executives will not and cannot perform this role. Their incentive is to avoid the formal constraints and numerous clearance points that impede implementation of their policy or program initiatives.

Chief executives can benefit greatly from program innovation cultivated from below. However, the drive of program executives to get things done—to be visibly successful—creates incentives to behave in ways that can threaten the fiscal, ethical, or legal integrity of the organization as a whole. Chief executives should subject program ideas to a higher test than a program executive would. Chief executives should not act like the fox—knowing many things, pursuing many ends, often unconnected and even contradictory. Instead, they must, like the hedgehog, maintain their focus on that one big thing, the administration's overall performance. The foxlike behavior of President Carter, knowing all the details, seems to have contributed to his administration's political and policy failure.

Interviews with Carter and his aides indicate that his approach to the presidency was groping, ad hoc, and characterized by serial decision making.[5] He treated each decision as separate, with limited reference to any overriding strategic conceptions of policy direction. Carter did not perform the role of chief executive. He knew many details and tried many policies, but he had no strategic framework and failed to control his subordinates, as seen in the 1979 cabinet firing debacle. (After three years of failing to rein in several of his cabinet secretaries so that they would work smoothly with him, Carter abruptly and publicly fired several of them simultaneously.) Consequently, his administration had few policy or political successes, and he was denied a second term.

Ellen Schall, at New York's Department of Juvenile Justice, first focused on one big thing, bringing control and order to the chaotic agency. This enabled her to gain the mayor's support for her innovation of bringing social services into the agency's detention environment—the critical first step in revitalizing her agency.

Chief executives must question a program executive's proposed innovation: What if we get caught, both figuratively and literally? What if we spend too much money or run up a budget deficit? What if a tax increase is required? What if our methods are considered excessive or unethical or even illegal? What if our goals cannot generate broad support?

These questions need not always lead to a negative response, nor does asking them necessarily lead to excessive caution. Bold innovative actions should often be pursued even when there is some risk of failure. Potential or real costs and risks are not a reason to stop moving forward. In any event, the checks of analysis, oversight, and accountability do not ensure against all failure. They simply inform about the size and nature of the risk. Moreover, there are also great costs (some people would argue greater costs) in failing to innovate and act in the face of challenges. This is the other side of the dilemma of innovation and accountability and is characterized most dramatically by the behavior of the Carter administration. By contrast, Gordon Chase moved boldly and took risks in crises but faced no significant scrutiny from his political executive, Mayor Lindsay. Schall helped the Koch administration in New York City and Jackson the Dukakis administration in Massachusetts by bold risk taking that led to important innovations. But they did so as program executives under the watchful eye of an active chief executive.

Governor Dukakis and Mayor Lindsay: Different Chief Executive Performances, Different Political Fates

The Dukakis and Lindsay administrations, with their differing political fates, offer striking contrasts. They are explained in part by the way in which the roles of program and chief executives were played: Governor Dukakis's ability to perform the chief executive's oversight function in his second administration and Mayor Lindsay's failure to do so.[6]

In 1978, after four years as governor of Massachusetts, Michael Dukakis was defeated for reelection. Dukakis's first administration (Dukakis I) failed in part because of an improper balance between accountability and innovation; as a result, he used the next four years out of office to assess his performance and his future. After altering his executive style and his approach to managing, Dukakis was reelected to two more terms as governor and achieved an underdog victory for the Democratic presidential nomination.

In the second Dukakis administration (Dukakis II), he succeeded in implementing innovations, like the ET Choices welfare reform and tax enforcement reforms. These then became the centerpieces of his successful presidential nomination bid. Dukakis II succeeded because the man became a political manager: he focused scarce time and political capital on a modest number of problems, learned to compromise, and used marketing to get results and then to let citizens know what had been accomplished.

But Dukakis had become more than just a good politician. He sought to ensure results by careful executive oversight and control of his top managers, potential budget deficits, and budget expenditures. In all of this he performed the chief executive role. This contrasted with the unsuccessful Dukakis I, in which many talented program executives (including his banking and insurance commissioners) went off on their own without executive control and hurt rather than helped the administration. In Dukakis I, a threatened deficit produced both tax cuts and service cuts.

In Dukakis II, the governor first put in a tough nonprogrammatic administrator, Frank Keefe, as head of the state's Office of Management and the Budget. When Keefe had problems, he was not replaced with one of the successful program executives, as some advisers urged; Dukakis wanted a tightfisted controller there, not a program executive. To achieve gubernatorial control and initiatives reflecting his preferences—to balance innovation and accountability—he created a new governor's office with separate oversight staffs for human services, economic development, and education. One of his most successful department heads explained this executive control: "Entrepreneurs like me and the other aggressive program advocates around here might be dangerous without someone like Michael to rein us in."

Dukakis's ability to perform the chief executive's oversight function explains some of the striking contrasts between the Dukakis and Lindsay administrations and their political fates. Lindsay pursued less pragmatic policies that were rarely implemented effectively. But he was also unable to control his subordinates, especially many of his bold and innovative entrepreneurs, whose programs were often very expensive. Unlike Dukakis, he did not have a tightfisted executive run his budget bureau. These failings contributed to New York's huge budget deficit.

Should one of Lindsay's entrepreneurial program executives, like Gordon Chase, have performed these oversight functions of the chief executive? We suggest that it would not have been wise for Chase to pursue the role of chief executive. If he had, he would probably have been much less successful at implementing his many innovative programs. Almost no individual can be effective at both management roles. Instead, the mayor's office and the budget bureau should have been performing the chief executive's functions.

But in the Lindsay administration, the budget bureau, historically biased toward cutting, became an activist institution advocating expenditures in specific policy areas. In an interview, the director of the bureau characterized it as "activist": "We were always looking for innovative programs." Another of Lindsay's top aides concurred: "If the mayor and his staff liked a program, they moved forward on it."[7] The bureau abandoned its role as a watchdog accountable to the taxpayers, who want to stretch their dollars across the range of all city services. When the mayor and his staff evaluated new program proposals, they failed to consider the opportunity costs. Moreover, they neglected to aggregate the costs and effects of individual programs for the administration as a whole. They focused instead on the merits of individual programs.[8]

The cost of some of these very expensive programs was one of the contributing factors to the city's near bankruptcy and the demise of Lindsay's political career. Lindsay sought the Democratic presidential nomination but, unlike Dukakis, did not win.

The Pentagon Procurement Scandal: Failures of the Executive

The case of Secretary of the Navy John Lehman and the late 1980s Pentagon procurement scandal aptly illustrates the utility of our anatomy of management roles. Secretary Lehman faced an enormous obstacle to developing innovative policies: a rule-bound oversight and regulatory process. As a program executive of innovation in the procurement process, Lehman responded with creative subversion of oversight mechanisms so as to achieve better results. But no one in the Pentagon (neither the top executive, Secretary Caspar Weinberger, nor Lehman himself) nor anyone at the presidential level performed the necessary reining-in role of a chief executive. Thus there was insufficient accountability and oversight to balance the innovation. Consequently, these innovative policies ultimately resulted in the abuse of power by Pentagon consultants and the scandal described earlier that embarrassed both the Pentagon and the Reagan administration, and were a net liability for both.

The Need for a Balanced System

The inherent tensions between the functions of chief executive and program executives are clear, but we have seen that both are necessary. A balanced system is needed, one that nurtures innovation while subject to the guidance of oversight and accountability. But what does this mean in practice? We will suggest how to institutionalize this with illustrations from the private and public sectors.

This balance is achieved in settings where a culture of action flourishes, constrained by oversight. Innovations at the Massachusetts Departments of Revenue and Public Welfare were the successful result of an administration that achieved such a balance. The proper balance was absent in the Pentagon, where the procurement scandal was the result, and similar imbalances plagued the Lindsay administration. Thus despite the Lindsay administration's innovative project management approach and Navy Secretary

Lehman's procurement innovations at the Pentagon, in both cases balance was not achieved because the chief executive did not constrain the bias toward action with the interest of the administration as a whole. In the first, near financial bankruptcy resulted; in the second, the result was corruption and abuse of power.

Structural safeguards do not substitute for executive judgment and vigilance. Indeed, far from advocating increased formalism, our analyses concluded that there are heavy costs and needless waste of performance that accompany excessive dependency on rules, regulations, and structural safeguards. Steven Kelman's careful study of procurement at the Pentagon also revealed the limits of rules to ensure integrity and equity.[9] Discretion does not ensure corruption, nor do rules guarantee its absence. Indeed, Kelman argues that seldom do rules themselves protect against fraud and abuse. More sophisticated surveillance and investigative techniques can play a more important role in deterring abuse. Combined with more aggressive prosecution and punishment, he argues, increased room for managerial discretion can confront the straitjacket of regulatory overload on government performance and innovation.

The balance of the book will further explore managerial vehicles to overcome the impediments to action. Though we advocate increasing the scope of managerial discretion and freedom to initiate in public management, our goal here is to provide examples of ways in which highly structured and closely controlled organizations have built in room for risk taking and innovation.

The IBM PC and the Xerox Alto: Top Executives Balancing Innovation and Accountability

Private sector corporations that confront similar tensions have much to teach us. Thus we have observed the successful resolution at IBM and the dramatic and costly failure at Xerox, where a culture of control dominated. The success in the IBM PC case depended on the chief executive's maintaining the balance between action and oversight. The Xerox PC case illustrates how the chief executive's disproportionate emphasis on one element—control in this case—meant a failure to achieve either balance or innovation. This was true despite Xerox's PARC success at creating smallness within largeness.

The key contribution of IBM chief executives to this was in establishing and maintaining an environment that encouraged, nurtured, and then protected creativity. Further, this was achieved with no threat to organizational accountability and oversight. The concept of creating a PC at IBM and the radical strategy to carry it out bubbled up from the program level—IBM's Entry Systems Division at Boca Raton, an independent business unit (IBU) within the company. But the IBU owed its very existence to the chief executives at IBM. IBM Board Chairman Frank Cary wanted internal venture units set up inside IBM to introduce not only new products but also new cultures within the larger organization. As he put it, they were designed to "teach an elephant to tap dance."

To achieve both innovation and accountability, an organization needs a culture of action constrained by oversight, but not by a culture of control. However, Xerox, under McCoulough, developed a culture of control, unsupportive of risk or even innovation. In developing a culture of control, McCoulough did not understand the need for creating and supporting organizational structures and styles that also encourage creativity and innovation while maintaining accountability. Instead, the top staff was oriented toward controls and intolerant of error. Failing to see that a culture of control discourages experimentation and risk taking, Xerox did not promote innovation.

The decline of IBM in the late 1980s and early 1990s confirms our emphasis on the importance of maintaining a balance between accountability and innovation. By allowing accountability in the form of centralized testing procedures to dampen innovation, IBM ignored the lessons of its earlier success with its PC.

*Achieving Balance: Encouraging
the Unconventional Within the Conventional*

Balance between innovation and accountability means action constrained by oversight. But the next cases illustrate that it also means pushing toward the unconventional within a context in which not everyone in the organization is going "too far." Then we examine cases of program executives going too far without top executives reining them in—the Lindsay and Reagan administrations.

Investigation of big oil finds in Alaska, the North Sea, and Libya provides further evidence of how to institutionalize this balance. These operations went against the conventional strategy of their companies, and in every case there was a handsome payoff. But this strategy was part of a balanced system in which most explorations followed the conventional path. No oil company could survive if all its exploration activity went against the accepted exploration strategy.

IBM Laboratories' discovery of a new superconductor, for which its researchers won the 1987 Nobel Prize in physics, followed the same pattern as the oil finds. Their approach went against conventional thinking in the field. They were searching where experts least expected to find a new superconductor—in a ceramic that normally conducts electricity poorly. Colleagues called their ideas crazy. Their ideas were so unconventional that they kept the ideas secret from their bosses.

This worked for IBM because it was part of a system with the balance we have suggested. No oil company or manufacturer could survive if all efforts at innovation "went against orders." Unconventional strategies can only continue to be followed if they are part of a system in which *most* exploration efforts follow the conventional strategy. Otherwise the company might go bankrupt.

An Absence of Balance: No One Playing the Chief Executive Role

The Lindsay administration did not have this balance, and it went bankrupt, financially and politically. The problem was not the administration's bias toward action or even its high expenditures. The problem was that these were not complemented by executives and overhead agencies that were performing the function of analysis, oversight, and accountability. No person or agency was playing the role of chief executive.

The importance of a balanced system being brought about by a chief executive is evident in the case of Oliver North and the Iran-Contra scandal during the Reagan administration. Marine Lieutenant Colonel Oliver North was a top aide to President Reagan's National Security advisor. He became the point man in a scheme to extralegally fund the Contras in Nicaragua—government funding had been banned by Congress—by using the proceeds of sales of arms to Iran that the Reagan administration publicly said it opposed. An additional goal of creating better relations with Ayatollah Khomeini's Iran by selling the nation arms was to get them to help free U.S. prisoners in Lebanon. Though many people might support the goals of supporting the Contras and developing better relations with the Khomeini regime in Iran, the illegal and extralegal tactics that North used eventually wounded the Reagan administration and its foreign policy when these methods were exposed.

North was clearly an action-oriented program executive if not the classic macho manager. But in his single-minded pursuit, North and his colleagues did not consider alternative priorities or costs. Moreover, even if North's actions had been effective for bringing back the hostages from Lebanon, they were not carried out in conjunction with a concern for the administration's larger goals such as its fundamental political and policy existence.

No one was performing the chief executive function

of reining in these bold foreign policy entrepreneurs. No one asked about this and other potential downside risks such as how North's actions would play with other branches of government that the administration would need at some other time (as in a vote for Contra funding—the very cause that the administration was trying to further in all of this). No one questioned the potential consequences of disclosure—would this cause more damage for the administration's overall foreign policy concerns and political existence than could be compensated for by the gains of bringing back the hostages? This failure of oversight carried the potential for bringing down the entire administration. In fact, the Iran hostage affair greatly weakened the Reagan administration.

Conclusion: Shifting the Balance

Innovation and accountability must be jointly accommodated if the goals of productive yet equitable and honest government are to be achieved. Accountability is critical to ensure equity and integrity. And almost always the balance must be overseen by executives at the top (or their staff) rather than by program executives. But there is an even greater challenge for public management: to design systems and structures that allow the critical values of public performance—especially excellence—to coexist with those of democratic accountability. As we argue throughout, this is a tall order.

Although this chapter has emphasized the real dangers of unrestrained executive freedom and the benefits of oversight, we do not argue for increased reliance on formalism for resolution of these dilemmas. Recent experience with federal deregulation has dealt a hard blow for the forces of change. Scandals or simply uneven results associated with deregulation have led to the perception of a lack of control. As a result, there has been a backlash of increasing pressure to reinstate regulations to hold public officials accountable. But reassessing institutional demands and loosening organizational rules can be accompanied by increased accountability for performance. Improvements in performance at the Massachusetts Departments of Revenue and Public Welfare were accompanied by strong bureaucratic entrepreneurs who changed the opportunities for middle managers to exercise discretion while at the same time holding them accountable for results. Similar strategies were successful at the Massachusetts Bay Transit Authority, which is analyzed in Chapter Six.

The costs of rule-bound public management are high indeed in innovations and initiatives forgone. Rules also impose high costs through the toll they take on talented individuals discouraged and cynical about improving public performance. Efficiency and quality of public services are not the only values on which government performance should be judged. But they are surely important values, increasingly desired by a weary public.

Nevertheless, the importance of ensuring the integrity of our public institutions is also critical both substantively and symbolically. But our analyses of innovative public managers' success suggests that the formal vehicles used to achieve that goal impose social costs that often are too high.

Increasingly, the lessons we must teach aspiring managers and executives will be how to shift the balance. Our lessons must emphasize the systemic means to loosen the stronghold of these constraints on managerial discretion. And they must also emphasize the creative and entrepreneurial opportunities to assert managerial initiative in over-regulated environments. It is to these issues that we devote the balance of this book.

Notes

1. "Ideal types" abstract a pattern from reality. Few program executives or chief executives reflect all aspects of these models, but they are generally accurate composites.
2. A significant exception was Ed Tetelman of the New Jersey Department of Human Services and his school-based model. Commissioner Drew Altman was an important champion of the concept of integrated school-based services and brought in Tetelman to realize his initial conception. Altman, however, was ultimately accountable to the governor. In some ways, therefore, he played the dual role of both program executive and chief executive.
3. James P. Walsh and Robert D. Dewar, "Formalization and the Organizational Life Cycle," *Journal of Management Studies* 24 (1987): 215–231.
4. Martin A. Levin, Bonnie Hausman, and Sylvia B. Perlman, "Gordon Chase: The Best and the Brightest Doing Good Deeds in New York City," paper presented at the Association for Public Policy Analysis and Man-

agement Research Conference, Chicago, 1985; Charles R. Morris, *The Cost of Good Intentions: New York City and the Liberal Experiment, 1960–1975* (New York: Norton, 1980).
5. Erwin Hargrove, *Jimmy Carter as President* (Baton Rouge: Louisiana State University Press, 1988).
6. The analysis of the Dukakis administration is based on David Osborne's *Laboratories of Democracy* (Cambridge, Mass.: Harvard University Press, 1987), chaps. 5–7; and Martin A. Levin, "Learning How to Manage Dukakis' Ups and Downs," *Los Angeles Times,* August 21, 1988, p. 7. The analysis of the Lindsay administration is based on Morris, *The Cost of Good Intentions;* Diana Gordon, *City Limits* (New York: Charterhouse, 1973); and Natalie Cippolina, "New York City Politics and the Cost of Good Intentions," *Public Interest,* Summer 1981, p. 87.
7. Levin, Hausman, and Perlman, "Gordon Chase."
8. Cippollina, "New York City," p. 87.
9. Kelman, *Procurement and Public Management.*

9

Cultivating Bureaucratic Entrepreneurs
Lessons for Success

The preceding chapters have documented a rich portrait of success and innovation in dozens of public enterprises. By exploring the nature of successes among a large group of bureaucratic entrepreneurs and highlighting their specific and replicable characteristics, we have identified a range of individual behaviors that are commonly related to innovative performance. But we must emphasize that even the most successful innovators operate in an environment that is fundamentally inhospitable to change, novelty, and initiative. Indeed, inertia is the most serious malady plaguing public organizations. As a result, achieving success often involves circumventing or subverting political and institutional obstacles to innovation. The ability to act is the most important single step toward creative initiatives.

Thus producing an environment conducive to action and innovation in public organizations may ultimately be the most important vehicle for improving public performance. Because talented managers are frequently unable to exercise creative initiative in the current environment, considerable progress is likely to accrue from concentrating our efforts on the means to remove, or at least loosen, their bureaucratic shackles.

Managers at all levels in a public organization have some degree of control over the variables linked to innovation. But initiative and change may face professional limits in our political culture. Some observers have argued for the need to alter political and institutional structure in order to create the conditions for innovation. But while awaiting this millennium, our research suggests that even within these constraints, there is a good deal that managers can do to improve their organizations. We focus on what entrepreneurial managers have done within the existing organizational environment.

If senior managers systematically build a culture that promotes and rewards innovation, the potential to unleash creative policy and managerial responses to organizational objectives is greatly improved. The route to change involves two systematic reorientations of traditional thinking. The first relates to the way public managers see their role; the second, to specific and concrete managerial vehicles used to increase organizational performance. Our analyses suggest that adherence to some basic principles can significantly improve the likelihood of successful innovation in public enterprises.[1]

The first part of this chapter will discuss some of these principles in an effort to identify the ways in which managers can create environments for change. The emphasis here will be on organizationally relevant activities that can improve the environment and the likelihood of success. These represent a range of activities that can be initiated by managers at various levels in the organization.

These activities most often relate to building, sustaining, and rewarding innovation. Managers—both those that play the role of chief executive and those that are program executives—must create an atmosphere that encourages creative thinking and risk taking by line workers.[2] These employees must feel free to break out of traditional constraints. Executives must create an atmosphere that is tolerant of mistakes. They must communicate support for new ideas and become familiar with the needs of line workers through management by wandering around. They should encourage the balancing of managerial discretion and accountability in the implementation of programs.

These strategies reflect on the executive's primary role: to set a clear organizational mission and well-defined goals. By promoting and rewarding initiative throughout the organization (incentives and creative awards), managers can develop an innovative culture to unleash creative policies. The benefits of working on the periphery must also be exploited.

The second part of the chapter will review the implications of our findings for the way in which future public managers are trained. How managers view their role and where they look for inspiration and ideas are often shaped by their training, their disciplinary biases, and the institutional norms they internalize. Current public policy programs often emphasize the wrong skills and expose students to limited interdisciplinary perspectives and professional norms. As a result, they often fail to acquaint future managers with the kinds of behaviors that we have found to be most important for successful performance.

Indeed, too much training or experience in a particular policy area may distract executives from the larger picture. Being very knowledgeable of a policy area's approaches may cause a manager to be too closely connected to them. In fact, the advantage of being an outsider to an agency's policy area is indicated by the success that these perspectives seem to have brought to Jackson, Schall, Chase, and Ruckelshaus, as well as Glynn at the transit agency. It seems to have freed them from conventions and encouraged them to be boldly innovative. This is a familiar outcome in other fields. From architecture to film, outsiders have produced innovations because they did not know the bounds of the envelope. For example, the skyscraper was developed in the nineteenth century in Chicago, away from New York (the center of American architecture) with its Parisian Beaux Arts orientation. Many of the leading builders in Chicago had backgrounds as engineers (especially in bridge building) rather than as architects. Similarly, Orson Welles's many film innovations seemed to flow from his experience in a different medium (radio) and thus were not constrained by film's traditional approaches. As Chapters One and Three note, there are many examples of this pattern in science.

We conclude by reemphasizing that creating an environment that encourages innovation is even more important than leadership itself. In the final chapter, we emphasize that though management matters, it is not everything. Indeed, management can be overemphasized. Good management must be concerned with ends as well as means.

Generating a Culture of Innovation

Many characteristics of public organizations impede innovation. In Chapter Two we reviewed the reasons why it is so hard to get things done in government. Some of the constraints, such as civil service rules and political disincentives, are difficult to change in the short term. The lessons from successful executives demonstrate, however, that there are considerable opportunities to innovate despite the inherent obstacles. The next eight sections review how executives can create a better environment for success.

Tolerance for Error

As Chapters Two and Seven established, government operations increasingly attempt to ensure accountability by limiting managerial discretion. Fearful of media and political fallout, public sector managers are obsessively concerned with avoiding the appearance or the reality of failure. These fears are so great that, coupled with the tendency to equate good government with reduced managerial discretion, government policy makers are preoccupied with damage control.[3]

Nevertheless, lessons from our successful entrepreneurs and from a host of analyses of public and private enterprises where innovation flourishes argue that a tolerance for mistakes—as one of the executives in our study argued, a "high tolerance for well-conceived failure"—is a critical ingredient of innovative organizations. Because the material rewards for innovation in the public sector are few,[4] and the professional risks are often great, the absence of institutional support for initiative means that innovation is less frequent than it could be. A vigilant manager who communicates a consistent message of support, in addition to providing well-bounded authority for experimentation, can increase the willingness of other managers under his or her supervision to attempt creative initiatives.

Support for Initiative and Risk Taking

Senior managers interested in changing the incentives within their organization need to change the message about what is valued and will be rewarded while confronting structural characteristics that suppress initiative. This is also true in developing enterprises, where the executive can actually shape the initial value and reward system. The first job for an executive is to communicate down the line that new ideas are welcome. Management by wandering around is an effort to penetrate the organization, to understand the needs of middle managers and line workers, and to be alert to their ideas. Workers close to production and service delivery are often a fertile source of opportunities to improve performance. Indeed, the recognition that successful public and private enterprises are "close to the customer" is an understanding of this reality.

The success at IBM developed, we have seen, from a concerted strategy to identify an innovation, allocate resources for its development, and protect the nascent enterprise while it grew. Communicating to an organization that initiative and innovation are to be encouraged and supported requires having budgetary flexibility to respond to new ideas with significant promise. It also requires that executives take responsibility for promoting ideas, selecting those with particular merit, harnessing resources for their development, and ultimately shielding managers from the consequences of some failure. This attitude is key to changing organizational incentives.

Managerial Discretion for Implementation, Accountability for Performance

Gordon Chase was fond of saying that staff serves the line. Another critical principle for innovative policy and management, then, is giving line workers what they need to realize their objectives. Obviously, this means information and discretion, but it also implies support, resources, and tolerance for mistakes.[5] Successful bureaucratic entrepreneurs tend to develop organizational structures that allow for information sharing and cooperation across formal lines of responsibility. Rigid lines and territories discourage creative interplay among organizational units. Further, creative managers often need to search for resources and support throughout the organization to leverage innovative projects. A senior executive who creates opportunities for interactions and partnerships—through such mechanisms as task forces, working groups, and across-function teams—can greatly expand the opportunities for innovation. Particularly central here is developing a clear set of common performance goals among different organizational functions and holding line workers accountable for achieving these goals.

Considerable evidence supports the view that an executive's development of a well-understood organizational mission supported by clear goals and meaningful rewards maximizes performance. This is especially true if middle managers are held accountable to clearly defined targets but are given significant latitude and discretion in how they go about achieving them. Evidence from the creative management of ET Choices demonstrated that when middle managers in regional offices throughout the state were held to reasonable targets for numbers and quality of job placements but given significant discretion on the precise means to achieve them, performance was greatly improved, and management innovations were developed.[6]

The key to innovative policy and program development, as we have argued in earlier chapters, is a willingness to be guided by a clear mission and defined goals even when the means to achieve them are not well designed in advance. Managers must be given discretion to develop their own implementation plans but held accountable for meeting clearly specified goals.[7] Then executives can depend on analysis of operations to determine what works and what does not and use those lessons to inform continued efforts for improvement.

Emphasis on Analysis and Evaluation

Innovations depend on analysis and evaluation so that the means to achieve them can be well understood and successful approaches can be learned along the way. Managers should build in evaluation and analytical activities at critical junctures as innovative ideas are tested. The role of analysis in developing innovation is one of assessing field operations and refining programmatic design. Thus ET Choices, the Family Learning Center, and School-Based Services for Youth are typical examples of programmatic efforts that developed in stages. Indeed, ET Choices is often referred to as ET-I, ET-II, and so on to call attention to the critical changes made over the course of its first few years. Error correction through reorientation of programmatic approaches and goals should be continually sought through evaluation of feedback from operations in the field.

Informal assessments were continual and considerable as Steven Swanger sought the precise model capable of realizing his objective. Trying a Junior Achievement model of youthful enterprise in a bottle-and-can-collection business, he evaluated its impacts and after a year and a half abandoned it because he was convinced of its incapacity to allow kids to feel empowered. Then he tried other models connected to worksite monitoring, such as a Big Sister/Big Brother model. Finally, he adapted his Work Force employment prevention model. Even then he had regular feedback from the field to the main office to evaluate the impact of incremental changes in program design (such as different staff roles and program components). Refinement of program operations was shaped by field-based learning.

Wayne Fortin used systematic formal evaluation of each volunteer's efforts by emergency personnel and trauma victims to learn what worked and what didn't. This feedback was then used for staff training and program redesign. The ET Choices program used operations data regularly to assess success at meeting registration and employment goals and to provide feedback on management innovations. To evaluate the impact of a marketing campaign to attract welfare mothers to enroll, ET Choices organized focus groups of clients to assess program literature and communications. The effort significantly refocused marketing materials for clients by emphasizing different benefits of the ET Choices program.

Most innovative enterprises do not derive from conventional analysis of all program options or ideas ahead of time. But they are shaped, refined, and reoriented by continual formal and informal analysis and evaluation of program operations as they evolve. Bureaucratic entrepreneurs do not eschew analysis; they simply value it more highly after program development than before.

New Organizational Structures to Enhance Flexibility

Many of our program successes developed outside of large bureaucratic organizations, either as partnerships with public agencies or as freestanding nonprofits. In many respects, the size, flatness (lack of hierarchy), and age of the enterprises contributed significantly to their success. Indeed, the lessons from the less traditional public enterprises in our sample strengthen our conclusions about the needed managerial emphases in larger and more bureaucratic environments.

Starting something new, outside the conventional bounds of your organization, places you on the periphery. As we have seen, new initiatives often need protection from potential sources of opposition during the development stage. When the enterprise is located away from view and thus unable to threaten existing interests, it often has time to become effective before facing organizational scrutiny. Sandra Steiner Lowe identified this need for space and time as critical. Having some invisibility provides this time. Steven Swanger's Work Force was a social services intervention in a housing authority, peripheral to the agency's core business and poorly understood by housing managers. Swanger bought time and experience before going public with his youth employment and development initiative. By the time he did so, he had cultivated significant external constituents and a strong record of success.

Further, because large hierarchical organizations have more rules and constraints imposed at different levels and functions (budget, control, personnel), it is more difficult to amass resources and organizational support for new initiatives. Indeed, more potential opportunities exist for important interests to say no. New organizations have the luxury of establishing both the values and the structures to support their interests. As a result, they do not confront resistance to change. Moreover, they can often hire staff at the outset who support their missions and working styles. Ed Tetelman had his own enterprise within the New Jersey Department of Human Services charged with developing his school-based services initiative. He had a large but clear mission and a relatively small central staff. His personnel choices were tightly focused on attracting the necessary skills but even more specifically on identifying individuals who shared a particular predisposition for his mission and the values that supported them.

Barbara Levin needed a cooperative nonhierarchical structure to support her enterprise, which confronted traditional medical models. It was therefore critical to have professional, paraprofessional, and nonmedical staff working together around a specific set of "customer-centered" values. Flat, less hierarchical organizations are more able to adapt to changing ways of doing things. The needed flexibility derives in large part from the freedom to organize people, resources, and relationships in unconventional ways. These are major obstacles in larger, more hierarchical organizations, and therefore bureaucratic entrepreneurs must find creative ways to increase flexibility, communication, accountability, and rewards. Contracting out for some programmatic services often provides this kind of flexibility for circumventing hierarchical constraints. Gordon Chase used this approach in many of his initiatives.[8]

Creative Use of Rewards

Even though public bureaucracies often operate under rigidly defined systems of personnel management—civil service systems and/or public employee union rules—motivating personnel is a principal goal of effective public management. Material benefits may be an important means to encourage productive effort, but they are not the only or even the best means to do so. Public service is often so poorly regarded and appreciated that managers who invest at the outset in building the self-esteem of employees as they work out their organizational objectives can achieve enormous returns. Those who choose public service over private sector employment are more likely to be driven by values than strictly by income maximization.[9] This provides good managers with numerous opportunities to provide workers with important psychic and professional rewards when material rewards are constrained.

Self-esteem can be enhanced by giving managers and line workers a clear mission that provides a sense of value and imbues their work with a sense of purpose. Being part of an organization with an important social mission that you understand and internalize is highly self-affirming. Rewards can come from being part of an enterprise that is visible, has moral authority, and is doing good work. Many workers come to public service to make a contribution but soon learn how remote they are from their objectives. Managers who systematically look for ways to celebrate their enterprise and especially to celebrate their workers—rewarding them for performance that achieves the concrete goals developed to support the mission—can generate a willingness among the staff to go beyond what is ordinarily expected. Dozens of our entrepreneurs created environments where staff and workers had a clear sense of what their roles were, why they were important, and how they contributed to the mission and values of the enterprise. Glynn at the MBTA, Tetelman at School-Based Youth Services (he said, "All my staff does windows"), Fortin at Trauma Intervention, and Orente at the K-SIX Early

Intervention Partnership all pointed to a conscious and institutionalized approach to provide staff and workers with a strong sense of core values about their organization and the roles they played in contributing to the mission.

Rewards can come from obtaining both personal and organizational recognition for performance. Managers of public enterprises can use ceremony and publicity to enhance visibility and share credit with employees who contribute significantly to achieving the mission. Awards, commendations, and public displays can have great impact on morale. Further, as we saw in Chapter Six, rewarding good performance has the additional benefit of continually reasserting what is valued. Tom Glynn used awards and celebrations to reward behavior that supported the organizational mission. Ed Tetelman selected local directors of particularly well performing school-based programs to travel out of state for speaking engagements. The honor bestowed and the recognition associated with their performance contributed to morale and to establishing standards of performance. Sandra Steiner Lowe had the local board of supervisors present awards on a day of recognition to the doctors and others on whom she relied to support her effort to provide health care services to indigent youth. She sought and received TV coverage, which boosted the impact of the awards. But she also made it a point to drop personal notes and send flowers and baskets to express thanks for particularly meaningful contributions.

Because the behavioral incentives of managers in rule-driven organizations (shaped more by constraints than opportunities) are to be cautious and responsive, reward systems that allow for greater operational discretion and flexibility have multiple functions. First, they implicitly affirm the capability of individuals. When workers, managers, and the line staff feel empowered by both freedom to operate and accountability for results, they have incentives for initiative. Further, they are likely to feel a sense of efficacy and connection to the organizational mission when they are involved in a discrete and material way in setting and achieving its goals.

Rewards in the public sector are limited by laws, regulations, and union contracts. Indeed, creative use of available options is what most successful managers rely on. Because salary increases and bonuses may be limited, most public managers depend on finding other ways to recognize and reward achievement. Some measures may accrue to a particular unit, job classification, or office; others may relate to a single individual. Wayne Fortin promoted highly productive trauma intervention volunteers to permanent staff positions when they became available. The first and most important lesson is to become an advocate for your people. Robert Behn described the importance of this approach for Atkins and Glynn at the Massachusetts Department of Public Welfare.

But this is a critical approach for both middle managers and executives. Finding whatever leverage is available to improve the resource base, working conditions, caseloads, and promotional opportunities for your subordinates can establish you as a team leader rather than an adversary. This may be particularly important when union or civil service distinctions implicitly set up and reinforce hierarchical and adversarial conditions.

Executives must deal with outside constituents to generate program support. When those relationships are explicitly and visibly exploited for the support of successful and productive workers, executives generate the confidence and motivation of employees in fulfilling the mission. Thus using budget negotiations to generate new positions in order to reduce caseloads or to improve promotional opportunities for well-performing workers demonstrated Atkins and Glynn's willingness to fight for their people and give them what they need to do their job.

Finally, virtually all of our bureaucratic entrepreneurs depended for their success on establishing, nurturing, and sustaining often difficult and unconventional relationships between diverse organizations and interests. Internal reward and incentive systems (both material and psychic) and credit sharing are critical to increase motivation to meet new goals. The ultimate objective is to promote a sense of ownership of organizational goals and products among the people whose contributions are central to the success of the enterprise. Inclusion and developing shared values are two central vehicles that successful executives use to get their workers, both managerial and line, to want to do what the executives want them to do. When the critical contributors to success lie outside an executive's organizational boundaries, however, the challenge is greater and involves different kinds of actions.

Building External Constituencies

Most innovative enterprises we examined relied on new organizational arrangements both within and between organizations and sectors of the economy. Sandra Steiner Lowe's health care program for uninsured children depended, like Wasserman's obstetrical care for the indigent and Tetelman's school-based services for young people, on committed cooperative activity by multiple actors. Interest convergence, we have argued, was key to their success, and here we will explain how the particular mechanisms worked to bring about this convergence.

Some creative enterprises, Lowe's, Wasserman's, and Tetelman's included, were initially launched on the basis of a well-documented need or crisis. In these cases, the need for a solution was not in dispute; only the form it would take was. Getting the various external constituencies to agree on the need for a solution provides a point of departure for developing a consensual response. In these and similar cases, an initial crisis was evident, or the executive used research documenting the problem as a marketing tool to generate interest in action. Indeed, these vehicles often provided the first step in identifying relevant constituencies for action.

Whereas the impetus for joint action is often the generally recognized or aggressively marketed documentation of a problem, interest conversion requires either the fortuitous recognition that cooperation would provide benefits to each critical actor or a conscious strategy to convince central actors that joint action is in their interest. Different strategies succeed in different situations, and their appropriateness depends in part on whether the program innovator begins with a well-formed plan for problem solving or merely a well-considered process.

Ed Tetelman came to his efforts to gain the support and cooperation of state and local actors with a well-conceived concept. Deriving from school-based health services models, Tetelman's school-based initiative had a fairly clear prototype. His efforts to woo needed constituents, then, depended on selling them a particular product concept. (Even so, his model left room for considerable variation in program design to meet local conditions.) Conversely, Wasserman defined his role as creating a process for joint problem solving where traditional adversaries willingly joined together to develop a solution to a well-documented problem. His role was not that of a product champion but rather that of a facilitator who developed interest conversion by convincing the parties that they shared a problem that required a remedy and then by building the apparatus for collaboration. That led to an innovative response to the obstetrical care crises that involved all the participants.

Finally, two central skills appear to dominate executive success in enlisting support and cooperation with external constituents. The first comes from placing particular emphasis on communication. Most concentrate their efforts first on understanding and listening to diverse and often competing constituents with whom it is necessary to collaborate. Subsequent efforts to understand and accommodate the real problems of these participants then lead to successful solutions. Wasserman's carefully crafted solution to provide obstetrical care to indigent women grew from a real understanding of the difficulties that doctors and hospitals faced: financial losses and uncompensated liability.

Continual attempts to translate and explain a new initiative to diverse publics is central in marketing it successfully. Many of the programmatic initiatives we studied were innovative combinations of old things. Success in communicating the essence of the programmatic concept and its importance for meeting a critical social need is perhaps the most important ingredient in building needed external support. Steven Swanger's Work Force desperately needed parental support in the housing projects, yet most parents felt threatened by the program. Swanger's critical success came from articulating and communicating the essence of the program concept and capturing its message of youth empowerment and self-esteem. This was critical for allaying parents' fears and building their support.

Most of our executives sought every opportunity to describe and trumpet their programs. Early in the process of generating support, communication often centered on establishing the need for a particular programmatic response and on explaining its content conceptually. This may seem obvious, but translating a complicated set of programmatic elements into a clearly defined program concept understandable to nonexperts is a crucial step in dispelling cynicism and generating interest. Later, most executives use opportunities to meet and speak with various external constituents as a way to publicize their successes and gain additional political and budgetary favor.

Not all successful activities depend on the active engagement of multiple outside actors, but many do. This is particularly true when the innovation requires the creation of a public-private entity. Essential to selling a program idea is an articulate spokesperson who can identify what is unique in the idea and generate enthusiasm around it.

Finally, many program champions depend on exploiting previous relationships with important actors to garner support and further program development. Sometimes these prior relationships are related to the original program concept. For example, Wayne Fortin's Trauma Intervention Program was actually conceptualized from experiences he had had in a community mental health agency where he developed public safety programs with the police. His working relationships with the fire and police departments was key to his success in getting them to give his program concept a chance despite their early skepticism. Further, using existing relationships to build a core of program support may be central to launching a program idea that depends on multiple participants. Ed Tetelman suggested that knowing the primary actors in state politics from his law reform days in legal services was very helpful in launching his statewide initiative.

Media: Building Favorable Public Images

Getting external constituents to become program advocates (or at least reducing opposition) often depends on creating positive public images of one's agency or program. Executives who understand how to use the media for marketing and communications to external publics used similar techniques. Jackson, Chase, Atkins, and Glynn, among others, defined measurable goals that were clearly understood to represent success. Emphasizing quick and visible accomplishments, they used and cultivated press coverage of dramatic and symbolic events and messages. Jackson sought media attention for visually dramatic property seizures from wealthy tax evaders. Chase courted press coverage for large-scale visible program successes—methadone maintenance clinics, lead paint poisoning screening and removal, rat bite prevention, and others. Glynn used the governor's presence at his swearing in to attract press attention and at the same time trumpet his new organizational objectives and values.

At times, however, press attention can be unwelcome. Timing is critical. Because many innovations emerge from what may seem to be chaotic field trials, errors, and attempts at correction, considerable discretion must be exercised to protect incipient efforts until they are "ready for prime time." A combination of staying underground at the outset and looking quickly to identify measurable early indicators of program success are common strategies among bureaucratic entrepreneurs.

Interviews with dozens of Ford Foundation–John F. Kennedy School Innovations award winners indicated the significant value that the award itself played in generating and sustaining external constituents. The award presentation was a significant media event that helped stave off budget cuts for the Philadelphia Anti-Graffiti Network after the departure of Mayor Goode, a pivotal program champion. Similarly, Swanger's Work Force unemployment prevention program used the state's budget crisis, which resulted in defunding of the program, as a vehicle to publicize his efforts. Using his own funding crisis to tell what he described as a "sexy story" of success and loss, he was able to raise money from eighteen outside sources. The Ford award was a major focus of his media efforts to publicize the worthiness of his enterprise. Every other winner we spoke to also pointed to the importance of the media attention generated by the award in strengthening appeals for political and financial support.

The media are clearly strong allies in establishing program legitimacy, in building awareness of program success, and in dispelling cynicism about the capacity of public enterprise to bring about change or the worthiness of its clients. Whether media attention serves to destroy potential for creative public performance (by making public managers risk-averse) or to champion innovative activities, it is clear that careful and systematic attention to cultivating media relations and creating media events can help build constituencies.

Gordon Chase, a master at dealing with the media, reminds us, however, that the media are generally skeptical and that exposing the bad may make a better story than extolling the good. Nevertheless, in the end, public executives often get what they deserve, and organizing a media effort, getting the good news out, having command of facts, and telling the story in a straightforward, honest way are good approaches to the press. Another is anticipating bad news and preparing a response. The key is to manage the media function and to learn to use and respond to the press to promote one's organizational message and success.

Chapters Three through Six identified the approaches that successful bureaucratic entrepreneurs use to innovate. Seizing a good idea consistent with one's organizational mission and values is the beginning of programmatic activity, learning, and invention. A willingness to take risks and to act with a firm sense of direction even without a formal map was characteristic of many successful entrepreneurs. Recognizing good ideas and knowing when to act are crucial skills that can be learned but too often are not taught. In the next section we will critically analyze the prevailing models of training for public management and propose an alternative.

Education for Public Management: Development of Bureaucratic Entrepreneurs

We have just examined the key areas where executives focused their managerial efforts with significant success. Success is not the result of following a set of blueprints. Deciding precisely what to do is more likely to be shaped by knowledge about organizational capacity and performance as assessed in the field. Managing by wandering around, continual improvement through feedback, and the ready, fire, aim approach are all elements of the evolving and continually interactive strategy that creative public executives employ.

Thus a central question for the people charged with training future public managers is how to prepare them to recognize good ideas, adapt these to real environments (constrained by resources, politics, and organizational limitations), and implement the ideas opportunistically. If, as Louis Pasteur reminded us about discovery, "chance favors only the well-prepared mind," what kind of preparation ought we provide to aspiring public managers?

Educating Students for Success

Much controversy has surrounded the development of academic programs and scholarship on public management.[10] In the late 1960s, the field of public policy struck out on its own. It eschewed any connection with traditional training that emphasized scientific administration for career civil servants. It sought to move away from a model that was descriptive rather than prescriptive, that focused on institutions rather than choice and action, or that was dependent on the single discipline of political science.

The emerging public policy programs relied, instead, on microeconomics for their disciplinary core.[11] They distinguished themselves from the more traditional public administration programs by emphasizing what they thought of as an ends-driven rather than a means-driven focus, seeing their goal as decision-forcing and prescriptive. Decision making became the end for public managers in the new model, and policy analysis became their primary means. This departed from the traditional public administration focus on the implementation of politically generated decisions, flowing from their rather artificial distinction between administration (implementation) and policy (politics).

Successful entrepreneurial executives, however, have demonstrated a greater reliance on field-based learning and adaptation than on sophisticated prior analysis for programmatic and managerial innovation. Nevertheless, taking advantage of opportunities discovered only in the field requires an intellect capable of appreciating the opportunity when presented. Graduate management training can help develop this. Here we review the evidence on managerial behaviors related to success. Then we address its implications for the preparation that the academy can most appropriately provide and how this differs from existing approaches to training public managers.

Our findings have drawn a picture of individuals who are successful and innovative public managers by virtue of their abilities to understand quickly and to adapt to specific and contextual circumstances. They point to individuals who have skills others than formal policy analysis: those who can scan dynamic environments for useful and creative alternatives and can act quickly even under uncertainty to shape innovative policy responses in the field. They are individuals who can seize the unexpected and use it to their advantage.

Meaningful analysis occurs, more often, *after* the implementation of a policy or a program rather than before. Operational data generated from ongoing programmatic efforts become the subject for analysis rather than careful projections of the probable impact of alternative options.

These findings have implications for public management training that differ sharply from existing models. It may be desirable to reduce the role of academy-generated techniques such as formal policy analysis. Indeed, we found that most of the successful executives' learning occurred in the field through a process of iteration, adaptation, and post factum error correction. Action rarely springs from formal analysis of alternative options.

Moreover, much field learning is informal. Most executives come to their agency without blueprints. Most face vague and diffuse mandates, making success dependent on an ability to fashion new, personal missions. The process used to define and shape an organizational or programmatic mission often consists of knowledge gained and opportunities sighted by wandering around, informally listening and looking.

These findings lead us to conclude that this is both how innovative executives operate and how they ought to operate. It is a more effective and more realistic approach in light of the bounded rationality and general cognitive limits of more synoptic and comprehensive approaches.[12] Analysis-based choices fail most often because they simply cannot accommodate all the contingencies that can occur in the field. Changing politics, behavior, technology, or natural phenomena cannot always be taken into account or anticipated.

These findings also have significant implications for the likelihood of producing innovation: because successful managers use skills that can be learned, the prospects for innovation may be far better. Our challenge is to determine how to teach them.

How Executives Acquire Competence:
Learning from Analysis and from the Field

Our findings raise a critical question: Can graduate education in public policy be useful for creating these kinds of public managers, and if so, what kind of education is most useful? The educational backgrounds of the innovators in our sample are diverse. Public policy, law, medicine, education, social work, little formal education—each was equally likely to produce an innovative manager. Though few of our subjects had any single disciplinary perspective in common, all drew for their inspiration on a similar breadth of knowledge and experience that crossed disciplines, sectors, and institutional settings.

The approach most dominant in public policy education has been the policy analysis or policy planning model. It stresses the importance of an orderly, sequential, rational approach to problem solving prior to program design and implementation. Analysts are asked to identify the nature of the problem to be addressed, generate a set of policy options, and analyze their relative merits on the basis of explicit and quantifiable criteria. Outcomes of any policy choice should be anticipated, and programs should be designed to promote predicted outcomes. Program initiatives are generated in accordance with the lessons of analysis and implemented according to a careful and controlled plan subjected to intense prior scrutiny.[13]

Recent literature in both private sector and public sector management has been proposing a very different and contrasting model.[14] These studies, and our own analysis of innovative executives, suggest that the development of successful enterprises was not neat and orderly as prescribed by the policy analysis model. Indeed, rather than emerging from a systematic process of rational analysis of alternative choices, most effective and innovative initiatives develop as a result of experiential learning that derives from experimentation at the implementation stage. Good ideas are tested quickly in the field and subjected to evaluation and feedback from informal operational experience. Most implementation experience, and the error correction that it permits, depends heavily on the operational data generated. This process is messy and disorderly, yet practical and realistic.

Formal analysis, contrary to the reigning paradigm of public policy schools, was more helpful after implementation. As we noted in Chapter Four, it served an evaluative function by exposing the deficiencies of poor options. All this has very different implications for how managers ought to behave and how students of public management ought to be educated.

Charting the Agency's New Mission: Past Practice, Analysis, and Learning in the Field

The successful managers we studied gave direction to their enterprises. They defined the agency's mission, developed an organizational culture that could generate change, and rewarded behavior that supports the process. Thus while successful managers may muddle along testing, evaluating, and redesigning their approach, they do not wait for random accidents of nature to determine the fate of their enterprise. Rather they opportunistically pick up resources lying around, seize advantages, even in crisis, and take risks.

The guidance for this managerial opportunism seems to come from a combination of sources. First, it comes from their basic understanding of the behavioral models of management and the state of the art in particular policy areas. This is usually derived from a knowledge of past practice—in that agency but more often in diverse institutions and fields. Sometimes it is based on policy analysis and evaluation of the work in that field of endeavor, as well as historical analysis and the literature's evaluation of past practice.

The successful managers who developed Massachusetts's ET Choices program, for example, did a lot of learning on the job through an adaptive, trial-and-error process of ready, fire, aim. But they brought with them a basic conceptual model of welfare reform, a behavioral model of human motivation, and a knowledge of programmatic models of how to assist the dependent poor. Their program was not a product of inspirational insight or a shot in the dark. They had internalized two decades of analysis on employment and welfare programs.

But the conception was also shaped by what the executives almost immediately began to learn in the field about their agency. This was achieved more through an informal, adaptive, trial-and-error process than through formal policy analysis.

Tolerance for Mistakes

As noted in Chapter Four, these findings differ significantly from those suggested by formal models of program development and policy analysis. They point to qualities of management that emphasize risk taking, flexibility, and opportunism. Successful innovation was marked by a willingness to act without a complete plan and to make mistakes. Not only was a tolerance for mistakes and misfires necessary, but it was also desirable because the lessons learned facilitated continual error correction.

Learning through error correction is a process from which innovation emerges. Indeed, error correction has also been an important engine in scientific discovery. In his grand intellectual history of the development of molecular biology, Horace Judson tells us that molecular biology's great development proceeded by error correction and a willingness to throw out incorrect hypotheses. Analysis—careful analysis—is important in science. But Francis Crick tells us that boldness, overly simple hypotheses, and a willingness to throw out the errors is just as essential. Important in science, risk taking, evaluation, and correction were also central to the success of Jackson, Chase, Atkins, and dozens of other bureaucratic entrepreneurs.

Formal Learning in the Field

Learning in the field can be formal and informal. Formal learning comes from traditional evaluation and analysis, which can be taught in school. Formal program evaluation techniques seek, whenever possible, to maximize the conditions of good scientific inquiry. Students of program evaluation learn how to adapt the tenets of scientific inquiry to their work. Hence the principles of random assignment, control groups, and care to control field conditions are highly valued. But successful executives rarely use formal program evaluation. It is costly and so slow that often the results come too late in the political process to be useful for the design of new initiatives. Although managers need to be intensely aware of the limitations of informal and unscientific analysis of program operations, they must learn to compensate for these necessary methodological shortcomings of data generated for quick but useful operational feedback.[15]

ET Choices, for instance, did not undertake a formal evaluation until several years after the program was implemented, and they did not agree with internal and external calls for one. This was despite the fact that the program's two principals (Atkins and Glynn), as well as their staff (including their own quite capable policy analysis and evaluation shop), were well trained in formal analysis. Indeed, Atkins had started his career as part of the Department of Defense's Program Planning Budgeting System staff. Glynn held a doctorate in social policy. Formal program evaluation, however, would have been time-consuming and would have impeded their efforts at continual tinkering as it would have required holding all program elements constant during the period of inquiry. Further, it would have required withholding services from otherwise eligible clients. Atkins and Glynn were interested not in evaluating whether to continue or terminate ET Choices but how to make it work better. So they undertook a management improvement study instead.

Some executives are wary of the process of formal analysis and evaluation lest it threaten their agendas or political support. Others simply recognize the costly commitment and the lost opportunities incurred as a result of meeting social-scientific protocols. It is not necessarily a lack of belief in the validity of such efforts that inhibits their use but rather a realistic appraisal of the managerial and political constraints they impose.

Informal Learning in the Field

Most of the field learning among our successful managers was informal. They came to their agencies with no blueprint. Indeed, most faced vague and diffuse mandates at best. Much of their success came from their ability to create new and personal missions for their agencies. Under Ira Jackson, for example, the Department of Revenue's narrow and conventional mission was transformed into a new, broader one. First it was "honest, firm, and fair tax administration." Then it moved to the even more ambitious combination of increased enforcement and tax amnesty.

Under Gordon Chase, the Health Services Administration's broad, diffuse mission took on much greater specificity with his program management approach, which took on missions such as dealing with lead paint poisoning, children being bitten by rats, and prison health care in city prisons (the latter was actually under another agency's jurisdiction). Chase also crafted the new mission for the HSA that its program should treat the entire universe of the problem (all heroin addicts) and not just a pilot or demonstration program. William Ruckelshaus transformed the diffuse mandate that Congress gave him into a clear mission: pollution abatement through legislative enforcement.

These new missions were in part shaped by the personal model these managers brought with them of the nature of the problem and an underlying theory of cause and effect. We noted this as being the case with ET Choices. But the personal model some brought more often was rather diffuse. When Jackson came to the DOR, for instance, he knew very little about revenue agencies or even about management. (His previous public service had been on a mayoral staff, specializing in speechwriting and issues.) Perhaps his most focused preconception relevant to his agency was his personal distaste for corrupt government.

Chase had no background in health policy when he came to the HSA and was in fact strongly criticized for that. His most focused preconception relevant to the agency was a strong social conscience and a sense of indignation. He had the very vague personal ambition to "help a lot of people." Later that would be an element behind his expansion of the HSA's mission to treating the whole universe of the problem. But that developed only after learning in the field by having his nose rubbed in the reality of problems: he learned much from prison riots and suicides that were in part the result of inadequate health care and from heroin addicts overdosing while they were on long treatment waiting lists.

Ruckelshaus had almost no background in environmental policy or management. His most focused preconception relevant to the Environmental Protection Agency was his earlier field experience, as a former state assistant attorney general, in solving problems through legal enforcement approaches.

Training Managers to Be Hedgehogs Rather Than Foxes

We have not emphasized the importance of formal learning for successful practitioners. How important is formal training? That depends, we suggest, on the specific nature of that formal training and on the kinds of managers we seek.

We have emphasized the importance of informal learning to innovative executives. But formal training may be valuable since it prepares managers to know what to look for. As Pasteur wisely reminds us, "In matters of observation, chance favors the prepared mind." All things being equal, it is better to have more knowledge rather than less. Formal training may also be valuable because it can prevent executives from making obvious mistakes. Further, it will expand their knowledge of the breadth of options and choices that they might pursue. Finally, it will improve the general character of the options they pursue.

Thus in addition to experiential learning, the intellectual foundations of such formal training for executives should consist of teaching that focuses on the following areas: (1) general knowledge of human behavior and human nature; (2) welfare economics and, in particular, analysis of market failures and cost-benefit analysis; (3) some social science theory on cause and effect and the nature of evidence; and (4) knowledge of programmatic approaches and exposure to broad policy areas and options, including policy history.

Education for public management should therefore be less technical than broad, emphasizing both policy and management theory and practice. But of more significance than the particular curricular elements is the perspective that these students internalize about their roles. Managers should be taught a sense of professional identity. Policy analysts rely on the strengths of their techniques and methods. Bureaucratic entrepreneurs must define themselves more in terms of their broad purposes. Instead of identifying themselves with a specific set of techniques, these managers need to define themselves in terms of fulfilling specific missions, most of which ought to be self-initiated.

To prepare these managers to assume value-driven agendas, they must be exposed to managerial techniques and approaches within particular contexts. Appropriateness and value must be seen as dependent on the opportunities and constraints imposed by specific environments. That is the kind of training a manager gets on the job. Success depends on selecting the appropriate approach for a given situation. To be useful, academic training must attempt to simulate these experiences through the use of good case material, role playing, or faculty-generated relationships for students with managers in operating organizations. Management practices can be taught and learned; knowing which ones to use in which situations takes more experience. It is these kinds of experiences that graduate education must simulate through creative pedagogical techniques.

Further, successful entrepreneurs in government distinguish themselves by the range of environments, both institutional and disciplinary, on which they draw. Using old stuff in new ways requires a knowledge of how old stuff was used in old ways. Instead of specialization, these findings suggest the value of a broad exposure to different policy areas, sectoral practices, and disciplinary perspectives. Instead of training specialists, education for this new breed of bureaucratic entrepreneurs ought to be broad and rich. Experiential learning, even if simulated in the

Emphasis on narrow analytical objectives may inadvertently prevent some public policy schools from training managers to be hedgehogs. Students need the right curricular emphasis and the right message. In part this derives from the culture of an institution and the values it imparts to students about what is important and who they are. Policy schools have historically paid only lip service to the value of public management education, while real status in the institution has been conferred on the analytically and technically nimble.

And policy-specific graduate training, like public health, social welfare, or urban planning and housing, may even be doing a worse job. Struggling to maintain its relevance in an increasingly crowded field of professional-degree-granting schools, policy-specific training gains a comparative advantage from its monopoly position in a relatively narrow area. Even so, each area maintains its own set of deeply held biases and orientations. These in turn can be disabling to the entrepreneur looking for broad sources of inspiration and opportunities for action.

Some programs, such as Harvard's Graduate School of Business, seem to do a better job of providing students with a sense of professional identity while training them as general managers. With an interdisciplinary approach and broad exposure to multiple areas of management practice, graduates report (and employers confirm) confidence in and ability at general management.[17] Public policy programs have not as yet taken the reins away from the policy-analytical economists in order to emphasize and celebrate the importance of public management. Indeed, slow-to-ity to concentrate their efforts and resources on the one big thing.

What is the implication for training managers? Managers' training ought to emphasize teaching them to think in terms of larger themes and missions for their agencies. It ought to put more emphasis on knowledge of managerial techniques and organizational arrangements than knowledge of specific programmatic approaches and policy options. The many little things that the fox knows and that managers must also know (such as details about a policy strategy or a particular agency or a detailed knowledge of a particular analytical or research methodology) are perhaps best learned along the way.

Indeed, too much training in a specific policy area or in a single discipline (say, law or economics) may prevent managers from focusing on the larger picture. It may distract them from developing the appropriate mission or vision for their agencies. Too much familiarity with the approaches of a particular policy area may mean that the new manager will be too wedded to convention or to institutional and disciplinary biases. Too much detailed knowledge of the trees, so to speak, may distract from developing an appropriate view of the forest.

The fact that Jackson, Schall, Chase, and Ruckelshaus, as well as Glynn at the transit agency, were all outsiders to their agencies' policy areas may have actually helped them. Unbridled by norms of the field, they had more license and more incentive to develop new and personal visions for their agencies. And in each instance, the agency desperately needed a new vision.

classroom, can then depend on students' ability to scan broad environments for inspiration and lessons.

It is also important to remember, however, that although formal learning at school is influential, its effects are often felt later—in Eugene Bardach's felicitous phrase—in a delayed and sometimes even serendipitous manner.[16] Bardach suggests that formal learning may only truly occur many months (for example, after a summer internship following a year of classwork) or even years after the analysis or skills were formally taught in class. The learning often takes root only after the recipient has had experience in the field. It is only then that the lessons of school come to have meaning, when they have a specific referent within an individual's own direct experience.

But let us remember that the successful executives in our study tended to act like hedgehogs rather than foxes. "The fox knows many things; the hedgehog knows one big thing." These successful managers acted as if they knew one big thing. They developed highly focused visions of one big thing, such as immediately establishing the agency's credibility through an emphasis on action—almost any immediate and visible action—or bringing immediate and visible enforcement suits or emphasizing the agency's honesty and power by enforcing the law against its own employees.

They did not act like the fox, pursuing many things simultaneously. Pursuing multiple objectives would engender conflict and dilute managerial focus. Whether pursuing different and perhaps contradictory treatment strategies, enforcement strategies, or client groups, foxes lose the abil-

respond professional and academic organizations have only begun to treat public management scholarship with proper seriousness as a respectable field of inquiry.[18] Nevertheless, there is new attention to its role in the curriculum as the study of best practice. Our research contributes significantly to the body of knowledge of best practice.

Finally, all these findings on how learning takes place among successful managers leave us with a hopeful conclusion. Because bureaucratic entrepreneurs are not simply born with these talents but rather have learned them, the prospects for increasing the incidence of innovation are very good. But we must arm our aspirants with these effective strategies, inspire with these stories of success, and teach them to learn from their own experience.

Notes

1. Parallel suggestions for the private and public sectors are made by several leading authors. See Rosabeth Moss Kanter, *The Change Masters* (New York: Simon & Schuster, 1983); Rosabeth Moss Kanter, *When Giants Learn to Dance* (New York, Simon & Schuster, 1989); Gordon Chase and Elizabeth Reveal, *How to Manage in the Public Sector* (Reading, Mass.: Addison-Wesley, 1983); Thomas Peters and Robert Waterman, *In Search of Excellence* (New York: HarperCollins, 1982); Robert D. Behn, *Leadership Counts* (Cambridge, Mass.: Harvard University Press, 1991; Alan Altshuler and Marc Zegans, "Innovation and Creativity: Comparisons Between Public Management and Private Enterprise," *Cities,* February 1990; Peter Drucker, *Innovation and*

Entrepreneurship (New York: HarperCollins, 1985); Jay Galbraith, "Designing the Innovating Organization," *Organizational Dynamics,* 1982, pp. 5–25.
2. Almost all of the analysis in this chapter applies to *both* chief executives and program executives. Hence, we refer to both by the general terms *executives* and *managers.* (We have used the latter terms rather interchangeably throughout the book.) In the few instances of this chapter in which there are differences in our analysis according to whether an executive is a *chief executive* or a *program executive,* we make this distinction by explicitly using these two full terms.
3. Altshuler and Zegans, "Innovation and Creativity"; Michael Barzelay and Babak Armajani, "Managing State Government Operations: Changing Visions of Overhead Agencies," *Journal of Policy Analysis and Management,* 9(3), 1990.
4. It is clear, however, that personal rewards are substantial for successful innovators. Our research demonstrates the importance of a personal sense of mission or purpose and the related psychic rewards that are associated with a manager's willingness to take risks in the pursuit of excellence in public management.
5. Rosabeth Moss Kanter, "The Organizational Climate for Innovation," in Barbara H. Moore, ed., *The Entrepreneur in Local Government* (Washington, D.C.: International City Management Association, 1983).
6. Behn, *Leadership Counts.*
7. Clear specification of goals requires identifying nondistorting ways to operationalize them that allow each

unit to participate in choosing the right measure and the level to which it will be accountable.
8. Chase and Reveal, *How to Manage.*
9. J. R. Rawls and others, "A Comparison of Managers Entering or Reentering the Profit and Nonprofit Sectors," *Academy of Management Journal,* 18, 1975, pp. 616–622.
10. See Lawrence E. Lynn, Jr., "Public Management: A Survey," *University of Chicago Working Paper Series,* 92, 1992.
11. These arguments and conceptions were revealed in several curricular conferences sponsored by the Association for Public Policy Analysis and Management for its member institutions and in papers commissioned for them. For a review, see Lynn, "Public Management," Donald Stokes, "Political and Organizational Analysis in the Policy Curriculum," or Richard Elmore, "Graduate Education in Public Management," *Journal of Policy Analysis and Management,* 6, 1986, pp. 44–55.
12. For details of this more general argument, see the work of Nobel Prize winner Herbert Simon and the more popular, policy-oriented work of Charles Lindblom.
13. For a standard statement of policy analysis approaches, see David C. Weimer and Aidan R. Vining, *Policy Analysis Concepts and Practice* (Englewood Cliffs, N.J.: Prentice Hall, 1989); and Edith Stokey and Richard Zeckhauser, *A Primer for Policy Analysis* (New York: Norton, 1978).
14. Behn, *Leadership Counts;* Peters and Waterman, *In*

Search of Excellence; Gifford Pinchot, *Intrapreneuring* (New York: HarperCollins, 1985); Kanter, *Change Masters;* Albert O. Hirschman, *Strategy for Development* (Boulder, Colo.: Westview, 1988); Martin A. Levin and Barbara Ferman, *The Political Hand* (Elmsford, N.Y.: Pergamon, 1985); Olivia Golden, "Innovation in Public Sector Human Services Programs," *Journal of Policy Analysis and Management,* 9, 1990; Aaron Wildavsky, *Speaking Truth to Power* (Boston: Little, Brown, 1979).

15. We are not arguing against the need for high-quality social science research on program initiatives. We are, however, arguing against exclusive dependency on this kind of research for management initiative. Academy-generated research ought to provide a body of literature that helps managers initially choose some strategic programmatic directions. Its absence should not, however, needlessly constrain experimentation with new strategies or impede the informal learning process. Social scientists do research, but managers have operational needs that depend on different time frames, contexts, and priorities.
16. Eugene Bardach, "Delayed and Serendipitous Learning," paper presented at the Association for Policy Analysis and Management Research Conference, Chicago, 1985.
17. See annual survey on the nation's top business schools in *Business Week.*
18. Lynn, "Public Management."

▌ *Conclusion* ▌

Pointing the Trains in the Right Direction
Public Management Is About Values

As we have argued throughout, this book is about more than leadership. We seek to develop an environment that makes innovation both possible and probable, that stimulates innovation by freeing talented executives to exercise their creative abilities. This approach is more generalizable than an emphasis on individual leadership abilities and thus more transferable.

More important, therefore, than leadership is changing the incentives in public sector organizations. Too often they discourage executives' innovations in the interest of oversight. They must be replaced with ones that reward risk taking. Yet we also seek to develop an environment that ensures that democratic accountability and oversight are maintained while innovation is being pursued.

This points to the inherent dilemma in the roles of chief executive and program executive: getting things done versus maintaining democratic values. Given these tensions, a balanced *system* is needed, one that cultivates innovation combined with the guidance of oversight and accountability. To institutionalize this system, both program executives and chief executives are needed. But balancing innovation and accountability depends most on the role exercised by the executive at the top.

Management Matters

Drawing lessons from successful bureaucratic entrepreneurs, our most compelling conclusion throughout has been that management matters. Policy success depends on it.

The stories described here have helped us explain how attention to management can lead to success. Successful bureaucratic entrepreneurs are action-oriented. They act and adapt, using existing practices as foundations for new programs. They turn seemingly insurmountable obstacles into opportunities by using crises to give them creative license. They trust learning by doing and trial and error to produce some quick successes, which they then use as public capital for their next steps. Successful innovation is marked by a willingness to act without a complete plan and to make mistakes. This tolerance for mistakes contributes to a process of continual error correction. Managerial innovation is an iterative and adaptive process.

Pursuing these strategies requires changing the basic decision rules for moving forward. Executives can benefit significantly from analysis ahead of time, but there is more to fear from the paralysis of analysis than from action. Developing a clear vision of objectives and moving forward rapidly with continual scrutiny and vigilance is the proven strategy for success. This is a far cry from the public policy schools' recommendation that public managers use policy analysis. But we have found learning in the field more realistic.

Our intent is not to present maxims for innovation. This book is about real life, not theoretical principles. So our lessons were drawn from actual success stories. For example, we witnessed Ellen Schall's success in bringing innovation to New York City's juvenile justice agency by changing its tension-filled warehousing of juveniles awaiting trial. She used old stuff in new ways by delivering social services to the youths while they were in detention. Instead of waiting for weeks or months for the juvenile judge's recommendations, she started a process to evaluate each child's needs and provide educational and rehabilitative services immediately after the kids were arrested.

We saw how in creating the now nationally renowned Employment and Training Choices program, Massachusetts Welfare Commissioner Charles Atkins and Deputy Commissioner Thomas Glynn assembled old stuff in new ways and thereby redefined a new mission for their department: not merely providing clients with timely welfare checks but developing routes out of poverty. They merged training and employment with support services, including child care and transportation.

Gordon Chase, with his bias toward action and his ready, fire, aim eschewal of prior analysis, provided another vivid lesson for success. As head of New York's Health

Services Administration, he opportunistically used the city's heroin crisis to soften resistance to his bold and controversial creation, the nation's first methadone maintenance program.

The primary lesson of our book for beleaguered public managers is that innovating and pursuing an ambitious public agenda do not depend on exceptional executive abilities. They depend on learning from success and using concrete strategies and approaches.

But most actors, from intellectuals to top executives, tend to neglect the importance of implementation. The Clinton administration, full of intellectually oriented policy makers, risks a similar omission in its tendency to focus more on ideas than on management and follow-through.

The Day After an AIDS Vaccine Is Discovered

At the start of the book, we identified key point decisions that confront the Clinton administration as it faces the AIDS crisis. Our goal there, as it is here, is to underscore that public policy outcomes rely on skilled attention to management. For an increasingly ambitious policy agenda at the national level, such as the Clinton administration's, a focus on the management necessities of any policy action will be paramount.

AIDS provides a sobering example. President Clinton has spoken eloquently about the AIDS crisis but has focused exclusively on policy choices, expressing first, the need to reshape national policy and give more attention and money to AIDS prevention and treatment and, second, the need to end discrimination against and mistreatment of people who have AIDS or are HIV-positive.

Policy ideas are, of course, important prerequisites. But President Clinton has not acknowledged the need for sound management of these breakthroughs to implement them fully as policies, that is, the management of the line decisions to implement the point decisions. Nor has he yet acknowledged the paradox that after spending billions of dollars on an AIDS vaccine, the day after its discovery we will face major and predictable management problems that will limit the vaccine's immediate effectiveness.[1] The discovery of an AIDS vaccine will not be the beginning of the end; it will only be the first step in a complex series of decisions and actions.

The discovery is not the cure. It never is, as we have seen, whether the silver bullet is for AIDS, swine flu, or heroin addiction. Our analyses of all these cases have shown, among other things, that insufficient attention to management is just as likely in conservative as in liberal administrations. Bright staff people of all political persuasions are equally likely to assume that having good ideas and power are enough to achieve good policies.

Policy objectives set the goals of an administration. But implementation of an AIDS vaccine will occur in a highly complicated policy space with broad and competing constituencies. Thus the major implementation problems must be anticipated beforehand. Scientists, medical personnel, patients and their advocates, insurance companies, pharmaceutical companies, and myriad levels of government and competing public agencies must be given incentives to make their interests converge more clearly. This requires that implementation problems be anticipated and planned to the point of designing the policy vehicle for immunization beforehand. The irony is that while billions may be spent on developing an AIDS vaccine, these putatively less difficult management obstacles are capable of subverting a quick and effective immunization program.

The Stroke-of-the-Pen Myth: Clinton's Policy on Gays in the Military

Just as the cure is not sufficient, neither is the stroke of the pen. President Clinton's proposal to lift the ban on homosexuals in the military illustrates what we call the "stroke-of-the-pen myth." This proposal, wise as it may be, is merely the end of the beginning: it sets in motion a complicated process that must be followed by a well-managed series of implementation decisions including complex activities of assemblage, coordination, and bargaining among many independent actors. Because of the special nature of the military, the implementation of Clinton's initial decision to lift the ban will be difficult and slow. It will be neither automatic nor routine.

Following his election, President Clinton's policy revealed a lack of focus on the line decisions and the management needed to make point decisions a reality. During the campaign, he criticized the Pentagon ban on homosexuals in the military. He said that if elected, he would lift it, and he would do it rapidly, with a stroke of the pen—an executive order, a quintessential point decision.

At his first postelection press conference, he said he would sign such an executive order. Eloquently stressing the need to have the best people in the military, he argued for judging an individual's conduct and not sexual orientation. This was immediately met with many complaints in the military, from the chairman of the Joint Chiefs of Staff, General Colin Powell, on down. Some opposition may have been prompted by homophobic attitudes, but most, such as General Powell's, seemed based on genuine management concerns. Sensitive to the complexity and the difficulty of implementing this change, many critics pointed to the high degree of intimate living and working situations in the military and the unusual importance of good personal relationships and morale among military co-workers. Implementing a nondiscrimination policy capable of responding to these concerns requires careful attention to management.

For the purposes of analysis, let us assume that lifting the ban is a wise policy. The president must immediately anticipate the critical implementation decisions necessary to turn this initial decision into an effective policy. The administration must construct, and then learn from, a detailed scenario for the series of line decisions that are required.

To help with this, they must analyze previous comparable policy changes. In the late 1940s and the 1950s, for example, policy changes haltingly brought about racial integration of the military. It did not occur quickly or easily. It resulted from a complex series of activities requiring assemblage, coordination, and bargaining among many independent actors in an environment generally unfavorable to the policy. If we are to have effective integration of homosexuals in the military, the Clinton administration must recognize that management is the most challenging part of policy making. A policy that fails to anticipate and plan for the inevitably difficult implementation steps is bound to face considerable obstacles. Full results will not be achieved by the stroke of a pen.

Despite the central role of management in policy success, it is critical to remember the limits as well as the potential of effective management to create productive and socially desirable change. The recent history of public debate on government gridlock has produced a backlash of admiration for action. But we must distinguish between getting things done and choosing the right things to do.

Management Matters, but It Is Not Everything

Management matters. But despite the fact that it is too often neglected, it is not everything. Indeed, management can be dangerously overemphasized. Good management, like good policies, must be concerned with ends as well as means, with doing the right things as well as getting things done. But uncritical strategies, pursued in the rush to get things done, can impose far greater costs than inertia and delay. Our findings emphasize the strategies for getting things done, but there is no more important concern than doing the right thing.

A Backlash of Admiration for Action: Management by Guts

People in government feel a great deal of frustration over the difficulties of implementing policies given our political system's fragmented formal and informal structure of power. In the past decade or so, these frustrations have led to a backlash of admiration for action. The result has been a sometimes uncritical search for strategies that can get things done and a bias toward action without sufficient consideration of the costs of this emphasis.

In California, for example, a group of state administrators recently sponsored a weekend workshop called "Management by Guts." The workshop's first session illustrated this bias and the frustration from which it seemed to spring. People entered the workshop carrying placards of their favorite proponent of "management by guts." One of them was Joseph Stalin.

A less extreme form of this overcompensatory emphasis on action is the behavior of the executives in this study. Their route to innovation often took the form of creative subversion: they often worked around formal rules and bureaucratic regulations, short-circuited organizational clearance points, and gathered enough informal power to surmount implementation obstacles, often operating outside the formal bureaucratic chain of command.

President Bush and the "Vision Thing"

The most striking recent instances of this dangerous overemphasis on management and action have come at the national level, perhaps because of frustration with poor economic performance and alleged policy inaction and gridlock.[2] In reaction to this poor performance and inaction, there have been an overemphasis on management and action and insufficient concern with ends. President

Bush was not adept at articulating the ends of his administration. But he shrugged this off as not being important, saying, in a now-famous statement, "I'm not good at the vision thing."

Ross Perot: Making the Trains Run on Time—But in What Direction?

In 1973, Jeffrey Pressman and Aaron Wildavsky's now-classic book, *Implementation,* first cautioned the new public policy schools about the difficulties of effective implementation or, as their subtitle put it, "How Great Expectations in Washington Are Dashed in Oakland or Why It's Amazing That Federal Programs Work at All." But Pressman and Wildavsky also emphasized that ends are most important, warning that "a fast train is worse than a slow one if it takes you in the wrong direction."[3] But with Ross Perot's 1992 presidential bid and his emphasis on getting the trains to run on time, we have a graphic case of the fallacy of thinking that management is everything.

Perot acted as if all our major policy problems are merely problems of technical implementation, problems about which there is little disagreement and just a need for action by a good mechanic. During the campaign, one writer observed that "a President Perot would be a sort of Mechanic in Chief—as he often puts it, 'under the hood of the car, working on the engine.'"[4] He presented himself not as a visionary but as a doer, someone who should be made president not so much for any specific ideas on how to fix the nation's ills but simply because he was good at fixing things. He would make the trains run on time.

CONCLUSION

In a presidential debate, Perot flatly asserted that the ends of policy are not the problem and not in dispute:

> *The American people are hungry for action.* . . . Please understand, there are great plans lying all over Washington that *nobody ever executes.* It's like having a blueprint for a house you never built, and don't have anywhere to sleep. Now, the challenge is to take these things and do something with them. Step 1. You want to put America back to work? Clean up the small business problem. Have one task force work on that. The second, you've got your big companies that are in trouble including the defense industries; have another one on that. Have a third task force on new industries in the future. . . .[5]

We explored the consequences of compromising democratic values in Chapter Seven. Here we emphasize the importance of sensitizing practitioners and aspiring public servants to the profound value dimensions of their work. Being a successful bureaucratic entrepreneur is not simply resolving difficult technical problems of implementation. It also requires an ability to develop value-driven agendas that are worthy of implementation.

More than Implementation: Getting the Trains to Run in the Right Direction

Management is broader than the process of implementation. Management is not value-free. It is a political endeavor concerned with ends as well as means. Policy is always being made in the management process. We have shown that policy is created when carrying out line decisions, as well as in making point decisions. Managers have personal and political agendas that distinguish their role from that of an administrator carrying out the objectives of others. The process of implementation is concerned with how to make the trains run on time. Its focus is on means.

Management, by contrast, is a broader problem with profound political dimensions. Managers are also concerned with means, but they are first and foremost concerned with what direction the trains are going to run in—ends. Thus they must be both right and effective. They give direction to their enterprises, which are driven by a set of values. They create the agency's mission.

In this age of frustration with government, this overemphasis on action—and the concomitant lack of sufficient concern for ends—is widespread. But we must emphasize values and ends just as much as means.

We must ask public sector executives to try to make the trains run better and faster. But even more important, we should require that they concern themselves with where they are going.

To help them with this emphasis on direction and ends, we urge executives to consider questions of values and virtue along with those of power and action. We urge them to heed the advice of Aaron Wildavsky:

> [Pay attention] to questions of virtue as well as questions of power. . . . Always take the high ground: emphasize moral aspects of public

policy. . . . One cannot overemphasize political and organizational factors, because, although [analysts] love to talk about politics, they apply economics. The theory that comes with the handy applicator is the one they will try to use. Besides, economic solutions seem more practically proportioned to the kinds of problems [at hand]. . . . Warm the [agenda]! It's cold out there, and people enter the public sector to warm themselves with the thought that they will . . . make useful contributions to society. It is wise, therefore, to engage them early about larger as well as small questions. Life throws up many moral dilemmas in public policy—from the death penalty, to abortion, to police strikes, to affirmative action. Being right may well be more important than being effective, but effectiveness sometimes does increase the capacity to get rightness taken seriously. Striking a balance between the two is connected to the growth of moral consciousness. I should add that the criteria for decision embodied in many analyses (such as equity, efficiency, and equality) are essentially moral, and the ability to decide which are appropriate under different circumstances is an important part of an analyst's moral education.[6]

Management is fundamentally a political endeavor. It is value-driven. Hence it is also a moral endeavor. We therefore need to be concerned with the moral education of

ment. These have paradoxically increased the competition for policy development rather than deadlock. All this has contributed to more innovations rather than less, and they have developed more rapidly than in the past. There have of course been some significant exceptions to this rush of innovative policies; efforts at deficit reduction, for example, have moved slowly. But this, as Aaron Wildavsky and other contributors persuasively argue, reflects genuine societal disagreement rather than inherent institutional deadlock. Furthermore, as the essay on entitlements shows, within the aggregate budget deficit deadlock there has been a great deal of change: some entitlements (such as revenue sharing) have decreased greatly, while others (such as Food Stamps and WIC) have increased greatly.
3. Jeffrey Pressman and Aaron Wildavsky, *Implementation* (Berkeley: University of California Press, 1973), p. 137.
4. "For Perot, a Time of Need," *New York Times,* July 9, 1992, p. 1.
5. "Transcript of the Second Presidential Debate of 1992," *New York Times,* October 20, 1992, p. 22.
6. Aaron Wildavsky, *Speaking Truth to Power* (Boston: Little, Brown, 1979), pp. 413–414.

a new generation of public managers. As we emphasize and redefine the role of management as value-driven, we must also be careful to provide the moral education critical to assuming these new roles. Reawakening the question of values among executives will produce a generation of managers equally concerned with means and ends.

Notes

1. For the complete argument, see Martin A. Levin, "The Day After an AIDS Vaccine Is Discovered: Management Matters" (APPAM Presidential Address), *Journal of Policy Analysis and Management* 12 (1993): 438–455.
2. See the essays and the conclusion in *The New Politics of Public Policymaking,* ed. Marc Landy and Martin A. Levin (Baltimore: Johns Hopkins University Press, 1993), for the contrary argument that rather than policy gridlock, we have in recent years had an unusually large and rapid flow of innovative policies, ranging from the Tax Reform Act of 1986 through two immigration reform laws, the Disabled Americans Act, renewals of the Civil Rights Act, the Clean Air Act, and Superfund. These writers argue that in large part, these innovative policies have been produced by the confluence of "weak parties and strong ideas." They suggest that weak institutions, especially weakened political parties and a more highly fragmented Congress, have created a policy vacuum. Into this vacuum have rushed strong ideas propelled by increasingly independent policy entrepreneurs in large part stimulated by weakened institutions, such as political parties, and divided govern-

Index

A

Accountability: as constraint to innovation, 10-12, 14-17, 37, 213-220; and empowerment, 194; of managers and executives, 37-38, 275-276, 308-309n.7; and oversight, 37, 227, 234, 243-246
Action bias, 6-7, 14, 29-30n.3, 160-162; backlash against, 318-319
Adams, R., 225
Adoption programs, 134-135, 141, 154
Airline deregulation, 45-47
Allegiance, fostering of, 191-195
Altman, D., 266n.2
Anti-Graffiti Network (Philadelphia), 118, 119, 143-144, 166, 289
Apple Computer, 83-84n.24, 203
Arcata, California wetlands program, 101-102
Aspin, L., 232
Atkins, C., 5, 100-101, 134, 183, 284, 299
Awards. *See* Ford Foundation–John F. Kennedy School Innovations in State and Local Government awards

B

Bardach, E., 41, 304
Behn, R., 90-91
"Bootlegging," 223, 224
Brown, L., 179, 209n.8
"Bureaucracy Problem, The," 10
Bush administration: emphasis on management, 42, 81-82n.9, 319-320; and privatization, 43-44

C

Cambridge Public Housing Authority (Massachusetts), 18-20, 117, 142, 164, 170n.9, 277, 279, 287, 289-290
Cary, F., 66, 260
Carter administration: airline deregulation, 45-47; political and policy failures, 252-253
"Catalytic government," 26, 31-32n.13
Centers for Disease Control (CDC), 55, 56
Chase, G., 7, 34-35, 98-99, 112, 116, 119-120, 138-140, 144-145, 152-153, 156, 159, 161, 162-163, 164, 165, 217-218, 230-231, 290, 300, 301
Chief executives, 239-266; guardian role, 246-249, 252-253; as "ideal type,"

327

239, 266n.1; innovation role, 242; management role, 239–242, 271, 308n.2; and organizational culture, 182–184; policy analysis role, 240–242, 243, 245–246; staff oversight role, 249–254. *See also* Public executives
Civil Aeronautics Board (CAB), 46
Clinton administration: AIDS crisis handling, 314–316; and media, 249; policy on gays in military, 316–318
Commitment, fostering of, 191–195
Community policing, 179–182, 209n.8
Computer industry. *See* IBM; Xerox
Conservative administrations: government size and scope in, 77; lack of management in, 54–55. *See also specific administration*
Constituencies, external, 284–288
Creative subversion, 14–15, 38–40, 79, 216–220; in private sector, 221–227
Crisis, as impetus for change, 132, 285
Culture. *See* Organizational culture

D

DARE. *See* Drug Abuse Resistance Education program
Darman, R., 44
Decision-making process, public participation in, 38. *See also* Policy analysis
Defense Audit Contract Agency, 81–82n.9

Deficit reduction, 324–325n.2
Deinstitutionalization, failure of, 47–48
Deregulation: airline, 42–47; S&Ls, 42–43, 46, 81n.7, 228–229
DOR. *See* Massachusetts Department of Revenue
Drug Abuse Resistance Education (DARE) program, 133, 135
Drug programs, 118–119, 133, 135, 138–140, 144–145
Dukakis administration, 165, 251, 254–256

E

Eakins, J., 154
Economic Development Administration (EDA), 50–51
Education, public management, 291–296, 301–307; and experiential learning, 303–304; and morals, 323–324; and professional identity, 302–303
Electoral imperative, 57
Employee credibility, fostering of, 192–193
Employment and training programs. *See* Massachusetts Employment and Training Choices Program
Empowerment, 194, 283
Enterprises, new, development of, 172–173
Entrepreneurs, bureaucratic, 149–169; action bias of, 6, 14, 29–30n.3, 88, 122n.3, 132–135, 137–138, 160–162; characteristics of, 150–151, 168, 273–274; and media, 288–291; as opportunist, 7; as outsider, 224, 272, 305;

and political structure, 269–270; and risk taking, 158–159; underground strategy of, 222–225. *See also* Public executives

Environmental programs, 110–111

Environmental Protection Agency (EPA), 99, 110–111, 119, 128–130, 156–157, 162, 194–195

Errors, tolerance for, 135–138, 273–274, 297–298

ET Choices. *See* Massachusetts Employment and Training Choices Program

Evaluation. *See* Program analysis

Evolutionary tinkering: and character of innovation, 88–89, 91, 110–112, 128; in natural sciences, 92–93, 123–124*n*.11

Executive staff, 249–254

Executive talent, scarcity of, 10–11, 213, 235–236*n*.1. *See also* Chief executive; Middle manager; Program executive

Experiential learning, 303–304

F

Family Learning Center (Michigan), 103, 130, 154

Federal Aviation Administration (FAA), 46

Field-based learning: formal and informal, 298–301; versus prior analysis, 292–296, 298–301

Ford administration, 55

Ford Foundation–John F. Kennedy School Innovations in State and Local Government awards, 5, 24, 94–97, 101–103, 289

Ford Motor Company, 200, 210–211*n*.24

Fort Worth's Storm Drain program, 102, 114, 130

Fortin, W., 172, 277–278, 283, 288

Fry, A., 222

Funding, need for oversight, 251

G

Gaebler, T., 26, 31–32*n*.13

General Electric, 223, 226

Glynn, T. P., 5, 100–101, 134, 174–175, 179, 183, 184–195, 202, 208*n*.1, 210*n*.9, 282, 284, 289, 299

Goals: and accountability, 275–276, 308–309*n*.7; diversity of, 69–71

Golden, O., 123

Goldmark, P., 233

H

Harvard's Graduate School of Business, 306

Hiding-hand principle, 162–163, 230–231

Hierarchy, as constraint, 226

Hirschman, A., 162

HSA. *See* New York City Health Services Administration

I

Iacocca, L., 224–225

IBM, 12–13, 64–67, 260–261; "bootlegging" at, 223–224; creation of mission, 195–198; "performance shootouts" at, 226–227

Illinois Department of Public Aid (DPA), 102

INDEX

Illinois QUIP program, 102, 114, 141–142
Implementation, 320
Independent business units (IBUs), creation of, 196
Innovation: character of, 103–120; through evolutionary tinkering, 88–89, 91–93, 110–112, 128; iteration and adaptation in, 128–132; as new context for old stuff, 112–116; as novel service and skill assemblage, 116–120; speed and action emphasis in, 138–140
Innovations in State and Local Government awards, 5, 24, 94–97, 101–103, 289
Interest convergence, 140–145, 284–288
Intrapreneuring, 220
Iran-Contra scandal, 263
Iranian hostage rescue, 49–50

J

Jackson, I., 6–7, 93–98, 111–112, 114–115, 136–137, 151–152, 156, 160–161, 163, 165, 289, 300, 301
Jacob, F., 88, 121–122n.2
Johnson administration, Great Society program, 235–236n.1
Judson, H., 298

K

Kahn, A., 46
Kanter, R., 203
Keefe, F., 251, 255–256
Kelly, R., 181
Kelman, S., 9, 259
King, A., 76
Koch, E., 165–166
Kodak, 203

L

Lehman, J., 218–220, 232, 248, 257–258
Levin, B., 20–22, 172, 280
Lindsay administration, 165, 254, 256–257
Line decisions, 34, 40–47, 50; and assemblage, 41; failures of, 47–51; joint action in, 50–51; management of, 315–318; versus point decisions, 40–41
Lipsky, M., 90, 122n.6
Lowe, S. S., 74
Lowe, W., 64–67, 83n.24, 196–197, 282

M

McCardell, A., 200, 201
McCoulough, P., 61–62, 199–201
"Management by Guts," 318–319
Management by wandering around, 135–136, 148n.4, 274
Managers, middle: accountability of, 275–276; advocate role, 283; culture management role, 207. *See also* Public executives
Massachusetts Bay Transit Authority (MBTA), 174–175, 208n.1; culture management at, 184–195
Massachusetts Department of Public Welfare (DPW), 100–101
Massachusetts Department of Revenue (DOR), 6–7, 93–98, 111–112, 114–116, 118–119, 151–152
Massachusetts Employment and Training (ET) Choices Program, 5, 29n.2, 100–101, 117,

137-138, 277, 278, 299. *See also* Welfare reform
Media: management of, 288-291; oversight role of, 252; power of, 249-250
Michigan's Family Learning Center, 103, 130, 154
Mission: creation of, 151-155, 158, 195-198, 303; and field-based learning, 296-297; redefinition and communication of, 5, 184-188, 200-202; as self-esteem enhancement, 281
Monroe County (Tennessee) Maternity Center (MCMC), 20, 114, 130-131
Montgomery County (Maryland) Meeting Obstetrical Needs of Indigent Women, 143
Multiple cultures, management of, 196-197, 202-203, 206

N

National Narcotic Border Interdiction System (NNBIS), 53
Natural sciences, innovation in, 92-93, 123-124n.11
New American Political System, The, 76-77
New Jersey Department of Human Services, 22-24
New Jersey School-Based Youth Services (SBYS), 118, 143
New York City Department of Juvenile Justice (DJJ), 102, 153, 165-166
New York City Health Services Administration (HSA), 7, 34-35, 98-99, 116, 119-120, 138-140, 144-145, 152-153, 156, 159, 161, 162-163, 164-165, 217-218, 230-231
New York Department of State, 102, 113-114

New York-New Jersey Port Authority XPORT program, 115, 131-132, 154-155, 161-162, 233-234
New York's Nova Ancora program, 102, 111, 141
Newman, R., 139, 217
North, O., 263-264

O

One Church, One Child, 134-135, 141, 154
Organizational culture, 171-207, 273-290: constraints on change, 175-176, 208n.2; as culture of action, 234, 260-261; as culture of control, 12, 199-203, 234, 260-261; executive management of, 182-184, 204-207; inappropriate controls in, 199-200, 211n.24; marketing strategy in, 183-184; multiple, management of, 196-197, 202-203, 206; and new vision, 176, 181-182; shared values in, 177-178
Organizational decisions: as teaching vehicle, 188-190; and values reinforcement, 190-191
Osborne, D., 26, 31-32n.13
Ouida, H., 131, 154-155, 161-162, 233-234
Outsider status, and innovation, 224, 272, 305
Overregulation, 227, 228-229
Oversight: and accountability, 37, 227, 243-246; budget, 251; executive, 246-249, 252-253, 255; media, 252; and Pentagon procurement process, 219, 231-233; regulatory, 228-229
Owens-Corning, 224

P

Palo Alto Research Center (PARC), 61–62, 200–203
Pennsylvania's Timber Bridge Program, 101, 111
Pentagon: military ban on homosexuals, 316; procurement scandal, 218–220, 231–233, 257–258
Performance, and managerial accountability, 275–276
Perot, R., 320–321
Peters, T., 29–30n.3, 221, 223, 226
Philadelphia's Anti-Graffiti Network, 118, 119, 143–144, 166, 289
Pinchot, G., 220–225
Point decisions, 42–47; defined, 40–41, 50; versus line decisions, 33–34, 36, 40–41
Policy analysis: and decision making, 2–3, 33–36, 40–41, 243; versus field-based learning, 298–299, 310n.15; formal, 89–91, 292–294; teaching of, 2–3, 292–296. See also Program analysis
Policy gridlock, 319–320, 324n.2
Policy implementation: impediments to, 35–36; line decision management in, 314–318; political disincentives in, 57–60
Political system: and fragmentation of power, 75–77; and policy implementation, 13–14, 36, 57–60
Potter, R., 203
Powell, C., 317
Pressman, J., 41, 50, 320
Private sector: approaches, public sector use of, 112–116; creative subversion in, 221–227; innovation-accountability balance in, 234–235; interest convergence and partnerships with, 1–2, 140–145; oversight mechanisms in, 60–61, 220–221; success measurement in, 71–72
Privatization, 43–44, 52, 68, 84n.28; of education, 71–73
Professional identity, development of, 302–303
Program analysis: as constraint on innovation, 215, 220–221; formal and informal, 276–278. See also Policy analysis
Program executives: abuse of power, 250; management role, 15, 239–240, 271
Project managers, 207. See also Program executives
Public education: institutional constraints on, 69–72, 84–85n.31; versus private education, 71–73
Public executives: accountability, 37–38, 215–216, 308–309n.7; and agency mission, 151–155; constraints on, 68–75, 213–216; education for, 291–296, 301–307; political support for, 163–167. See also Chief executives; Entrepreneurs, bureaucratic
Public health programs, 7, 20–22, 114, 130–131
Public housing programs, 18–20, 117, 142

Q

QUIP program (Illinois), 102, 114, 141–142

INDEX

R

"Ready, fire, aim" approach, 6, 29–30n.3, 88, 122n.3, 132–135, 137–138
Reagan administration: and deregulation, 42–44, 47; Iran-Contra scandal, 263–264; government size and scope during, 77; and privatization, 68; S&L debacle, 42–43, 228–229; war on drugs, 52–53, 133
Rehabilitation programs, 102
Resource allocation, constraints on, 72–75
Rewards: and mission reinforcement, 192–193; personal, 274, 280–284, 308n.4
Risk taking: bias toward, 250; disincentives to, 72–75; in innovative culture, 274–275
Ruckelshaus, W., 99, 110–111, 128, 156–157, 162, 194–195, 300, 301

S

Saint Louis CARE program, 101, 111
Savings and loan (S&L) debacle, 42–43, 46, 81n.7, 228–229
Schall, E., 5, 117, 153, 165–166, 253, 254
Schlesinger, L., 186–187
Self-esteem, and mission, 281
"Skunkworks," 226–227
Social science research, role of, 310n.15
"Stroke-of-the-pen myth," 316
Structure, nonhierarchical, 278–280
Swanger, S., 18–20, 117, 142, 154, 164, 177, 277, 279, 287, 289–290
Swine flu vaccine program, 55–57

T

Taylor, R., 202
Tetelman, E., 22–24, 118, 266n.2, 279, 282, 286, 288
Texas Instruments, 226
3M Company, 222, 225

U

Underregulation, 15
Unemployment prevention programs, 142

V

Values, and public agenda, 69–70, 321–324

W

Wasserman, M., 155, 159, 286
Waterman, R., 29–30n.3, 221, 223, 226
Weinberger, C., 248, 258
Welfare reform, 134, 183. *See also* Massachusetts Employment and Training Choices Program
Wheeler, J., 90
Wildavsky, A., 41, 50, 320, 322–323, 325n.2
Wilson, J. Q., 10, 135
Work Force. *See* Cambridge Public Housing Authority

X

Xerox Corporation, 12, 61–64, 66–67; culture of control, 199–203, 234, 260–261
XPORT program. *See* New York–New Jersey Port Authority